Grey Wolves

FOR MARGARET

Grey Wolves

THE U-BOAT WAR 1939–1945

PHILIP KAPLAN

Skyhorse Publishing

Skyhorse Publishing books may be purchased in bulk at special discounts for sales promotion, corporate gifts, fund-raising, or educational purposes. Special editions can also be created to specifications. For details, contact the Special Sales Department, Skyhorse Publishing, 307 West 36th Street, 11th Floor, New York, NY 10018 or info@skyhorsepublishing.com.

Skyhorse® and Skyhorse Publishing® are registered trademarks of Skyhorse Publishing, Inc.®, a Delaware corporation.

Visit our website at www.skyhorsepublishing.com.

10 9 8 7 6 5 4 3 2 1

Library of Congress Cataloging-in-Publication Data is available on file.

Jacket design by Jon Wilkinson

ISBN: 978-1-62873-727-1
Ebook ISBN: 978-1-62914-076-6

Printed in the United States of America

CONTENTS

INTRODUCTION

Submariners are a race apart, even from their comrades who serve in surface vessels. Early in the Second World War, an elité force of German submariners known as the Ubootwaffe nearly perfected the underwater tactics of the First World War U-boats to successfully sever Britain's transatlantic supply lifeline. To the Allies, these enemy sailors were on a mission that was unequivocally evil.

A popular fiction persists that the U-boat men were all volunteers; they were not. But once committed to the Ubootwaffe, each man soon understood and accepted that he would be a proud part of a unique brotherhood. Doing so was essential; he was about to set out, in claustrophobic, unsanitary, hellish conditions, on a voyage—an adventure— that would challenge and stretch his mental and physical endurance to the very limits, one that he was unlikely to survive. And, if he did return, he drew little comfort from family or friends, trapped in the knowledge that another, possibly fatal patrol awaited him. The men of the Ubootwaffe were linked together as comrades, by the ever-present dangers of the enemy and the weather, and by their unity of purpose more powerful than that of any other sailors.

All submariners are brave, no matter what cause they are fighting for. The men of the Ubootwaffe were eventually beaten by the overwhelming industrial and technological might of the Allies. Of the 39,000 men who went to sea in the U-boats of the Second World War, 27,491 died in action and a further 5,000 became prisoners of war. Of the 863 German U-boats that sailed on operational patrols in that war, 754 were lost.

Those who passed the training had to be the sort of men who did not mind being unaware of where or why they were going when they sailed out of harbour, who had never known claustrophobia, who could live in close proximity to forty other men for up to three months at a time and who could spend four hours on watch, lashed by icy winds, their eyes stung by salt spray, strapped or chained to a deck rail or wire to avoid being swept away, and learning the truth of the old sailor's adage that "water is pointed."

The men best suited for life aboard a U-boat were those who could sleep well in a bed that was still warm and redolent of the man who last lay in it, and who could stay in dreamland through the hissing of the inlet valves, the odd gurgle of the bilge-pumps and the pounding of the pistons, and who would only be awakened by the sound of depth-charges or the warning klaxon. They were those who could tumble out of bed and scramble aft or forward like pieces of human ballast when the commander ordered "Take her up!" or "Dive!", who would be ever keen for action, who could stay motionless and silent for hour after hour while the depth-charges boomed around them and hurled the boat about, and who never worried when their muscles began to atrophy from insufficient exercise.

As the days went by, they got to know one another and their officers, and began to realise that, although they were all individuals, each was now a part of something more—a unit that was going to war. This was the touchstone that helped them to become the sort of men they had to be. Not so much for love of country, nor yet for love of family, but out of loyalty to the men they had trained, messed and sailed with, and with whom they now shared their lives and fate.

A U-BOAT GLOSSARY

AA Anti-Aircraft, weapon or firing.

AAF (U.S.) Army Air Force.

Abaft towards the stern of a boat or ship.

Abt Abteilung / department or division.

Adressbuch U-boat code book used in disguising ocean chart grid positions in radio transmissions.

AGRU Front Ausbildungsgruppe Front / a technical testing branch to evaluate submarines and crews before releasing them to operational duty.

Alarm! emergency dive order on a U-boat.

Angle-on-the-bow variance between line of sight on a U-boat, and the compass heading of its target.

Aphrodite German device used to confuse radar by reflecting impulses.

Armed Guard U.S. Navy gun crew serving aboard a merchant ship.

ASDIC acronym for the British Anti-Submarine Detection Investigation Committee; the name given to a device housed in a dome under the hull of an anti-submaring vessel and used in detecting the presence of submerged submarines.

ASV airborne microwave radar (10 and 3 cm).

ASW anti-submarine warfare.

Athos radio detection antenna.

Bachstelze (water-stilt) autogiro-like device towed on a cable behind a U-boat to improve the field of vision of the 'flying' lookout.

Bali a radar detection aerial.

Bauwerft a ship-building yard.

B-Dienst Funkbeobachtungsdienst / German radio-monitoring and cryptographic intelligence service.

BdU Befehlshaber der Unterseeboot / Commander in Chief, U-boats (referred specifically to Admiral Karl Dönitz, but also in reference to his staff or headquarters.

Betasom the Italian submarine command based in Bordeaux.

Biscay, Bay Atlantic bay extending from northwestern France to northern Spain; the area in which the main German U-boat pen shelters were located.

Biscay Cross nickname of the early radar detection aerial used on U-boats.

Bletchley Park the British Government Code and Cipher School located in a large country house in Buckinghamshire, north of London.

Bold a device used by U-boats to confuse ASDIC.

Bombe a linked series of Enigma machines, devised at Bletchley Park.

Boot a German boat or warship; the commander is not a staff officer, and the second-in-command is called First Watch Officer, i.e. on a submarine.

Bootskanone gun on the foredeck of a U-boat.

Bow forward end of a vessel.

Bow caps small doors at the outside ends of a submarine's torpedo tubes.

Bows forward exterior hull of a vessel.

Bunkers exterior fuel tanks on a U-boat.

Calibre the measurement of gun and shell size, taken from the internal diameter, or bore, of the gun barrel, i.e. a five-inch shell is not five inches long, but five inches in diameter.

Casing a submarine's outer skin of light plating, which encloses the ballast tanks and pressure hull.

Cipher a secret letter-substitution communication code system.

Conn steering responsibility for a boat or ship.

Conning tower the observation tower or platform of a submarine; on a U-boat it contained steering controls; on type ix U-boats it contained the attack periscope eyepiece and torpedo deflection calculator.

Contact pistol torpedo detonator that explodes on striking a solid object.

Control room Zentrale the U-boat diving control facility, located below the conning tower and bridge.

Convoy a precise assembly of merchant ships organised in columns and escorted by warships.

Corvette A highly manoeuvrable armed escort ship, smaller than a destroyer.

Cypern a type of radar detector.

DD U.S. Navy reference to a destroyer-class warship.

DE a destroyer escort-class warship.

Decrypt a deciphered or decoded message.

Destroyer Germans used this term for all small vessels employed in combat protection and often included frigates and corvettes in this category.

Dienst duty.

Dienstgrad rank.

Dienstelle headquarters.

D-maschine diesel engine.

Displacement the weight of a boat or ship, as measured by the amount of water displaced when placing the boat or ship in water.

Dräger Tauchretter underwater escape apparatus for U-boat crewmen (made by the firm Dräger).

Eel (Aal) U-boat nickname for a torpedo.

EK Eisernes Kreuz Iron Cross award.

E-maschinen electric motors.

Encryption enciphered or encoded message.

Englisch a common German reference term to everything Allied or British during World War Two.

Enigma the Schlussel M cipher machine (also used in reference to the machine's encrypted product).

Fächerschuss simultaneous spread or fan-launch of two or more torpedoes.

Fähnrich zur See Midshipman.

Fangschuss coup de grace or finishing shot.

FAT (Federapparat Torpedo) an anti-convoy weapon that travelled in a straight line for a predetermined distance and then zigzagged.

FdU (Führer der Unterseeboote) Flag Officer for Submarines.

Feindfahrt operational patrol.

Flak (Fliegerabwehrkanone) anti-aircraft gun.

Fliege Fly. A radar detector.

Flotilla small fleet of small vessels.

Flugboot German for flying-boat aircraft.

Fregattenkapitän Captain (junior).

Freya a radar detection apparatus.

Frontboot U-boat at sea that has entered an operational area.

Funk-Telegraphie (FT) German reference for Wireless Telegraphy radio transmission / reception.

Funker German Navy radioman.

Funkmess radio / radar detection.

Funkpeilgerät radio direction finder.

Great Circle shortest route, following arc of the earth's surface.

Grossadmiral grand admiral, corresponding to Fleet Admiral (U.S.)

GRT gross register tonnage, the total displacement of a ship.

Gruppe group.

HE (hydrophone effect) underwater sound such as propeller cavitation of a surface ship.

Hedgehog a type of anti-U-boat bomb thrown ahead of the vessel carrying it.

HF / DF (Huff-Duff) high-frequency / direction finder.

Hundekurve (dog curve) track taken by a U-boat in attacking a ship, to present the smallest possible profile to the enemy at all times.

Hydra cipher used by U-boats in establishing the daily setting of the Enigma / Schlussel M cipher machine.

Hydrophone underwater sound detection device.

Hydroplanes extended rudder surfaces on submarine hull that make the boat go up and down when it is underwater.

Jumping wire heavy cable with a cutting edge, stretched from bow to stern over the submarine's conning tower, to cut or deflect underwater obstacles such as nets.

Kaleu, Kaleunt diminutive forms of the naval rank Kapitänleutnant.

Kapitänleutnant Lieutenant Commander.

Kalipatrone Potash-cartridge respirator that absorbed carbon dioxide.

Keroman protective U-boat bunkers at Pointe de Keroman near the Lorient harbour entrance.

Kleine boot small training submarine, i.e. type IID.

KM (Kriegsmarine) the German Navy, 1935-1945.

Km kilometre.

Knot a ship's speed measured as one nautical mile per hour.

Konteradmiral Rear Admiral.

Korvettenkapitän Commander.

Krieg war.

Kriegstagebuch (KTB) German war diary kept by boats and ships at sea and by shore-based headquarters staffs.

Kurzsignale a U-boat's short signal radio position report.

Leutnant zur See Lieutenant junior grade.

LI (Leitender Ingenieur) Chief Engineering Officer.

Löwe Lion. Nickname for Karl Dönitz.

Luftwaffe German Air Force.

M.A.N. Maschinenfabrik Augsburg-Nürnberg AG, the manufacturer of diesel engines for the Type VII and IX U-boats.

Manoeuvring room electric motor room on U-boat.

Metox a type of German radar detector.

Milch cow nickname for a U-boat used for re-supply and re-fueling of other U-boats.

Mixers torpedo mates on a U-boat.

Naxos a radar detection device.

ObdM (Oberbefehlshaber der Marine) Supreme C-in-C of the German Navy.

Oberfähnrich zur See Ensign.

Oberleutnant zur See Lieutenant senior grade.

Papenberg column a shallow depth pressure gauge.

Paukenschlag to beat on the kettle drums—a code name for the initial U-boat attack on the United States.

Periscope extendable tubelike optical device containing prisms, mirrors, and lenses that enable a U-boat crewman to view the sea surface while the boat is submerged.

Radar radio direction and ranging.

Rake a patrol line of several U-boats across the path of a convoy.

Reichsmarine the German Navy, 1919-1935.

Ritterkreuz the Knight's Cross decoration.

Rohr torpedo tube.

Rudeltaktik technique of massing U-boats in a 'wolfpack' patrol line across a convoy's course and engaging ships of the convoy in a radio-coordinated attack.

Schlüssel M the Kriegsmarine version of the Enigma cipher machine.

Schnorchel / Schnorkel a valved air pipe that protruded above the surface and a allowed submerged U-boat to proceed on diesel power.

Schussmeldung a U-boat's 'shooting report', required after each action.

Sea cow nickname for large U-boats.

Sea force recorded in a U-boat's KTB on an ascending scale from zero to ten.

Soda-lime a chemical used to absorb moisture and carbon dioxide breathed into the air by the crew of a submarine during a prolonged dive.

Sonar acronym for Sound Navigation and Ranging (U.S.)

Spargel literally, asparagus; U-boat nickname for the periscope.

Special Intelligence decrypted wireless German radio traffic, from Bletchley Park in England.

Squid an Allied anti-submarine mortar weapon.

Standzielsehrohr the attack periscope sight in a U-boat conning tower.

Tetis a U-boat cipher used in wireless transmissions by new U-boats in training.

Tiefenmesser a U-boat's depth-pressure gauge.

Torpex a high-explosive mix of Cyclonite, TNT and aluminium flakes.

Trim the balancing of a submarine's weight and equillibrium underwater.

U-boat underwater boat, German submarine.

Ubootwaffe the German submarine fleet.

Verloren lost; sunk.

Vernichtet destroyed.

Versenkt sunk.

Vorhaltrechner a Siemens-made electro-mechanical deflection calculator in the U-boat conning tower that fed attack coordinates into the gyrocompass steering mechanism of the torpedoes in their tubes.

Wabos German nickname for Wasserbombe.

Wasserbombe German term for depth-charge.

Wanze a radar detection device.

Wehrmacht the German Army.

Weyer a U-boat's identification manual for the warships of all nations.

Werft shipyard or dockyard.

Wind force wind velocities were recorded in a U-boat's KTB on an ascending scale from zero to ten.

Wintergarten German nickname for the open, railed platform on the after part of a U-boat bridge. The British referred to it as a 'bandstand'.

Wolfpack *Rudel* in German; an attack technique developed by Admiral Karl Dönitz.

Working up the time allotted for officers and crewmen to familiarise themselves with their new boat prior to sailing on their first patrol in her.

Zaunkönig the German acoustic torpedo, also known as T5.

Zentrale the U-boat control room, directly below the conning tower and bridge, containing all diving controls.

THE LION

Karl Dönitz was the son of a Prussian family living in the Berlin suburb of Grünau. He was born in December 1891 and took after his father—instilled with the qualities required and expected in an officer of the Imperial German Navy, which he joined as a cadet when he was eighteen. Dutiful, patriotic, loyal and efficient in his work, the young Dönitz was soon rewarded for his enthusiastic, diligent and dedicated performance, with a commission as a naval officer.

From the beginning of the First World War, Dönitz served in a naval aviation squadron as an air observer, but by 1916 he had developed an intense interest in submarines, leading to his transferring to the Navy's U-boat arm and, by March 1918, advancing to command of *UB-68*. In October of that year, while submerged in the Mediterranean near the Sicilian coast, his submarine developed a malfunction which caused it to involuntarily surface. The boat emerged among a British convoy of merchant vessels being shepherded by several warship escorts which immediately sank it. Dönitz and most of his crew were rescued, captured and interned. He would spend the next ten months in a remote Scottish prisoner of war camp. Finally, he was declared mentally unsound and was invalided back to Germany, having undoubtedly pretended the condition.

A clever tactician, Dönitz's enthusiasm for the submarine weapon remained strong and he had spent much of his confinement working on plans for the development and deployment of the rudel or wolfpack battle technique—a concept he had learned about during the war—in which a group of U-boats operated together in a coordinated attack. The theory had long fascinated him, and inspired him to follow it to fruition. The rudeltaktik had been devised during World War One as a new and unique method of attack, grouping several submarines into a "wolfpack" to overwhelm the protective warship escorts of an enemy convoy. The method had proven difficult to implement in that war due to limitations in the capabilities of the available radios. Since then, however, the Germans had developed a range of ultra-high frequency transmitters which they believed would place their radio communications beyond the ability of the enemy to jam them. This, together with the highly capable Enigma cipher machine, made the Germans feel secure about their U-boat capabilities. Dönitz also supported the concept of attacking convoys at night from the surface or near the surface, minimising the ability of the British sonar to detect the U-boats.

From the postwar years of the 1920s, through the 1930s, Karl Dönitz promoted the values and capabilities of the U-boats, to all who would listen within the German Navy and elsewhere. In September 1933, he was made a Fregattenkapitän (full commander) and the following year was given command of the cruiser Emden, which was then operating a training ship.

In 1935, as a result of a new Anglo-German Naval Treaty revising some of the terms of the 1922 Washington Naval Conference Treaty, Germany was permitted to resume limited production of submarines, and the then German Navy Commander-in-Chief, Grossadmiral Erich Raeder, placed Dönitz in charge of rebuilding the Kriegsmarine U-boat arm. Dönitz quickly went to work, dedicating himself to planning the new force around his dream rudeltaktik, based on his firm belief that Germany's primary target in a future conflict would be the vital overseas supply lines, the lifelines providing food, fuel, and other resources to Britain from around the world. He reasoned that his U-boats were the only means for Germany to conduct a war on such trade in which the British enemy would transport its supplies by ships in convoy that were escorted and protected by warships. They were accustomed to the threat of lone U-boats, but he believed intensely in the capability of his new wolfpacks to elude the convoy protection and destroy the convoy supply ships. His theory called for a fleet of at least 300 submarines . . . fast, medium size, highly manoeuvrable boats of which, 100 would be on-station in the high seas, a further hundred would be either on the way to the convoys or on the way home after their patrols, and the final hundred would be back at base undergoing servicing and being re-equipped.

By November 1937, Dönitz was lobbying agressively for the conversion of the German fleet to a force composed almost entirely of U-boats. His philosophy of attack was to strike only at merchant vessels, relatively soft targets. He pointed out that, for example, destroying the British oil tanker fleet would deny the Royal Navy the supplies it needed to power its ships, thus depleting its capability and eliminating it as a threat at sea.

The boat Dönitz preferred for the task was the Type VII, a vessel of about 750 tons displacement and equipped with five torpedo tubes. It was suitable for mid-Atlantic operations, unlike larger U-boats, or the smaller, 250-ton boats whose usefulness was limited to activity in the

Baltic or the North Sea. The German head of state, Adolf Hitler, had a different view about preparedness for battle at sea, however. Politically, he believed that the British and the French would not go to war with Germany unless their global wealth was threatened. He projected 1945 as the date by which his navy and Ubootwaffe would have to be ready for the sort of submarine campaign that Dönitz had in mind.

Dönitz, felt that he could work with the Nazi regime if they could avenge the humiliation of Germany in the Versailles Treaty at the end of the First World War, and ultimately bring victory to the German Fatherland. "I am a firm adherent of the idea of ideological education. For what is it in the main? Doing his duty is a matter of course for the soldier. But the whole importance, the whole weight of duty done, are only present when the heart and spiritual conviction have a voice in the matter. The result of duty done is then quite different to what it would be if I only carried out my task literally, obediently, and faithfully. It is therefore necessary for the soldier to support the execution of his duty with all his mental, all his spiritual energy, and for this his conviction, his ideology are indispensable. It is therefore necessary for us to train the soldier uniformly, comprehensively, that he may be adjusted ideologically to our Germany. Every dualism, every dissension in this connection, or every divergence, or unpreparedness, imply a weakness in all circumstances. He in whom this grows and thrives in unison is superior to the other. Then indeed the whole importance, the whole weight of his conviction comes into play. It is also nonsense to say that the soldier or the officer must have no politics. The soldier embodies the state in which he lives; he is the representative, the articulate exponent of this state. He must therefore stand with his whole weight behind this state. We must travel this road from our deepest conviction. The Russian travels along it. We can only maintain ourselves in this war if we take part in it with holy zeal, with all our fanaticism."

He continued preparations for the possible employment of his wolf-packs by sending a selection of his best young U-boat commanders on an exercise patrol around the Shetland Islands and down to the French Atlantic coast.

With the outbreak of war in 1939, Grossadmiral Raeder assigned Dönitz the task of blockading all of Britain's UK ports. Dönitz undertook the job but was soon in the position of having to persuade Raeder of the extreme vulnerability of the U-boats to attacks by land-based aircraft in such actions, and that his boats would be far better deployed out in the Atlantic, cutting Britain's supply lifelines, and beyond reach of the aircraft. At that time, Dönitz could only muster twenty-two ocean-going submarines, with seldom more than six on station at any given point in the six months after he was given the task. The wolfpack concept would have to wait.

His crews wanted to please the Lion, as they referred to Dönitz, and despite their limited numbers, managed to locate and sink more than 300,000 tons of British merchant shipping between January and April 1940, for the loss of thirteen U-boats. The German shipyards were unable at this stage to keep pace with replacement of the submarine losses. But Dönitz, who was now BdU or Befehlshaber der U-boote, Commander-in-Chief, Submarines, was heartened by the French surrender which gave him access to key harbours on the Bay of Biscay coast and the Channel coast where slave labourers employed by the Todt organisation built several bomb-proof U-boat pen shelters. Their locations virtually halved the transit time for his boats to their Atlantic action stations.

With the development of the Biscay pens, results improved dramatically for Dönitz's Atlantic raiders. Between June and October—a period known among the Ubootwaffe as *die glückliche Zeit*, the happy time, the U-boats sank 274 British merchant ships for a total tonnage of nearly 1,400,000, with just six U-boats lost. The losses for Britain were significant.

In the next two years of war, the German Minister of Munitions Albert Speer managed to produce prefabricated parts in dispersed factories, enabling much faster production of U-boats. At the beginning of 1942, ninety-one U-boats had become operational, with 212 being operational by the end of the year. By April of 1943, 240 were operational. A total tonnage of more than two million was sunk (432 merchant vessels) in 1941. A combined tonnage total of more than 4,300,000 resulted for the year when the overall total of 1,299 merchant ships sunk was considered. It included sinkings caused by aircraft, surface ships, and mine fields.

Dönitz was forbidden by Hitler to act against the United States, which was providing all possible aid to Britain at that time, in spite of the U.S. position of neutrality in the war. Then, on 1 September 1941, the U.S. Navy Commander-in-Chief, Admiral Ernest King, ordered American warships to join with the British and Canadians in convoy escort duty. In the next few days the USS *Greer*, a destroyer bound for Iceland, received a warning from an R.A.F. aircraft that a U-boat was near the American warship. What followed was a three-hour chase by the destroyer, with depth-charges and torpedoes exchanged and nothing conclusive resulting. Dönitz believed that the *Greer* had taken the offensive, while President Roosevelt told the U.S. public that the U-boat commander had been guilty of piracy.

With America's entry into the war on 7 December, Dönitz's pent-up anger at the U.S. was released and he ordered five long-range Type IX U-boats and sixteen widely separated Type VIIs on the attack against American vessels. He called the operation *Paukenschlag*, "beat on the kettle drums", and, of the submarine attacks that ensued along the east coast of the United States, he noted: "Bathers and sometimes entire coastal cities are witnesses of the drama of war, whose visual climaxes are constituted by red aureoles of blazing tankers." In the months up to June 1942, more than 300 Allied ships, including many tankers, had gone down, victims of the German torpedoes unleashed by U-boats ranging south from New York harbour to southern Florida and the Caribbean. These results prompted the U.S. Army General George Marshall to comment: "I am fearful that another month or two of this will so cripple our means of transport that we will be unable to bring sufficient men and planes to bear against the enemy in the critical theatres to exercise a determining influence on the war."

While Paukenschlag continued along the U.S. east coast, the great Atlantic convoys of the Allies proceeded practically unmolested, so savage and intensive was the Dönitz campaign against the Americans. He sat in his chateau at Kernéval near the massive U-boat facility in the inner harbour of Lorient, giving orders to his submarines by radio, moving them like chess pieces, telling his commanders to keep him apprised of their positions and to give him descriptions of the weather they where they were. He plotted their positions on the grid of the huge wall map in his elegant headquarters and directed their attacks, mustering them into packs in response to their convoy sightings. He anxiously anticipated their action reports of the sinkings they achieved and the estimated tonnages they had accumulated. It was quite a time for the Lion of Lorient. A substantial amount of this radio traffic was overheard by the British, however, and was soon deciphered by their code breakers at Bletchley Park.

Dönitz was convinced that if his U-boats could attain a monthly average of at least 800,000 tons of enemy shipping sunk, it would starve Britain and choke off her ability to wage war. As it was, his boats were accounting for a monthly average of 650,000 tons sunk, imposing a devastating effect on the British. In one of the ironies of that war, Admiral King, who was anything but an Anglophile and had little regard for the Royal Navy in particular, was involved in a long-standing feud with General Henry 'Hap' Arnold, head of the U.S. Army Air Forces. Their feud though, was easily matched on the other side by that of Dönitz and Reichsmarschall Hermann Göring, the Luftwaffe chief.

In a major event for the German Navy, on 30 January 1943 Hitler replaced Grossadmiral Raeder with Karl Dönitz as Commander-in-Chief. Hitler had been greatly disappointed with the performance of his pocket battleship *Lutzow* and heavy cruiser *Hipper* when, going against a Russian convoy off Norway on 31 December 1942, they had been held off by five Royal Navy destroyers, and finally driven off by two RN cruisers, without sinking a single ship. He ordered that the two warships be paid off as of no further use to the Reich, reprimanded Raeder and sacked him. This resulted in new prestige for the U-boat arm of the Kriegsmarine but, to some extent, weakened the operational relationship between the head and the U-boat commanders at sea, when operational command and control passed to Dönitz's Chief of Staff, Rear Admiral Eberhardt Godt, who, while enthusiastic and zealous, lacked the Lion's touch. In this climate of command change, seventeen new U-boats were being commissioned each month and Dönitz was pressing Speer for more. In April 1943, more than 400 U-boats were operational and it seemed that a German victory in the Atlantic was near.

Then, in what may have been the only significant tactical error committed by Admiral Dönitz in the course of the war, he ordered his boat commanders to sail on the surface when running to and from their battle stations and engage in combat with enemy aircraft if they were attacked. His decision was based on the logic that the boats would make the transit much faster on the surface, and the deck-watch lookouts would be more efficient and reliable than the Metox detector, which was largely ineffective at warning of the Allies' latest airborne radar. But now it seemed that the hostile aircraft of the Allies were everywhere. The Catalinas, Sunderlands, and Liberators of the Allied maritime air commands had extended their reach further into the Atlantic, and carrier-borne aircraft, released from their role in support of the Allied campaign in North Africa, were suddenly available in support of convoys all the way to their destinations. The cost: twenty-eight U-boats were sunk by the aircraft and fifty-seven Allied planes were brought down. It spelled the end of 'happy times' for the Ubootwaffe and the turning of the tide in the Atlantic war. In May, forty-one U-boats were sunk with the loss of most of their crewmen, including Peter Dönitz, younger son of the Admiral. It was a time of great concern for the German submarine service, with losses becoming unsustainably high. Admiral Godt now gave serious consideration to recalling all of the U-boats to base, but it would appear to be an open admission of defeat. Besides, there was only sufficient berthing for 110 boats in the Biscay pens. Godt and Dönitz instead opted for a strategic redeployment, withdrawing the wolf-packs to the relative safety of the Azores.

Dönitz now clung to the promise of new and impressive advances coming to the Ubootwaffe—improved sonar, the electronic compression of radio transmission, the snorkel, wire-guided torpedoes, and the new generation Type XXI and XXIII submarines. When these innovations were available he would take them back to the Atlantic and continue the battle. In the meantime, he tried to sell Hitler on putting his boats to work landing storm troops on the North African coasts, or mining the main Egyptian ports. The enraged leader reacted furiously to the admiral's suggestions: "The Atlantic is Germany's first line of defence in the West. The enemy forces tied up by our U-boats are tremendous, even though the losses we inflict are no longer great. I cannot afford to release those forces by discontinuing our U-boat operations." When the U-boats did begin returning to the Atlantic, often as not they were the hunted. More and more, they were on the defensive. The impressive technical innovations awaited impatiently by the Lion arrived in due course, but by the time they did, the Allies had already developed the means of defeating them. The merchant vessels of the Allied convoys were arriving safely in ever greater numbers and it was becoming clear to both sides that Germany was losing.

No more would Dönitz personally greet his commanders on their return from patrols. There were no more dockside embraces, no more awarding of medals, and no more handing out bouquets. No brass band welcomes, no more lovely, smiling nurses on the piers.

By late April 1945, the Third Reich was in utter chaos. Hitler was operating from the Führerbunker underneath the Reich Chancellery gardens in Berlin. In those last days of the Reich, those who had been close to the German leader were vying to succeed him in power. Heinrich Himmler, the head of the SS (Shutzstaffel), had been negotiating to surrender German forces to the Allies; his offer was declined. Luftwaffe commander Hermann Göring, meanwhile, had the temerity to contact Hitler by radio to ask the Führer for permission to assume leadership of the Reich. Hitler immediately expelled both men from the Nazi party. One of the few people he still trusted was Karl Dönitz, whom he appointed his heir and Head of State. After Hitler's suicide, the Lion took charge briefly and he acted quickly to rid himself of people like Himmler, propaganda minister Josef Göbbels, and Martin Bormann, Hitler's private secretary. A week later German General Alfred Jodl, representing the German High Command and Grossadmiral Dönitz, signed the act of unconditional surrender of all German land, sea and air forces in Europe to the Allied Expeditionary Force and to the Soviet High Command.

Between November 1945 and October 1946, a series of war crimes trials were held in Nuremberg, Germany, in which one of the principal defendants, Grossadmiral Karl Dönitz, was charged with waging unrestricted submarine warfare against neutral shipping, among other counts. These included 1) conspiracy to commit crimes against peace, war crimes, and crimes against humanity; 2) planning, initiating and waging wars of aggression; and 3) crimes against the laws of war. While he was convicted on counts 2 and 3 and sentenced to a ten-year prison term, he was not punished for his conviction on the unrestricted submarine warfare charge because the United States and Britain had also committed the same breach. He served his prison term confined at Spandau in what was then West Berlin.

Dönitz spent the rest of his life quietly in the town of Aumühle in Schleswig-Holstein, northern Germany, where he wrote his memoirs and corresponded, mainly with German naval history enthusiasts in America and elsewhere. He died there in December 1980. Both of his sons were killed during the Second World War. Peter, the younger son, was a watch officer in the submarine *U-954*. He died when his boat was sunk in the North Atlantic on 19 May 1943. His older brother Klaus was killed on 13 May 1944 when his torpedo boat, *S-141*, was destroyed in a raid on HMS *Selsey* off the English coast.

To Dönitz, his young U-boat commanders were the bravest of the brave: "I was fascinated by that unique spirit of comradeship engendered by destiny and hardship shared in the community of a U-boat's crew, where every man's well-being was in the hands of all and where every single man was an indispensable part of the whole. Every submariner, I am sure, has experienced in his heart the glow of the open sea and the task entrusted to him, has felt himself to be as rich as a king and would change places with no man."

"And pleas'd th' Almighty's orders to perform. / Rides in the whirlwind and directs the storm.
—from *The Campaign* by Joseph Addison

THE CREW

What was it like being a member of a U-boat crew in the Second World War? A common misconception exists that all submariners were volunteers. This was not so. Many young Germans became underwater sailors through the age-old military method of selection: "I want three volunteers—you, you, and you." But the recent 'volunteer' quickly learned that he had entered an elite, close-knit corps in which he would serve with great pride.

They would serve in an environment that was claustrophobic, foul-smelling and unpleasant. They operated in the often unfriendly sea with its chlorine, potassium, magnesium, flouride and strontium—toxic and threatening to one's health and safety. That unpredictable, constantly changing sea in its nature and movement, from calm and silent to clamourous and turbulent, changing in density and temperature and continuously impacting on the performance and behaviour of their boat. Far more than most military men, the underwater sailor was in touch with the deep, dark, deadly secrets of the sea. If he cared about his life, he soon learned to treat the element in which he moved and functioned, with respect.

To paraphrase Winston Churchill, Britain's wartime leader, our submariners were gallant maritime adventurers, while those of the enemy were ruthless murderers, skulking under water to slaughter helpless sailors. In fact, all submariners were trained to do a job that was expected to ultimately lead to depriving the enemy of its ability to make war, a role and goal they shared with bomber air crew who were often criticised and condemned as "terror fliers" and "assassins of the air." New recruits of the Ubootwaffe underwent stiff and rigorous training, initially in the form of arduous physical conditioning, marching, and classroom lectures in the early months, followed by specialised training in seamanship and submarine technology. In the course of their training they were required to take and pass a range of tests that would screen and eliminate all candidates deemed unsuited to withstanding the hazards and privations that came with U-boat warfare.

The successful trainees were those who were unphased by the cramped, oppressive interior of a submarine, the stench of life in a metal tube in close proximity to forty other men for ninety days or more at a time, standing watch on the "wintergarden" of the conning tower in brutal winds and icy salt spray, strapped or chained to a deck rail or wire to avoid being swept away. In *Bloody Winter*, John Waters wrote: "The North Atlantic is where the seaman takes his graduate course in weather, and the curriculum is tough." The graduates had no problem accepting practices such as hot-bunking, sleeping in a bed that was still warm from the man who last occupied it . . . sleeping soundly through the pounding of the pistons, hissing of the inlet valves, and the gurgle of the bilge pumps. They were those able to keep silent and motionless for hours while the boat lurched and groaned as depth-charges blasted around the hull.

They would be the ones who could adjust to rotting food, soggy, sweating surfaces, damp, dank clothing that could never be properly dried, queueing at the one and only toilet, and dealing with the inevitable outbreaks of rashes and lice.

The candidates first entered the "narrow drum" where they would live, work, and likely die, on a visit to one of the yards building U-boats, in Kiel, Bremen, Hamburg or Wilhelmshaven. There they familiarised themselves with the dials, handles, wheels, gauges, and the systems they would have to understand. They would then meet their fellow submariners, the officers and their commander on whose decisions their lives would depend. Just before their boat was completed and fitted out, the shipbuilders gave them a formal luncheon prior to turning the boat over to them for the working-up exercises.

Learning about their new boat included the testing of the hydroplanes, the trim and ballast tanks, and the pressure hull at depth. Sailing in the Baltic Sea, they spent hours practicing the re-loading of torpedoes, dummy launches, testing the diesel and electric motors, the radio and sonar, and the armament of the boat. In all of this intensive practice and instruction, the notion of actually taking the boat to war began to sink in—the reality of their situation impressed them now as never before. They began to understand the essential truth of the unit that each man was a part of and the bond between them that might keep them alive. They came to know and value the crucial interdependency of submarine crew members and respect it.

Few U-boat crewmen were likely to survive the twelve patrols required of them before being re-assigned to non-combatant duties. But if awards and decorations are any indication of the value the Kriegsmarine placed on the contribution of the Ubootwaffe officers to the war effort, fewer than five percent of the total commissioned naval strength received nearly half of all the Knight's Crosses awarded in the entire navy. In the Ubootwaffe, a Knight's Cross was normally handed out to a commander when he had sunk 100,000 tons of Allied shipping. When his achievement was 150,000 tons, he received the addition of the Oak Leaves, and those few who exceeded this total had the award of the Swords. Only two men received the award of the Diamonds, or Brilliants, in World War Two—Kapitänleutnant Albrecht Brandt and Kapitän zur See Wolfgang Lüth.

Even with the special rates of pay, the best of rations, the medal, adventure and glory—U-boat warfare was certainly not for everyone. As one Second World War submariner recalled: "Lying deep in the Atlantic, gasping for breath, simultaneously shivering with fear and sweating like a pig, listening to the sound of the Asdic bouncing off the hull ever louder and faster, hearing it fade when the hostile destroyer was almost overhead, knowing that the depth-charges would be sinking down towards you"—all that horror might be more than nerve and fortitude could stand, just as an airman, high over Germany in the bitter cold, rocked by flak bursts, blinded by the search-lights and hunted by the fighters, might suddenly decide that that kind of life was not for him. "Lack of moral fibre" was how the R.A.F. described the condition; the U.S. Army Air Force, less harshly, called it "combat fatigue". Both in the bombers and the U-boats, the solution was the same—remove that man from the crew as rapidly as possible, before he infects the other members.

Most of the submariners tolerated and endured the hazards, the discomfort, the claustrophobic life, while somehow adjusting to the extraordinary fear, and they did so repeatedly on the patrols when they encountered an enemy they seldom saw. They clung to the thought that they were doing this for Germany, and were comforted by the photographs they carried connecting them to their families and girl friends. They were spurred by the trust of their commander and the reliance upon them by their crew-mates, and the belief that through their efforts this war would not end like the one their fathers fought, but in triumph for the Fatherland.

But with ever increasing losses, ever more replacement crews required, and tens of thousands dying on the Russian Front, the Lion was no longer able to choose from the cream of German manhood for the Ubootwaffe. If he could, he would have chosen a high percentage of trained craftsmen, metal workers and machinists, men able to relate to a U-boat's working parts, to carry out repairs at sea and make replacements, but such artisans were rare now and needed in the war industries.

Many of the new recruits did not meet the requirements of the submarine arm. Many were callow youths, with little understanding of what awaited them, of being at the mercy of the elements and no conception at all of the reality of naval combat. The majority of officers being trained to command early in 1944 had been posted from redundant surface ships. Nearly all had no submarine background. Most who should and would have formed the next generation of U-boat commanders—those who had sailed with the early aces as 1st and 2nd officers—were dead.

Increasingly, new lower-rank U-boat officers were staunch Nazis, scornful of the crew's favourite jazz gramophone records because such music was non-Aryan or, worse still, American. These officers frequently lectured the crews on subjects like the way forward for National Socialism, not that useful when the next hunting Allied warship or aircraft came along. The new recruits soon grasped to realise the harsh reality of their situation: beaten soldiers could surrender or retreat, airmen had parachutes and stricken surface sailors had access to lifeboats, but a U-boat's liferaft held less than half the complement, and the personal escape-suit, out in the Atlantic, would be about as helpful as a clear understanding of the way forward for National Socialism.

In combat, the optimist believes that, although some of those around him will probably be killed, he will somehow survive. Since the time of bows and arrows, this euphoric belief has heartened nearly all fighting men—except those who went to war in submarines. They knew that when their craft was breached, deep down in the sea, the fate of one would be the fate of all.

THE IDEA

They looked dangerous and they were. The Kaiser's submarines in the First World War, and Hitler's in the Second, are history's most feared and best remembered vessels for making war at sea. Their deadly story started in 1914 with the sinking of three British Royal Navy cruisers, torpedoed and destroyed. This shocking event, happening as it did to what was then the world's greatest navy, marked the real beginning of undersea warfare. It continued with a fury in the 1940s, with the great U-boat campaign and the Atlantic convoy war against Britain's merchant fleet which nearly brought starvation to the British.

How does history record the appearance of the world's first working submarine? Actually, it was just a submersible and was created in 1620 in the otherwise undistinguished reign of King James I of England. The king was invited by the Dutch inventor, Cornelius van Drebel, to go for a short ride in his oar-driven vessel on—and briefly under—the filthy waters of the Thames. The record goes on to acknowledge the initial offensive use of a submersible craft when an egg-shaped, wooden, one-man boat designed by David Bushnell and called the *Turtle*, attempted an unsuccessful attack on HMS *Eagle* in New York harbour during the American War of Independence. The inventor failed again when he tried to sell *Turtle* to Emperor Napoleon, who at the time was involved in a major sea campaign, an activity in which he was no more effective than that other dictator, Adolf Hitler, in later years.

It was not until 1864, during the American Civil War, that the thirty-foot Confederate submarine *H.L. Hunley* (named for her builder), hand-cranked by her crew of eight, managed to approach and sink the 1,200-ton Federal sloop *Housatonic* off the coast of South Carolina. Her torpedo was fired on the surface, but the *Hunley* had come to her target under water and successfully demonstrated the capability of such a vessel. *Hunley* herself then sank like a stone.

Eleven years passed and the New Jersey scientist John P. Holland, walrus moustache, rimless glasses, high wing-collar and black frock coat, designed and built a vessel that would be the model for all subsequent submarines until the age of nuclear power. The *Holland I*, with a crew of three, was powered by a steam engine when operating on the surface and by electric battery-driven motors when submerged. She was steered by a conventional rudder, and her depth was controlled by water ballast tanks, and later by hydroplanes mounted on each side of the bow to provide an element of longitudinal control.

His next effort was *Holland II*, developed in 1881 and also known as the *Fenian Ram*, in recognition of the Irish revolutionary party that, for reasons of its own, was sponsoring Holland, who was an Irish émigré. Thirty-one feet long and displacing nineteen tons, *Holland II* was powered by an early model of the internal combustion engine, was armed with a pneumatic nine-inch bore cannon, and fired a six-inch torpedo under water. It would be a further twenty years before the U.S. Navy accepted the *Holland II* and by then, five such Holland submarines were under construction for the Royal Navy by the British firm Vickers. Their development as serious weapons of war led to the D and E classes of submarine, the first relatively reliable and quite formidable submersible vessels. They were equipped with diesel engines, twin propellers, saddle tanks, radio, and guns. By 1914 the Royal Navy had the largest submarine fleet in the world—seventy-four boats—ready for action from the start of World War One.

No such progress was being achieved in Germany. Wilhelm Bauer, whose promising submarine design would later cause his country to claim him as the true inventor of the vessel, had received little encouragement from his government or the German Navy. Being an army man, his credibility as a submarine originator failed to impress the German admirals, as did his initial experimental launch in 1851. Half a century later, Raimondo d'Equevilley, a Spanish engineer, who had been studying submarine design in France, convinced the German industrialist Friederich Krupp to build what would be the first of more than 2,000 German U-boats.

It was to be a struggle for both men. Grossadmiral Alfred von Tirpitz, the founder and commander of the Kaiser's Navy, believed that submarines might be of some use in coastal defence, but no more than that. His priority was the construction of a high seas battle fleet. It was not until late in 1906 that *U-1*, the first unterseeboote built by Krupp-Germania, was commissioned. It impressed the naval powers and, having come along later than the other submarine pioneers, German engineers had the advantage of being able to skip the early-phase experiments with steam power and gasoline for fuel, going directly into the use of heavy oil or paraffin. This resulted in a war boat that was at least as good as the Royal Navy's latest type. Even the German periscopes, a field in which the British had originally excelled, were superior.

With the end of World War One, all of the combatant countries were designing and building larger, more powerful, better-armed submarines. In fact, Germany's plans then included sailing a fleet of large, cruiser U-boats, each of 1,500 tons displacement, and armed with six twenty-inch torpedoes and a 150 mm gun, a vessel with a surface speed of 17.5 knots and a submerged speed of 8.1 knots, manned by a crew of forty-six, to the coasts of America. These plans were postponed for twenty-four years by the Allied victory in November 1918 and the Treaty of Versailles banning Germany from building, buying or borrowing any kind of submarine. Having suffered more from submarine attack than any other nation, Britain wanted world-wide abolition of the vessels, but was unsuccessful in that advocacy and proceeded with development of her own submarine war fleet of E, M and R class vessels in the 1930s.

The relatively new threat posed by the submarine propelled the early development of anti-submarine countermeasures. The British scored the first significant breakthrough in the area with their 1917 invention of the sonar detection apparatus. They called it ASDIC, after the Allied Submarine Detection Investigation Committee, under whose auspices it had been originated. The device transmitted a narrow beam of sound waves which traveled great distances through water, at four times the speed at which they pass through the air, to sweep around the target vessel. These sound waves produced an echo return from any object in their path, the range of which could then be calculated from the time interval between the emission of the pulse and its return to the receiver. Asdic provided a good basic indicator of the range and heading of a submerged U-boat up to a distance of about three miles, but only a rough indication of depth. Other limitations stemmed from the beam being directed at an angle, making the result relatively unreliable at short distances. Also, the Asdic operator had to be sufficiently skilled to differentiate between the echo return from an actual U-boat and from various other responses including those caused by ocean debris, fish, plankton, rough water, and even by sea layers of different temperatures.

One of the first items on Adolf Hitler's agenda after assuming power in Germany during 1933 was the secret resumption of U-boat design and construction which he ordered the following year. In March 1935, he openly repudiated the WWI Treaty of Versailles. Sentiment in some British circles was that the terms of the treaty had been unduly harsh, and a new accord, the Anglo-German Naval Agreement of 1935, was made, under which Germany was permitted to rebuild her navy to a strength not to exceed thirty-five percent of that of the Royal Navy (forty-five percent re submarines, a ratio later extended to 100 percent).

By that time, the Germans had six U-boats commissioned and many more on the way. As German encroachment on the Saar, the Rhineland, Austria, the Sudetenland, and Poland loomed, the purge of German Jewry was proceeding—a brutal, self-destructive programme that, with its subsequent exodus of intellectuals and scientists, was to cost the Third Reich dearly.

In years of development and evolution, the fundamental design of the U-boat barely changed from the familiar long, tubular shape formed by a steel outer casing containing the ballast and the saddle fuel tanks. The inner pressure hull, three-quarters of an inch thick, held the engines, the batteries, the control room, the torpedoes, the crew accommodation, and the working areas. The ballast tanks could be either emptied under pressure from an air compressor when the boat was to surface, or flooded with sea-water to submerge and control its depth. As the diesel fuel oil was consumed, sea-water could be let in through the bottom of the fuel tanks, both to reduce buoyancy when the boat was submerged and to prevent the tanks from collapsing under pressure when it went deep.

Steering was through conventional stern rudders, and the attitude was controlled by pairs of hydroplanes mounted fore and aft. The control room was amidships, with a hatch above it giving access to the conning tower and bridge.

The diesel engine-room was abaft the galley, with an array of valves and switches, levers and turn-wheels, tubing, cranks, and gauges. The relatively silent electric motors were located in the stern, their batteries' life was long enough to keep the boat in motion underwater at an economic speed for about twelve hours; then, until the advent of the snorkel air pipes, the boat had to be surfaced to recharge the batteries with the diesels.

The main weapons were torpedoes, each weighing a ton and a half, and launched through tubes in the bow and the stern. Mines could be carried in addition to, or instead of torpedoes, and were discharged in the same way. Pairs of anti-aircraft Oerlikon machine guns were mounted on the afterdeck, and the bigger ocean-going boats were also armed with 88- or 105mm cannon forward of the conning tower.

Formidable as the U-boat was, it had some fundamental weaknesses as a fighting vessel. The small surface area of the rudders—and the screws being close together—tended to make the turning circle wide; it had a comparatively low speed and limited defences, was highly vulnerable to counter-attack, and its range of action was greatly restricted when submerged. Below fourteen metres—the full length of the periscope—the U-boat was entirely blind, and dependent on sound-locating hydrophones for an indication of its enemy's location.

Another operational shortcoming was that the range of vision from the boat's bridge was much less than from that of a surface warship or, indeed, a merchantman. Some interesting efforts were made to improve on this, including posting a look-out in a bos'n's chair lashed to the top of the attack periscope. Another was to "fly" the look-out in an autogiro-like device called a Bachstelze or water-stilt, on a length of cable.

On the plus side, the U-boat was fundamentally seaworthy. It had a low frontal silhouette, making it difficult to spot. It was able to achieve surprise—a basic principle of warfare—and, alone among warships, it could hide. This last advantage was, however, offset to an extent by the extraordinary added weight of the electric motors and fifty-ton batteries required to propel it when submerged.

German engineering professor Helmuth Walther, had been working on a way to produce steam for a turbine engine from a heated mix of hydrogen peroxide and oil since 1937, but despite pressure from Admiral Dönitz for an accelerated construction programme, it was several years before the Walther engine entered production. By VE-Day only four of the engines had been completed. Until then, two propulsion systems were always required.

Obviously, submarines were designed and intended to operate under water, but for the half century of their operational history they traveled and fought mostly on the surface. In fact, until the 1940s, they seldom dove deeper than their own length. Sonar detectors and depth charges were then much less effective then they later became. Before the more advanced development of ship- and airborne radars, U-boats were forced to dive more often and to stay down longer. Then the advent of the snorkel made it possible to run the diesel engines at a depth where only the mastheads were detectable by radar or visually.

Designed as a simple wind scoop to provide a submarine with ventilation when it was submerged, the snorkel, or "snort", as the U-boat crews called it, was a Dutch invention. An example was acquired by the Germans when they occupied Holland, and they soon exploited it for war use. They adapted the ventilator tube to bring air to the engines and added a longer tube to serve as an exhaust, raising and lowering the tubes, initially with a winch and later by hydraulic pressure. In theory, a U-boat had no need to surface throughout a patrol, and one boat actually established a record remaining submerged for sixty-six days. But there were problems. The exhaust tube spray was visible for miles, compromising the submarine's location, and in a heavy swell the water pressure could block the outlet and cause an accumulation of carbon monoxide in the engine room. When sea water covered the induction tube, a float valve automatically closed it causing the diesel engines to suck the air out of the boat, leaving none for the crew.

In a submarine, the weight distribution of fuel, weapons, stores and provisions was crucial to stability. Submarines have a greater tendency to roll than surface vessels. A load of iron bars in the keel virtually guaranteed that the centre of gravity was low. No matter what forces were applied to it, either by nature or enemy action, no U-boat was ever known to have capsized. One of the Royal Navy's top U-boat killers, Captain Donald MacIntyre, once set the bows of HMS *Hesperus* against the beam of *U-223* and put on speed. The submarine rolled over, righted itself and was back in Saint Nazaire, only slightly damaged twelve days later.

While on the surface, U-boats were more stable in the longitudinal plane than in the lateral, and vice versa when submerged. To maintain the trim—the boat's balance in the water—the levels in the trim tanks and the movement of the crew were rigidly controlled. The Chief Engineer even required a daily report from the cook about the disposition of the food on board. A "stopped trim" was the most difficult to achieve, but if the Chief got it absolutely right, a pencil that was lying athwartships on the navigator's table would stay exactly where it had been placed.

U-boats were built around the torpedoes, engines, diesel tanks and batteries. The remaining space was for the crew, their kit and the provisions and was always at a premium. Every officer and rating had his own tiny share of it for working and sleeping. All left over space was used for storing food—carefully packed according to its shelf-life. Fresh food would always be consumed first, followed by tinned and dried commodities. Huge smoked hams and strings of sausages—growing more disgusting with mold by the day—hung over every deck; lockers intended for personal possessions were crammed with cans and packages of food. Men who liked eggs never needed to stint themselves: there were always enough to be eaten raw, boiled, scrambled or fried, with, before, and after every meal. A U-boat man was fed with more and better rations, albeit in less comfort, than any other member of the German armed forces in World War Two.

On an operational patrol at sea the environment in a U-boat quickly became nearly intolerable—noisy, damp with condensation, reeking of diesel oil, galley fumes, sweat and human waste. The crew slept in folding cots fitted to the bulkheads and the walls and in the torpedo rooms, with only enough cots for half the complement to sleep at any time—the other half took over "hot bunks" when they came off watch. Water was reserved for drinking and cooking. And personal hygiene was never a priority.

On 3 September 1939, Grossadmiral Erich Raeder signalled to his Kriegsmarine officers "Britain has declared war and we have no alternative. Total engagement. Die bravely." The British Admiralty's order to all Royal Navy ships carried the same import but without the melodrama: "Commence hostilities at once with Germany."

FISH, EELS, AND MIXERS

The silent torpedo was the primary weapon at sea in both world wars. Torpedoes were known as "fish" in the Royal Navy, while the men of the Kriegsmarine called them "eels". The German technicians who loaded and serviced them were called "mixers."

The first prototype torpedoes were developed in 1870. They had a fourteen-inch diameter, an eighteen-pound explosive charge and were able to run for about 200 yards at a speed of six knots. In 1872 English engineer Robert Whitehead perfected an improved torpedo with a charge four times greater than that of its predecessor. It had gyroscopic stabilization and a range of 1,000 yards. Torpedo development continued through and after World War One and the technology had advanced considerably by the beginning of World War Two, when the weapon had become much more than a sea bomb . . . a vessel in itself. Launched by compressed air, it had rudders and hydroplanes, a guidance system, propulsive power, and it could travel at a speed of forty knots.

But torpedoes then were less than predictable and at times erratic and prone to occasional misbehaviour. The torpedoes launched by U-boats in 1939 and the early 1940s were prone to other and more serious defects, as was shown in a report radioed to U-boat headquarters in Wilhelmshaven by Kapitänleutnant Günther Prien, patrolling off the coast of Norway in *U-47* on 16 April 1940.

"2242 hours, fired four torpedoes. Shortest range 750 yards, longest range 1,500 yards. Depth setting for torpedoes—12 to 15 feet. Ships stretched in a solid wall before me. Result nil. Enemy not alerted. Reloaded. Delivered second attack, on surface, after midnight. Fire control data precise. Thorough inspection of all adjustments by Captain and First Lieutenant. Four torpedoes. Depth setting as for first attack. No success. One torpedo off course exploded against cliff . . ." There were many similar reports from U-boat commanders, both of premature explosions and of failures to explode at all. At the time, all available U-boats were deployed in support of the Wehrmacht's Operation Weser, whose aims were to occupy Denmark and, subsequently, to drive the British Army out of Norway. But the Ubootwaffe had failed to sink a single ship in the region. With such extensive weapons failure, Dönitz elected to withdraw his boats pending an investigation of the torpedo faults. Two months later the British Army withdrew from Norway, with a far greater impact on the outcome of the war, for it resulted in the resignation of the British Prime Minister Neville Chamberlain and his replacement by Winston Churchill.

The torpedoes at fault were twenty-five feet long, weighing 3,000 pounds, with an 800-pound high-explosive charge that was detonated on impact by a firing pistol in the nose. The engine was driven by a compressed air tank aft of the warhead, which in turn sent power through a gearbox in the stern to turn two contra-rotating propellers (the two-way rotation countered the weapon's tendency to spin). The other components of the mechanism—the gyroscope and the balance chamber—were between the engine and the gears.

While most submarine commanders preferred to be within a mile of the target when they fired, the torpedoes could be launched at a range of three miles. The lower limit, as recommended in the manuals then, was 300 metres—about a thousand feet. The course, speed and range, as observed by the Commander or the 1st Officer, whichever was at the master sight on the bridge, was passed through the Torpedo Bearing Transmitter (TBT) and integrated with the U-boat's own course and speed by a high-speed electronic calculator and was then automatically fed into the weapon's guidance system. Pointing the U-boat at the target was not necessary. Having been fed all the targetting data, the torpedo steered itself.

On command the torpedo tubes were flooded, the aiming officer set the master sight's cross hairs on the target and the calculator's warning lights indicated that it was doing the sums. The red lights went out, the white "ready" light came on and firing could start. Keeping the cross hairs on the target, the aiming officer called "Fire!" and pressed the button. As the torpedo left the tube, the U-boat jolted slightly, and the hydrophone operator, listening on his headphones, reported "torpedo running". The appropriate trim tank, bow or stern was then flooded to replace the weapon's weight and maintain the boat's trim. The mixers stood ready in the torpedo rooms with chains and trolleys to reload the tubes on the aiming officer's command. If the aim had been true, they would shortly hear the thump of the detonation, followed by explosions and the sounds of metal rending as the target ship went down. Most U-boat crewmen never saw their target.

In its tube a torpedo was safe until it had been armed. The charge would not detonate until the spinner in the nose brought the firing pin in line with the percussion cap. Korvettenkapitän Prien and his colleagues sometimes experienced problems with the contact pistols on their torpedos, even the latest version of which had some inherent faults: not only was the operation of the device peculiarly complicated, the explosive charge would sometimes fail to fire if the torpedo struck the target at an acute angle—which it sometimes did.

Using the target vessel's field of magnetism to activate the firing mechanism, when launching a torpedo designed for magnetic detonation, the depth setting on the torpedo computer was less crucial than with impact detonation, due to an explosion underneath the hull being as effective as a hit below the water line—usually enough to break a ship in two. But even with magnetic torpedoes the results could be unpredictable. On 14 September 1939, in the grey North Atlantic, three magnetic torpedoes fired at the British aircraft carrier *Ark Royal* from *U-39* exploded prematurely. The carrier's destroyer escort, guided by the water plumes of the explosions, found and sank the U-boat—the first to go down in World War Two. About two years later, though, *Ark Royal* herself went down in the western Mediterranean off Gibraltar—when struck by a magnetic torpedo fired from the submarine *U-81*.

In fact, U-boats using magnetic torpedoes in the Norway campaign were no more successful than those employing contact detonation. When asked about this, the German Torpedo Inspectorate claimed that the magnets were being affected by the pull of the North Pole, or by the heavy loads of iron ore in the Norwegian mountains, or maybe both. One or both of these influences may have had an effect, but the more likely cause of the magnetic pistol failures was the de-magnetizing process, "de-gaussing" or "wiping", which had been applied to many British ships as a protection against magnetic mines. Dönitz then ordered his commanders to use contact pistols.

Torpedo troubles continued for the men of the Ubootwaffe. Another problem related to faulty operation of the weapon's balance chamber, which controlled the crucial running depth by means of a hydrostatic valve. While designed to be airtight, the chamber was not, and the torpedoes—which caused the greatest damage when they hit the hull as low as possible—were frequently hitting too high or too low, or passing several feet below the keel and doing no harm at all. The problem frustrated the U-boat crews for two years, and Dönitz was extremely displeased. He believed that the trouble lay with the Torpedo Experimental Institute, whose staff, he later wrote, "adopted an uncritical attitude towards their own achievements." Grossadmiral Raeder, on being told of the situation, ordered an inquiry that concluded that over thirty-four percent of the unsuccessful torpedo launches were due to weapon failure. These findings led to the court martials of four senior members of the Institute's staff.

The continuing evolution of the weapon led next to replacement of the compressed air bottle with an electric motor, powered by a battery. Though these "E-torpedoes" needed much more maintenance than the air-driven "A-torpedoes", they did not leave a trail of luminescent bubbles in the water—which could alert the master of a merchant ship to take evasive action or guide an escorting warship to their source.

When making an attack, commanders were encouraged not to think in terms of economy (by the torpedo section of the Kriegsmarine U-boat Manual). When attacking a worthwhile target, they were instructed to fire a salvo, even at close range, to be sure of hitting the target. If the range was above a thousand yards, they were told to fire a "fan" of three or four torpedoes. The experienced commanders, however, employed the methods that they found worked the best for them: some always fired a salvo, others were more frugal. The motto of Otto Kretschmer, the highest-scoring ship-killer by any measure, was "One torpedo, one ship down".

Admiral Dönitz was deeply concerned about the torpedo failures that some commanders continued to report. According to his analysis, of 816 Allied ships attacked and hit by torpedoes between January and June 1942, forty percent went down after one hit, and a further thirty-eight percent needed two or more, but twenty-two percent continued sailing after being hit by up to four torpedoes. More modifications were urgently ordered and, by the end of 1942, the depth control mechanism had been redesigned and a new magnetic pistol had been introduced that would also fire the charge on impact. By late August 1943, an acoustic guidance system had been developed for the T-5 torpedo, known as the "Gnat" to the Allies and Zaunkönig "Wren" to the U-boat force. This required less accuracy in determining the aiming angle because, once fired into the target area, the acoustic homer steered towards the loudest sound. But, if the range happened to be incorrectly set, a Gnat might settle for the sound of it's launcher's own propellers and come back like a boomerang. At least two U-boats were believed to have been sunk by their own returning Gnats.

The FAT (*Flachenabsuchender Apparat* Torpedo) and the LUT (*Lagenuabhängiger*) became available in late 1942. These were surface-running weapons programmed to travel for the entire range before turning onto the target vessel's course. They would then weave to and fro until they either scored a hit or ran out of power. This development was intended to overcome the problems associated with accurate aiming in rolling ocean waters, and to cut down the aiming time, since every moment on a steady course with the periscope in view worked to the advantage of the prowling Allied escort ships. Although tactically sensible, this hit-or-miss idea would have been scorned by such marksmen as Kretschmer, Prien, and Schepke. By then, though, they were no longer in the hunt.

Whatever their type or model, the torpedoes all needed regular and frequent attention. Every few days the long, grease-smeared monsters were hauled out of their tubes by chains, pulleys, hoists, and the muscles of the boat's mixers, for all of their systems to be checked—batteries or air bottles, engines and gearboxes, hydroplanes and rudders, gyroscopes and firing pins.

As German scientists and engineers struggled to improve the U-boat arm's torpedoes, boffins in Britain, and later in America, were hard at the task of developing new countermeasures for use in the Allied warships and maritime aircraft. The main anti-submarine weapon had always been the depth-charge and would remain so. Depth-charges from ships or aircraft would account for more than forty-two percent of all U-boat sinkings, but those in use at the beginning of the war were just as antiquated as the early torpedoes of the U-boat arm, and the method of delivery—being dropped through chutes in the warship's stern—had never been changed. The new ship-launched weapons, however, were designed to be thrown instead of dropped, and to reach the target area before asdic contact was lost.

The "Hedgehog", a multi-barrelled mortar that fired a salvo of twenty-four "water bombs" in a circular pattern of about 130 feet in diameter ahead of the target on its estimated course, was the first depth-charge launcher to be used in action in 1941. Its mounting was manually adjustable to allow for the rolling of the ship. Its bombs, each with a thirty-two-pound charge of Torpex—a new explosive powerful enough to crack a U-boat's hull at a range of twenty-five feet—were designed to sink quickly and detonate on impact. Asdic contact was only broken if the weapon hit—when it no longer mattered. The Hedgehog's rate of kill steadily increased to twenty-eight percent by 1944—nearly five times better than the rate achieved by dropping weapons from the stern.

After Hedgehog came "Squid", a weapon that entered service in 1943 as a complement to Hedgehog. Squid was a three-barrelled mortar that fired three full-sized depth-charges, time-fused and aimed to explode in a triangular pattern around the target. While Hedgehog's contact fuses meant that near-misses did not detonate and so caused no damage to the U-boat nor consternation to the crew, a hit by one of Squid's 300-pound explosive charges would destroy the U-boat. A near miss would be enough to force it to the surface, where the warship's guns would finish it off.

Later still, a proven minesweeper instrument for combating acoustic mines was adapted to counter the acoustic torpedo. Housing a small but very noisy engine which sounded like a pneumatic drill, the "Foxer" was mounted in a dinghy and towed astern, to attract the torpedo's sonar sensor.

The skill, courage and stamina of the opposing combatants would still play their part—man versus man, U-boat versus warship—but in the Atlantic Ocean they would not decide the outcome of the battle. That was to be waged between the offensive and defensive technological devices, sonar senders and receivers, radar searchers and detectors, magnetic guidance and demagnetizers, acoustic sensors and bafflers. It was a fight to be decided by men and women in design offices and factories, and there the Allies always held the upper hand.

THE GOODS

It has always been a primary task of the Royal Navy to keep Britain's sea lanes open. She has never been a self-supporting nation, always requiring a huge volume of imports for her survival. In the 1930s, at least a third of her food, including wheat, butter, cheese, and meat, was obtained and shipped in from overseas sources. Her farmers relied on imported fertilizers. The bulk of her timber and steel came from North America and many of her other essential materials were imported by sea from all over the globe. She bought iron ore from Norway and Africa, cotton from the Americas, Egypt and India, wool from Australasia, nitrates from South America, rubber from Malaya, zinc and lead from North America and Australia, and oil from the United States and the Dutch West Indies. It required more than 3,000 merchant vessels—freighters and tankers—to bring the more than 4 million tons of these resources to Britain each month during the Second World War.

Germany's U-boats had come close to bringing the British to the brink of starvation in World War One and would have done so if not for the enormous efforts of the Royal Navy, with magnificent assistance from Commonwealth and Empire nations and from the United States. Karl Dönitz had participated in that campaign and vowed to do better the next time around. The main target for Germany's U-boat arm the next time would be the Allied merchant shipping plying the Atlantic routes, without which the British could neither eat, run their industries, nor continue the fight. Laden or empty, those ships would have to be sunk.

At the outbreak of World War Two, the strength and the power of the Royal Navy was not what it had been two decades earlier—the policy of disarmament in the 1930s saw to that—but it was still a match for any other navy and formidable enough to deter the Germans from the sort of set-piece sea battles that the older admirals still saw as the only proper way to fight a war. Grossadmiral Erich Raeder, though, was forced to agree that the primary target for the Kriegsmarine had to be British imports from wherever they might be coming.

Even with the toll taken of Allied merchant shipping by Germany's U-boats in World War One, the Royal Navy seemed to have forgotten most of the lessons of that conflict. The First Sea Lord, for example, considered that the next major threat would come from German surface warships. Even his superior, Winston Churchill, as First Lord of the

Admiralty, said that the U-boats' early successes "need not cause any undue despondency or alarm". The requirement for organised convoys, with naval protection, as practiced by Britain since the 14th century, and as demanded by Churchill himself in the early days of World War One for ships carrying troops and freight from Australasia to Europe, was largely ignored when World War Two began.

As soon as it was detected, a slow merchant ship sailing alone, was always going to be easy pickings, while ships in convoy could offer at least some sort of mutual protection. The best pace of a convoy though, was always limited to the speed of the slowest vessel in it, and convoys were slow and difficult to manage in situations requiring evasive action. Convoys needed escorts—warships to protect them and to discourage and deal with attackers. This posed a particular problem for the Royal Navy, which did not have enough suitable vessels or trained crews to undertake the vitally needed escort duties.

Air cover to hunt down and destroy enemy surface warships threatening the convoys was another problem. The R.A.F. was stretched virtually to capacity in both the defence of Britain from German invasion and in trying to take the war to Germany, albeit with bombers near to obsolescence. Furthermore, the degree of co-operation between the Navy and the Air Force at the time was not what it might have been; it would be two long years before they would fully co-operate in protecting merchant shipping. In the early days, the Navy's Fleet Air Arm flew many sorties against German surface ships, taking off in single-engined Fairey Swordfish biplanes from flight decks grafted onto freighters. Their navigation was by compass, rule and sextant, and their aircraft lacked the range, armament and the effective search radar to locate and attack the U-boats.

Once formed, the so-called "fast convoys" were certainly not fast; and the slow convoys were very slow indeed. A fast convoy's passage from North America to one of Britain's northwest ports was normally more than fifteen days at an average speed of nine knots; the slower vessels took fully four or five days more. Once Hitler's fellow fascist Benito Mussolini's navy began to threaten the Mediterranean, shipping from the east had to sail the long route around the Cape of Good Hope into the Atlantic, and a passage time of many weeks.

Operating the convoys was never easy. There were the difficulties in assembling the freighters and tankers at the departure ports, fueling and provisioning them, seeing that they sailed together, remained in proper position and maintained communication. At most of the ports of destination, installations, facilities and procedures were set up for the regular day-to-day arrival of individual cargo ships for berthing and unloading; not for the reception of thirty or forty such vessels at a time. None of this, of course, was of any concern to those in command of the U-boats, whose only interest was in locating the convoy vessels, torpedoing them, and leaving them and their cargoes on the bottom of the cruel sea.

"Undoubtedly the greatest strains of the war at sea fell on the shoulders of the masters and deck officers of the tramp ships. Their charges were slow and manoeuvred like the lumbering barges they were. Station-keeping in convoy was for these men an unending ordeal. On a dark, moonless night it required nerves of steel and the eyes of a cat; in poor visibility or stormy weather it was an impossibility. They straggled, they romped and they veered, becoming the easiest of targets for the stalking U-boats. The men in the engine-room suffered the tortures of the damned, never knowing when a torpedo might tear through the thin plates of the hull, sending their ship plunging to the bottom before they had a chance to reach the first rung of the ladder to the deck. Burdened, as they so often were, with heavy bulk cargoes, the tramps sank like punctured tin cans filled with lead shot. For those who took to the life-boats or rafts, the process of dying was more prolonged. Lacking protection from the sun and storms, and striving to exist on rations measured in ounces per day, many eventually succumbed to exposure, starvation, thirst or sheer mental exhaustion."
—from *The Merchant Navy Goes To War*, by Bernard Edwards

In Britain, at the Submarine Tracking Room of the Admiralty, U-boat positions, as indicated by the various contributing sources—radio intercepts, reports from secret agents in enemy bases, air and sea sightings—were all carefully plotted and the convoys accordingly rerouted or diverted. In those early days of the Atlantic war, there was always a shortage of escort ships and long-range aircraft, and in the mid-Atlantic gap between fifteen and twenty degrees west, called "the graveyard" by the Allied merchant seamen and the "black pit" by the men of the Ubootwaffe, the main defence against the U-boats was the lightweight armament of the cargo ships themselves.

Never an easy existence, the routine of the merchant seamen; they had to get used meals of corned beef and hard tack, catch a few hours' sleep between their watches, if they were lucky, and live with the impossibility of ever being dry. In wartime, though, there was the threat of being torpedoed, mined, and machine-gunned a thousand miles from land.

Their worst, most frightening time came in the summer and autumn of 1940—the period that came to be known in the Ubootwaffe as die *glückliche Zeit*. It was at the height of this 'happy time' on Saturday, 5 October, that convoy SC7 sailed from Sydney, Cape Breton Island, Nova Scotia, en route for the Clyde. The convoy was the seventh of the slower convoys—those with a speed of only six knots. It was made up of thirty-five ships, including three steamers that had been designed for sailing on the Great Lakes in America, along with various vessels re-claimed from scrapyards. Most of the ships were British, while some were from neutral Sweden, Norway, and Greece. They were carrying cargoes of steel, timber, oil, grain, sulphur, and iron ore, and were escorted by a single 1,000-ton Royal Navy sloop, HMS *Scarborough*, whose armament was depth-charges and two four-inch guns. For the first two days the convoy would also be accompanied by a seaplane and an armed yacht.

The convoy commodore was Vice-Admiral Lachlan MacKinnon, Royal Navy Reserve, sailing in the Liverpool-based cargo ship *Assyrian*. The convoy formation covered five square miles and was made up of three five-ship columns and five four-ship columns, the longer columns in the centre. Most of the tankers were in the middle ranks where it was believed they were less likely to be attacked.

The lake steamers and two of the Greek ships had vanished from the convoy in the early hours of the sixth day at sea. Five days later One of the lake ships, the steamer *Trevisa*, turned up some twenty-seven miles behind the convoy. *Trevisa* was sighted, quickly torpedoed and sunk by Kapitänleutnant Wilhelm Schultze in command of *U-124*. Fortunately, the destroyer HMS *Keppel* arrived in time to rescue all but six of the *Trevisa* crew members.

On the twelfth day out, as the merchant ships crawled past the south coast of Iceland, they were spotted by a bridge lookout of *U-48*, commanded by Korvettenkapitän Heinrich Bleichrodt, who immediately informed Dönitz at BdU in Lorient by short-wave radio. The admiral decided to muster six more U-boats that he knew could reach the convoy within the next twelve hours. They were: *U-46* commanded by Engelbert Endrass, *U-101* commanded by Fritz Frauenheim, *U-123* under the command of Karl-Heinz Mohle, the *U-38* of Heinrich Liebe, *U-100* commanded by Joachim Schepke, and *U-99* with Otto Kretschmer in command. He ordered the subs to assemble near the island of Rockall ahead of the convoy and await attack orders. In the middle of the night Bleichrodt elected to wait no longer. He sent three torpedoes, his targets being the freighters *Scoresby* and *Corinthic*, and the tanker *Languedoc*, sinking them all. His U-boat was then attacked by the escort *Scarborough* and by a Sunderland flying boat; he departed the immediate area, signalling BdU of his action.

By the evening of 18 October, all of the other six U-boats had arrived in the area of the convoy's track. The merchant ships were still in proper formation and were about to face the full fury of the *rudeltaktik* as envisaged by Dönitz. As well as the light of the full moon, the few escort vessels were firing starshells to further illuminate the area and, hopefully, help them find the U-boats which were now wreaking havoc with the merchant ships. The brightly lit sea displayed many masses of burning wreckage, palls of smoke, dozens of drifting lifeboats, and all of it in the orange glow of flaming oil slicks. In rapid succession, the timber and steel carrying *Beautus* out of Wales, victim of a torpedo from *U-46*, followed the Swedish pulp-wood-carrying *Convallaria* to the bottom, also felled by a weapon from the U-boat of commander Endrass. The next victim was *Creekirk*, her crew and iron ore cargo and, when the Dutch ship *Boekolo* came round to rescue survivors from *Beautus*, she was torpedoed and sunk. *Shekatika* met the same fate moments later, as did the largest vessel in the convoy, *Empress Miniver*.

Dönitz's wolfpack was hitting its stride, demolishing convoy SC7 at a breathtaking pace. The next vessel to fall was the steel-carrying *Fiscus*, torn to pieces in the continuing torpedo onslaught. Shortly after *Fiscus* exploded, the 1,500-ton Swedish pulp-wood carrier *Gunborg* was sent to the bottom. The crew of the Greek sulphur carrier *Niritos* came about in an effort to pick up victims from *Gunborg*, who waved them away, preferring to remain in their lifeboats. Their instincts proved correct a few moments later when a torpedo blew *Niritos* apart. In less than two hours the German wolfpack had attacked and sunk nine ships from the slow convoy.

Just after midnight the U-boats struck again. Fritz Frauenheim opened his account for the new day with a well-placed torpedo that sent the convoy flagship *Assyrian* and about half her crew down; her demise followed quickly by the apparent loss of *Blairspey*, torpedoed and abandoned at sea. Then, in rapid succession, a spectacular and fiery end came to the Norwegian timber carrier *Snefield*, the *Empire Brigade*, the British steamer *Sedgepool*, the Dutch tramp steamer *Soesterberg*, and the 10,000-ton Greek steel carrier *Thalia*. And the wolfpack subs weren't finished yet. The deck gun crew of the *Clintonia* fought a battle with two U-boats until she was torpedoed and then blown apart by the guns of the subs. With the dawn, just fifteen of SC7's merchant ships remained afloat and under way. Two of them were seriously damaged. None of the U-boats had incurred significant damage.

The convoy escort vessel *Leith* had picked up many merchant sailor survivors of the attacks and her surgeon worked tirelessly trying to save the lives of the worst affected among them. A few days later the ocean rescue tug *Salvonia* located and towed *Blairspey* to the safe harbour of Gourock. *Leith* took her load of survivors to Liverpool where they received medical treatment and were billeted. The arrivals were kept awake that first night by German bombers hitting the city in a lengthy night raid. Ironically, while the merchant sailor officers of the convoy ships that had been sunk continued to receive their pay, the merchant seamen did not, having been struck off the payroll when their ships were sunk.

Now another convoy, HX79 out of Halifax, was entering the Western Approaches. This convoy comprised forty-nine cargo vessels, and two armed merchant cruisers. They were accompanied by a Dutch submarine keeping station in the centre of the formation and the 5,000-ton rescue ship *Loch Lomond*. When the formation was within the Western Approaches, it was joined by four corvettes, a minesweeper, three anti-submarine trawlers, and the destroyers *Sturdy* and *Whitehall*. The wolf-pack of Admiral Dönitz was waiting for them as well.

Günther Prien joined the hunt in *U-47* and was the first commander to locate convoy HX79. He contacted the other U-boats of the pack, and those that still had torpedoes rallied in the evening of the 19th. Liebe sighted and sank the British steamer *Matheran* first, and the other subs soon attacked and disposed of two freighters and the oil tanker *Shirak*. Thirty-seven of *Shirak*'s crew were rescued by the trawler *Blackfly*. The next victim of the wolfpack attackers was the tanker *Caprella*, bisected by the strike of a torpedo. Prien then spent one of his last torpedoes on the motorship *Wandby*, which flooded and was abandoned with her timber and pig-iron cargo.

In a heroic effort to save the torpedoed and stricken tanker *Sitala*, which had been attacked by Schepke but was still afloat and apparently seaworthy, a group of engineers from the *Wandby* boarded *Sitala*. During the night, though, the tanker's bow plates failed and the engineers were promptly rescued by the armed trawler *Angle*. A further steel carrier, the 8,000-ton *Whitford Point*, received a torpedo hit that sank her, taking all but two of her crew to the bottom. In the early morning of the 20th, the final casualty of the attacks was the rescue vessel *Loch Lomond*, torpedoed and sunk at 7:25 am. Her crew and the merchant sailors she had saved were themselves saved by the minesweeper *Jason*.

In the action, thirteen ships of HX79 were attacked and sunk. Commanders Endrass and Schepke had each claimed three. The escort contingent of the convoy, while substantial, had been largely ineffectual for a number of reasons: there had been no standard briefing of the captains prior to sailing on the operation, the senior naval officer present had had no Atlantic escort duty experience, and the corvettes had sailed straight from the shipyard, their crews utterly inexperienced. The convoy ships had mostly been attacked by U-boats on the surface, rendering the Asdic echos ineffective, as were the depth- charges employed against the submarines. Inter-ship communications between the merchant vessels had depended upon loudhailers, signal lamps and flags. They had no radar and no means of listening to the radio communications of the U-boats. Thus, teamwork among the escorts and the merchant ships had been all but impossible. According to Paul Lund and Harry Ludlam in *Night of the U-boats*, "It was a story of inadequacy, unpreparedness and grim endurance on the part of the British, and cool, rewarding enterprise by the Germans . . ."

As the U-boats of that wolfpack did their business that night, yet another convoy was outbound from Britain and was attacked by U-boats that sank seven of its vessels. Their loss brought the total number of Allied merchant ships sunk in the past three days to thirty-eight . . . a thundering vindication of Admiral Dönitz's rudeltaktik and a bitter pill for those in London's Whitehall forced to reassess their thinking, planning, organisation, equipment, and tactics . . . a reappraisal too late to help the sailors of the merchant ship convoys that year. As one merchant ship master said, "Unless we get protection, we shan't find men to crew our ships."

Having refined the WWI concept of the wolfpack tactic to his satisfaction as a way to beat the Allied convoys, Karl Dönitz chose to experiment with the first field trial of the technique in June 1940. His notion was to assemble U-boats in patrol lines to hunt for convoys. When a convoy was sighted, the boat of the crew sighting the Allied ships would be assigned to follow the convoy, reporting its speed and heading to

Dönitz in Kernéval at BdU. Aware of the U-boats' positions each day, the admiral was then able to co-ordinate a wolfpack operation against the convoy by directing the nearby U-boats to form around the convoy, attacking with as many boats as possible during the night in an effort to overwhelm the convoy escort ships. In 1940, however, Dönitz lacked a sufficient number of U-boats in his command to establish the sizeable patrol lines he required, so the early wolfpack warfare had to be largely fought by small ad hoc groups of U-boats which produced the most successes when some among them were commanded by the higher achievers of the Ubootwaffe, men like Kretschmer, Schepke, and Prien.

In the spring of 1941 the number of operational U-boats available at sea to the admiral was great enough to enable him to establish the sort of patrol lines he needed. But, on 9 May the British captured an Enigma coding cipher machine and all of its accompanying documentation, when the corvette *Aubretia*, while escorting convoy OB 318 off the coast of Iceland, found and depth-charged the U-boat *U-110*, forcing the submarine to surface. The British B-class destroyer HMS *Bulldog* then approached and fired on *U-110*. The submarine's crew abandoned her in the belief that she was sinking. At that point, Sub-Lieutenant David Balme of *Bulldog* led a boarding party into the submarine, locating and removing the Enigma items, which were later turned over to personnel at the Bletchley Park facility in England where the German naval codes were eventually broken. The British Admiralty was thereafter provided with the Ultra message intercepts about German employment of the wolfpack tactic and were then able to re-route convoys around the known patrol lines.

With America's entry in the war in December 1941, the U-boat operations against the Allied convoys in the North Atlantic were restricted as Dönitz turned his primary attention to patrols off the U.S. east coast. Emphasis on wolfpack attacks in the Arctic Ocean against convoy ships on the Murmansk Run were continuing and would be pressed until the end of the war. The admiral resumed Atlantic wolfpack operations by mid-year 1942, his efforts producing big results until May 1943 when his boats were suffering very heavy losses and he had to withdraw them.

In the course of the war, Dönitz assembled and fielded nearly 250 wolfpack groups. The operations generally lasted a few days, but some continued for as much as a few months. In numbers these groups ranged from three or four boats to as many as twenty in the largest groups.

A newly developed technology, HF / DF, or "Huff Duff" as it was known, was proving to be of considerable value to the Allies, detecting

U-boats and commerce raiders during the Battle of the Atlantic. With a contact report, the first U-boat sighting a convoy (and then assigned to shadow the merchant ships) was then frequently located by the HF / DF system and quickly chased away by the convoy-escorting aircraft or warships. When wolfpack operations were resumed, the U-boats had been equipped with the new Gnat homing torpedoes, radar detection systems, and heavier anti-aircraft armament. Still, losses among the U-boat force were high and such operations had to be halted in the North Atlantic in March 1944, pending the arrival of the new Type XXI U-boats. As the situation worsened for the Dönitz' boats, he experienced gaps in his wolfpack patrol lines. Due to a policy of maintaining radio silence, notification of the loss of one or more submarines in a patrol line was sometimes days or even weeks late getting to the admiral at BdU.

(Action This Day)
City of Calcutta, due Lock Ewe March 2, is reported to be going to Hull arriving March 9. This ship must on no account be sent to the East Coast. It contains 1,700 machine guns, forty-four aeroplane engines, and no fewer than 14,000,000 cartridges. These cartridges are absolutely vital to the defence of Great Britain, which has been so largely confided by the Navy to the Army and the Air. That it should be proposed to send such a ship round to the East Coast, with all the additional risk, is abominable. I am sending a copy of this minute to the Minister of Transport. Another ship now of great importance is the *Euriades*, due Liverpool March 3. She has over 9,000,000 cartridges. I shall be glad to receive special reports as to what will be done about both these ships. —Prime Minister to First Lord and First Sea Lord 28.11.41, from: *The Second World War: The Grand Alliance*, by Winston S. Churchill

In November 1942 things began to change for the Allies with the appointment of Admiral Sir Max Horton to be Commander-in-Chief, Western Approaches. A high-achieving submariner of World War One, Admiral Horton had sunk the German cruiser *Hela* on 13 September 1914, the first enemy warship ever sunk by a Royal Navy submarine. Max Horton proved extremely effective in his game of bluff and double-bluff with Karl Dönitz, directing the merchant ship convoys along routes to avoid the attentions of the U-boats, as much as possible. In late May 1943, when Dönitz chose to withdraw his U-boats from the Atlantic following his most difficult and bitter winter, Horton signalled his ships,

"The tide of the battle has been checked, if not turned. The enemy is showing signs of strain in the face of the heavy attacks by our sea and air forces."

". . . and we only got two U-boats . . . two in five years. It seemed a lot at the time."
—from *The Cruel Sea*, by Nicholas Monsarrat

THE BOAT

"U-boats are those dastardly villains who sink our ships, while submarines are those gallant and noble craft which sink theirs."
—Prime Minister Winston S. Churchill

Three of every four German submariners died inside her. That was why she was known as "the iron coffin". With her sleek, shark-like fore end and her narrow tapered rear, she moved with an easy kind of grace and left those she didn't care for burning in her wake. She was the VIIC, by far the most numerous type of U-boat employed in her World War Two navy.

Some called her "the narrow drum", in reference to the tight confines of her long, slim hull, a space so slight and stingy that her crewmen seemed to spend half their time turning sideways to avoid one another when passing in the single aisle from her stem to her stern.

". . . her lines stood out . . . against the pale concrete wall above the low wharf. The casing was a bare metre clear of the oily surface. All the hatches were still open. The wooden planking which extended in one long forward sweep, flat and without sheer, to the bow; the conning tower and cumbersome-looking anti-aircraft armament, the slightly inclined stern, the steel cable and green china insulators of the jumping wire which ran down forward and aft of the conning tower. A picture of perfect simplicity: a VIIC U-boat, seaworthy as no other vessel afloat."
—from *Das Boot* by Lothar-Günther Buchheim

Her origins and heritage came from the UB III submarine of 1916 which operated in the First World War. Together with her sister ship, the Type IX, she reflected some of the qualities and characteristics of those First War submarines. Even with her greater range and ability to bring more torpedoes to where they were needed, and her improved armament though, the Type IX was subordinated by the VIIC, which did by far the lion's share of the work in the Atlantic battle against Allied merchant shipping convoys. More than 600 Type VIIC boats were built and they accounted for more than sixty percent of all the losses inflicted by German subs in World War Two. As one historian put it, she was "the most effective underwater fighting machine of all."

From the instant the commander ordered "Dive!", the VIIC could become entirely submerged in twenty seconds when operated by skilled personnel. According to the manual, the VIIC had an authorized safe diving depth of 100 metres or about 330 feet (later models of the Type VIIC were authorized for a maximum deep dive twenty-five metres deeper.)

Her dimensions measured 221 feet six inches in length, twenty feet six inches at her widest point, and she had a draught of fifteen feet. Her displacement was a svelte 769 tons. The Type IX, her more Rubinesque sister, displaced 1,120 tons and was thirty feet longer, and broader in the beam. Both types of boats were actually capable of going far deeper than the prescribed official safe limits, and did so on many occasions when avoidance of depth-charges left the crews no other recourse.

When cruising on the surface, the best speed the VIIC could make was eighteen knots, which was a shade slower than that of the Type IX, and somewhat slower than the Allied frigates and destroyers that often chased her. She was fast enough, however, to easily outrun the corvettes and sloops that accompanied most convoys as protective escorts. Progress underwater, though, was considerably slower, with an absolute top speed of just over seven knots, a match for most of the convoys she would chase. How far could she sail without refueling? 6,500 nautical miles was the normal range of the VIIC when carrying a typical fuel load of 113 tons of heavy diesel oil and running the two 1,400-hp engines economically at a ten-knot cruising speed. The range was cut considerably, however, if the boat was run for long periods at top speed. Underwater, running on electric power from the boat's huge and heavy batteries at only two knots, the range was reduced to a mere 180 nautical miles, and to just eighty nautical miles at a four-knot speed.

The Type VIIC first entered service near the end of the first "happy time". Equipped with four torpedo tubes in the bow and one in the stern, it could bring between eleven and fourteen torpedoes on a patrol, depending on the nature of the assignment and the range of the patrol. The Type IX boat had four tubes in the bow and two in the stern. It was capable of carrying up to twenty-two torpedoes. Other armament could vary, but normally included an 88mm gun in front of the conning tower, a 37mm and two 20mm anti-aircraft machine-guns mounted on the platform abaft the bridge, called the "Winter Garden" by the German crews. While this assortment of gunnery was sufficient for dealing with a merchant vessel or a low-flying aircraft, it did not stack up against the attentions of a corvette or a destroyer.

"The tiny, insignificant-looking submarines were being hurled high into the air by the mountainous swell, and then sent skidding down into the pits between the waves, where they would be covered by raging seas before emerging high on the crest of another wave, where they hesitated for a brief second while the water drained off them before plunging downwards again. Often they just drove through the waves, which broke over them in foaming torrents."
—from *The Golden Horseshoe* by Terence Robertson

The capability limits of the VIIC boats dictated their range of assignments basically to hunting patrols in the North Atlantic, the Baltic, Mediterranean and southward. The increased fuel capacity of the Type IX boats enabled them to roam far down the south Atlantic, off Africa and over to the Caribbean. In addition to duties on combat patrols, the IXs were sometimes used as supply ships, bringing fuel, ammunition, and provisions to other U-boats far at sea. The idea was to allow Type VII boats to remain on station in the area of a convoy for as long as deemed necessary. The presence of these "Milch Cow" boats to refuel and re-arm other subs in what were often lengthy and difficult transfers subjected both boats to potential attack by prowling Allied aircraft, for which they were sitting ducks.

The somewhat larger Type IX boat afforded a bit more crew space than that in the VIIC boat. The Type IX crews needed it as their patrols normally kept them at sea for as much as fourteen weeks. The Type VIIC crews were usually out for six to eight weeks. Still, there was no wasted space in either of the boat types. Food of various kinds was stowed, stuffed, or hung virtually everywhere.

The nerve centre of the VIIC was her control room. Twenty feet across and twenty-two feet long, the room sat beneath the conning tower and over the fuel and main water ballast tanks. It was amidships and was crowded with the myriad wheels, levers, knobs, switches, and gauges that guided her movements in all directions. It was there that the navigator plotted her course, and the boat commander directed her work and conducted her business. There the Papenberg depth gauge, the gyro and magnetic compasses, and the Zeiss attack periscope were housed. The combat centre was in the conning tower with the helm, the navigation periscope, the Siemans-Schukert torpedo computer which was linked to the bridge master sight and gyro compass as well as the fire-interval calculator. The helmsman could steer the boat from either the conning tower or the control room, turning the rudders by a pressure button. In emergency situations, he could steer the boat with a manual system in the electric motor room aft. U-boats had no windows. The helmsman always steered blind, maintaining and altering his course by the compass. Centrally located, the control room was separated from the fore and aft areas of the boat by heavy, concaved water-tight bulkheads.

A quick tour finds a crewman walking forward from the control room and immediately passing between the radio and sound rooms on the starboard side, and commander's tiny cubicle on the port. Next, he moves through the officers' quarters and the wardroom, past the twin lavatories, one of which is serving as an additional food store during the early days of a patrol. Then he enters the petty officers mess and on into the bow compartment or "bug-raum". This room is crammed with narrow cots on both sides and hammocks slung between them. The remaining space is occupied by reserve torpedoes chained above the cots and below the planks. Some of the crew dine on a folding table that can be set up in the centre of the room.

Our tour of the Type VIIC continues aft from the control room, through a combined utility room, the petty officers' quarters, past the small galley and the large air compressor, and into the electric motor room and the stern torpedo stowage area, and finally, into the diesel engine room, finishing with a look at the stern torpedo tube. Normally, ship's company in this boat was forty-four seamen, four commissioned officers—the commander, 1st and 2nd Officers, and the Chief Engineer—and ten Petty Officers whose responsibilities included the watches, engine rooms, electrics, the radio and control rooms. The crew comprised thirty technicians, torpedo men, engine room artificers, electricians, telegraphists, a coxswain, a quartermaster, and a cook. While the larger Type IX boats usually carried a qualified doctor, the Type VII crew had to make do with one of their number having qualified in first aid. The emergency equipment carried included inflatable life jackets, breathing tubes and masks, and a twenty-man rubber liferaft stowed in the outer hull forward of the bridge. There was certainly no room to swing a cat, as the saying goes, but the crew had to somehow make room to accommodate the occasional official observer, war correspondent, or recently-trained officer aboard to gain combat experience.

Strangely, one piece of extraordinarily unsophisticated kit found in the VIIC was a bulky wooden frame in the shape of a cross and containing a wire antenna which, in theory, could detect radar transmission pulses at a range of up to twenty miles. This crude device, known as the "Biscay Cross", was deck-mounted abaft the bridge and hand-turned by the telegraphist on his watch. When the man was able to distinguish those pulses from the other crackling noises in his headphones, he would be able to read off the bearing of the hunting enemy aircraft or ship. Functionally, the device had to be unmounted and brought inboard down through the conning tower when the boat was to be submerged. In an emergency crash-dive, it was likely that the device would be trampled under foot by the watch keepers as they hurried to get down the ladder and seal the hatch.

The Biscay Cross device was replaced on most U-boats during the summer of 1942, by the Metox, a radar detector that received signals in the short-wave bands. Metox, however, was suspected of having an undesirable side-effect. Submarine crews so-equipped were soon finding that their boats were attracting greater attention from enemy aircraft, indicating that the Metox system might be acting as a homing device. This appeared to be confirmed when a captured British airman stated under interrogation, ". . . we don't need radar to find you chaps; we can pick you up on radio." It was later discovered that the airman had lied—that the increased number of aircraft attacks on the U-boats was indeed due to Allied use of a new radar. Rumour and suspicion about Metox continued, however, and Dönitz ordered his crews to switch it off.

The drive to improve the performance and war capability of the U-boats continued in 1943 with the introduction of the snorkel, and of Bedbug, a new radar detector for the Type IX boats which was intended to replace Metox. Additionally, a system called Aphrodite was brought in which was a towed hydrogen balloon filled with strips of aluminium foil, similar to the "chaff" dropped by the Allied bombers to confuse enemy radar. But the attacks by Allied aircraft continued to increase in numbers and ferocity, as did the U-boat losses associated with them. No amount or kind of new technology seemed capable of changing this deadly trend.

LUSITANIA

To say that Americans were essentially isolationist when the First World War began, would understate. Clearly, a significant and catastrophic event would be required to shift public opinion in the United States and cause Americans to seriously consider entering that conflict. The incident that helped bring about that shift happened in May 1915 when the German submarine *U-20* encountered and sank the great 30,000-ton Cunard luxury liner RMS *Lusitania* as she sailed from New York to England.

From 1897, when Germany presented her newest ocean liner, the *Kaiser Wilhelm der Grosse*, everything changed on the Atlantic passenger run. Since 1840, the British had set the standard for fast, luxurious sea travel between England and the United States. In that year, the big British paddle steamer *Britannia* first sailed from Liverpool for New York and, for the balance of the century, Britain and Cunard maintained dominance on the Atlantic.

With the appearance of the new German liner, the British, who had always been a great sea power, were shoved aside. Not only were the Germans the new leader on the important Atlantic run, they were suddenly at the forefront of designing, building and introducing new, larger and more elegant liners over the next decade, assuring their continuing dominance in the field, while the British were simply unable to compete with the burgeoning German effort.

Britain's problem compounded when, in 1902, the American financier J. P Morgan began acquiring various transatlantic shipping lines including the Dominion Line, the American Line, the Red Star Line, the Holland-America Line, and the primary competitor of Cunard, the White Star Line. Soon, only Cunard, of all the major players in the ocean travel field, remained independent and out of Morgan's grasp, and he clearly wanted the British company.

Then, Lord Inverclyde, chairman of Cunard, had an idea about a way to right the situation for Britain. Opportunistically, Inverclyde planned to exploit British patriotism in that time of tight money and European political tension. He proposed an agreement to the British government, in which, if it would lend Cunard £2,600,000 at an interest rate of 2 3/4 percent, the money would be used to design and construct two magnificent new ocean liners, the *Lusitania* and *Mauretania*. Additionally, the government would be required to pay Cunard an annual subsidy of £150,000 to maintain the two liners in a condition allowing them to be adapted for naval use in time of war, and a further subsidy of £68,000 a year to carry mail. In return, Cunard would agree absolutely to remain a wholly-owned British company for the twenty-year duration of the agreement, resisting all efforts by Morgan to add the company to his holdings. Second, the two new liners would be available at any time for immediate takeover by the British Admiralty for war use. The government added some further requirements to the pact. Both ships were to be designed and built to accommodate the eventual fitting of twelve six-inch, quick-firing guns, and the engine and boiler rooms and rudder were to be located below the waterline. The coal bunkers were to run on both sides of the hulls to absorb enemy shells. Other than the engineers, all the certificated officers in the crews, and no less than half the balance of the crews, must be in the Royal Naval Reserve or the Royal Naval Fleet Reserve. Both Cunard and the British government accepted all the conditions and work began on the two new liners.

When the *Lusitania* appeared she brought a sea change to trans-Atlantic travel. Her dazzling speed, her luxury, and the unprecedented consideration for her passengers in all classes of travel, made a powerful impression on the traveling public. Even those who traveled in what was usually referred to as 'steerage'—those in third- class accommodation—enjoyed real mattresses, flush toilets, and much improved meals.

But the key decision for Cunard in the design stages of the ship was how to power her. She and her sister ship were intended to be the largest and fastest liners ever built. The existing reciprocating engine technology had virtually achieved the limits of its capability. The choice for the company officials was between the old, proven technology of that engine type, and the then-new steam turbine. Steam turbines had thus far successfully powered some British naval vessels, but had only been installed in a few passenger ships. The turbine appeared to be the only option able to produce the level of performance the new liners would need, but the risk of the relatively unproven engine seemed excessive. The Cunard board then elected to try a rather expensive experiment. They would build two new smaller sister ships of about 19,000 tons which would be identical except for their powerplants. One of them, the *Carmania*, would be driven by three propellers and turbines, while her sister, the *Caronia*, would have twin screws and quadruple-expansion reciprocating engines. The ships were completed and, in several months of trials, it was determined that the turbine-powered *Carmania* delivered better performance on the same coal consumption.

Lusitania and *Mauretania* were contractually required to achieve and maintain a cruising speed of at least 24.5 knots, essential for their goal of being record-breakers. The sea trials of *Lusitania*, the first of the pair to be completed, established that she would easily exceed that requirement, having steamed for prolonged periods at well over 25 knots.

There was just one significant problem that arose during the sea trials. When running at high speeds, the entire stern of the ship set up a truly unpleasant vibration, so violent that the spaces in that part of the liner were deemed uninhabitable. Massive, extensive renovations were needed and the ship had to be returned to her builders, the John Brown Company, for major alterations. The stern, which primarily housed Second Class spaces, had to be substantially strengthened through the addition of many new arches, pillars and beams. These renovations proved largely (though not totally) effective, and most, though not all of the vibration problem was cured. On arrival in New York following her maiden voyage, a newspaper reporter who had covered the crossing for his paper, complained about the "distressing vibration" when the ship was sailing at full speed. He said he could "scarcely write in the saloon." *Mauretania* too, was plagued with the vibration problem, though not as severely and not in the stern, but in the forward part of the superstructure, requiring her to also undergo some renovations.

More than 200,000 people gathered along the shore at Liverpool to watch *Lusitania*, the largest and fastest passenger liner of the day, steam slowly down the Mersey water after departing at 9:10 pm 7 September 1907 on her maiden transatlantic voyage. All hopes for a new Atlantic crossing record were dashed, however, when despite her extraordinary pace, she encountered intense fog a day out of New York, restricting her speed for the remainder of the crossing. Stylish and popular with her passengers, she was also one of the safest of vessels. As was the fashion then with the owners of such ships, she was promoted as "unsinkable", designed and constructed as she was with water-tight compartments and a double hull.

The famous Blue Riband, was an unofficial accolade given to the passenger liner crossing the Atlantic Ocean in regular service and recording the highest average speed. *Lusitania* did not achieve that recognition on her first Atlantic crossing, nor on her return journey to Liverpool. On her second crossing from England, though, she broke the transatlantic record held by Germany and brought the Blue Riband back to Britain. She was the first ship in history to cross the Atlantic in under five days.

The coming of war in 1914 brought a consideration by the British Admiralty of the possibility for employing the liner in the role of an armed cruiser, but that notion was shelved when her consumption of coal was determined to be too great for such an assignment. She was, however, engaged in the transport of American war materials to Britain, a role which regularly utilised a portion of her cargo capacity. She completed her 101st round trip between Britain and the United States, docking in New York on 24 April 1915, and preparations began for her return journey scheduled to depart on 1 May.

On 28 March, another incident had nearly propelled the United States into the war. Matters had begun heating up when an earlier British order was issued that all merchant vessels were to paint over their names and the names of their home ports and to sail under the flag of a neutral nation. If challenged by a submarine, they were ordered to immediately open fire or, if unarmed, to attempt to ram the sub. The Germans promptly responded to the issuance of these orders with a declaration from Kaiser Wilhelm that, as of 18 February 1915, the waters surrounding England and including the English Channel, were considered a war zone. Any merchant ship found in that zone would be destroyed immediately and without determining if that ship were neutral.

The British then responded with the proclamation of a complete embargo on all trade with Germany, denying her munitions as well as all other goods. The American response to the British embargo on the Germans came when President Woodrow Wilson and Secretary of State William Jennings Bryan protested what they saw as an act that would needlessly starve the German people. Many German-Americans in the U.S. feared they were about to become pariahs in their communities and some of them published an advertisement in New York newspapers on the shipping page immediately below a Cunard notice of the *Lusitania* sailing time. The ad ran on the morning of 1 May as *Lusitania* was ready to depart the city. It stated: "Notice! TRAVELLERS intending to embark on the Atlantic voyage are reminded that a state of war exists between Germany and her allies and Great Britain and her allies; that the 'zone of war' includes the waters adjacent to the British Isles; that, in accordance with formal notice given by the Imperial German Government, vessels flying the flag of Great Britain, or of any of her allies, are liable to destruction in those waters and that travellers sailing in the war zone on ships of Great Britain or her allies do so at their own risk." The ad, and, in particular, its adjacency to the *Lusitania* departure notice, whipped up the anxiety of the public, the passengers about to sail in her, and the enthusiasm of the press whose representatives turned out at New York's Pier 54 to cover the "last voyage of the *Lusitania*."

She sailed a few hours later than scheduled. Her captain, William Turner, fifty-eight years old, military in manner, taciturn, and cool, addressed the anxiety of the 1,257 passengers: "There is always a danger, but the best guarantees of your safety are the Lusitania herself and the fact that wherever there is danger your safety is in the hands of the Royal Navy." Furthermore, he told them that "the *Lusitania* was safer than the trolley cars in New York City."

In the early afternoon of 28 March, the SS *Falaba*, a 5,000-ton British passenger-cargo ship bound for Sierra Leone via the Canary Islands, had been steaming fifty miles off St David's Head in southwest Wales, when she was sighted and torpedoed by the German submarine *U-28* under the command of Kapitänleutnant Freiherr Georg-Günther von Forstner. Of 145 passengers and ninety-five crew on board, 104 died. One of them was a young American mining engineer, Leon Thrasher, who was returning to Africa. The attack by the German U-boat provoked substantial ill feeling towards Germany in the then-neutral United States. The American press put heavy emphasis on the story, denouncing the sinking as an act of piracy, and public pressure mounted for an American response to what many felt was a massacre of innocent civilians without warning. The *New York Herald*: "Not War but Murder". President Wilson wrote another note to the German government, knowing it would probably result in a declaration of war.

Numerous accounts of the *Falaba* sinking exist, including witness statements. In one such account, these statements purported to offer proof that commander von Forstner provided ample warnings and sufficient time for *Falaba* to offload her passengers and crew. The captain of *Falaba* chose instead to use that time in an effort to radio the position of the U-boat to a nearby armed British patrol vessel. The U-boat crew then attacked the merchant ship, igniting more than twelve tons of contraband explosives in her cargo hold. The Germans claimed that they had allowed twenty-three minutes for the *Falaba* crew to evacuate the ship, the British claimed that the time permitted for the offloading of the passengers and crew was only seven minutes.

Prior to the sinking of the *Falaba*, Americans had been largely ambivalent towards the war in Europe. Officially, the nation was neutral, at peace and reserving the right of trade with either side, determined to keep her ships sailing anywhere in the course of her business, despite the war. As trade between U.S. and German businesses became more and more difficult and dangerous in the circumstances, the situation began to change; British and French purchases of war-related materials from U.S. manufacturers was overtaking the value of American trade with Germany, as was the outrage in America over the continuing activity of Germany's U-boats. Still, the Wilson administration stood firm in its determination to keep the country from involvement in the "European war".

When the First World War had begun in August 1914, most British ocean liners were taken out of passenger service and made available to the Admiralty for possible use in the war effort. With the war, ocean passenger revenues had dropped dramatically. In an austerity measure, Cunard opted to save something on the costs of both coal and manpower by shutting down one of *Lusitania*'s boilers. How much money was saved with the decision is not known, but one effect on the performance of the liner was the reduction of her top speed from twenty-six to twenty-one knots.

There were 197 Americans aboard *Lusitania* on her early May crossing from New York to Liverpool, among them Alfred G. Vanderbilt, a thirty-seven-year-old multi-millionaire amateur sportsman.

Three German stowaways were discovered shortly after the ship sailed. They were arrested to be held for questioning on the ship's arrival in England. It has never been determined whether they were simply stowaways or German agents.

As the great ship eased into the Atlantic, she had a brief rendezvous with three Royal Navy warships that were patrolling the

U.S. east coast. As it happened, one of them was the Cunard *Caronia*, one of the two vessels built by the line to help determine which form of powerplant to use in *Lusitania*. *Caronia* had since been enlisted by the admiralty and bristled with guns in her new role as an armed merchant cruiser.

Each day at sea a lifeboat drill was conducted on *Lusitania*. A single lifeboat was involved, and the drill amounted to eight crewmen who would line up at the boat and, at the command of an officer, climb into it. There they put on and tied their life jackets. They then manned their oars. On a further command, they would climb out of the boat, take off their life jackets, and return to their duties. The procedure was later referred to by one of the surviving passengers as "a pitiable exhibition."

In the early morning of 5 May the U-boat *U-20*, had navigated down the west coast of Ireland and was then slightly north and west of Fastnet. The submarine was commanded by Kapitänleutnant Walther Schwieger, who was then searching for Allied troop transport ships, which were perfectly legitimate targets for the Germans. The *U-20*'s progress had been tracked for days by the British Admiralty, which had been monitoring the submarine's radio signals to her German base. Both the First Lord of the Admiralty, Winston Churchill, and the First Sea Lord, Admiral Sir John Fisher, had been kept informed of the U-boat's presence, as *Lusitania* steamed eastward less than two days from *U-20*'s position.

There was considerable variation between the cargo listed on *Lusitania*'s manifest for the voyage, and that rumoured to actually be in her holds. Officially, she was listed as carrying food stuffs, copper ingots, sheet brass, machinery, furs, hides, dental equipment, and auto parts, as well as 4,200 cases of small-calibre rifle ammunition, 1,248 cases of artillery shells, and eighteen cases of fuses. Rumour had it that she was bringing far more ammunition than was listed, for an actual total of six million rounds, and that the furs were actually highly volatile gun cotton. Further, there was, supposedly, upwards of six million dollars in gold bullion aboard. No one knows the truth.

As *U-20* was occupied with the attacks and sinking of three merchant vessels near Fastnet, evening on board *Lusitania* found Captain Turner preparing to go to dinner and an end-of-journey concert. His passengers were unaware that, in the six days since they had sailed from New York, twenty-two ships had been sunk in the war zone by U-boats.

A message arrived from the Admiralty at 8:30 pm with the warning "Submarines active off south coast of Ireland". Turner immediately ordered the ship's speed reduced to ensure she would pass Fastnet in the dark of night. He had the ship blacked out, had the lifeboats swung out on their davits, posted twice as many lookouts as normal, and had as many water-tight doors closed as was practical. He notified the passengers that, "On entering the war zone tomorrow, we shall be securely in the care of the Royal Navy." The German submarine had surfaced and was recharging her batteries. She was scheduled to begin her lengthy run back to Germany the next day, her fuel and provisions largely depleted and her torpedo reserve down to three weapons. Heavy fog had shrouded the area where *U-20* lay, but it began lifting by late morning of the 7th and Kapitänleutnant Schwieger took his boat down and out of sight. As he did so, the Admiralty sent another warning to all British ships: "Submarines active in southern part of Irish Channel. Last heard of 20 miles south of Coningbeg Light. Make certain *Lusitania* gets this."

Nearing Ireland, Captain Turner elected a change of course, bringing *Lusitania* a bit closer to land. At the same time, Schwieger had *U-20* under way on the surface at full speed for her German base. Her course would cross that of *Lusitania*. It happened just after 1 pm. The U-boat commander had enjoyed his lunch and was staring through his binoculars at a wisp of smoke on the horizon. The image grew slowly into that of the liner *Lusitania* and Schwieger yelled "Diving stations!'

At 1:40 pm Captain Turner, unknowingly, had *Lusitania* on a direct line to the U-boat. Schwieger spent the next half hour manoeuvring the boat into an ideal firing position for a torpedo shot at the liner. On Turner's ship, the second-sitting passengers were enjoying lunch when Schwieger launched a torpedo, whose use later appeared in his boat log entry: "Clean bow shot at 700 meters' range (G torpedo three meters' depth adjustment), angle of intersection 90 degrees, estimated speed 22 knots."

There was almost no time, from the instant Captain Turner was told by his Second Officer that a torpedo was approaching the liner, to the next instant when the weapon struck. Schwieger continued his log entry: "Shot hit starboard side right behind bridge. An unusually heavy detonation follows with a very strong explosion cloud (high in the air just in front of the first smokestack). The explosion of the torpedo must have been followed by a second one (boiler or coal or powder?). The superstructure above the point of impact and the bridge are torn asunder, fire breaks out, and smoke envelops the high bridge. The ship stops immediately and heels over to starboard very quickly, immersing simultaneously at the bow."

Lusitania was listing heavily to starboard now because of a secondary explosion, possibly of the munitions in the hold, ripping an enormous rent behind the bridge, flooding the nearly empty starboard coal bunkers. The bow area was greatly damaged and her foredecks were quickly beneath the surface. After the second explosion, the ship was no longer under the control of the helmsman, but continued forward on momentum, though she was going down by the bow. Steam pressure was dropping, seawater was flooding into the engine room, and the captain ordered "Abandon ship!"

More trouble for the crew occurred when they began trying to lower the lifeboats. Some of the lifeboats overturned when they contacted the water, owing to the continuing forward speed of the ship. Many of the passengers in them were hurled into the sea. Some were left helpless in the water while others were dashed against the hull of the liner. On the port side, a number of lifeboats were hopelessly damaged when they were lowered against the large rivets of the hull plates. In the terrible chaos only six of the ship's forty-eight lifeboats and collapsible lifeboats survived the launching. Relatively few of the passengers and crew managed to escape in them. The ship's wireless operator got off the SOS message: "Come at once. Big list. 10 miles south Old Head Kinsale."

In an effort to save his ship, the passengers and crew, Captain Turner decided to try for the shore and the slim possibility of beaching the great vessel. He also sought to slow her momentum, to allow those on board to evacuate more easily and safely. His efforts came to nothing, as the engines and rudder failed to respond. Even the dour Turner was moved by the tragic misadventures of the hordes of passengers and crew trying desperately, and mostly unsuccessfully, to launch the lifeboats. When he could no longer tolerate the sight of people being dumped from the lifeboats or crushed beneath them, he ordered that the lifeboat launching be halted temporarily, which produced immediate rebellion among the passengers. Another tragic incident occurred when a retaining pin was prematurely knocked out, sending a lifeboat sliding down the tilted deck into a crowd of helpless passengers, thirty of whom were crushed. The lifeboat then overturned and dropped its load of passengers into the water.

Of the most well-known passengers, one who could not swim and would not survive the sinking of *Lusitania* was the wealthy American Alfred G. Vanderbilt. After rescuing a woman, he gave his life jacket away and was never seen again.

Nothing could save the Cunard liner. The surface near her was littered with debris, clothing, anything that would float, and bodies. Now her deck tilted at an extreme angle. Anything, anyone not attached or connected to something slid into the railings or the sea. Everyone, it seemed, was trying to leave the ship, by any means that occurred to them. Diving from the slanting deck, climbing down ropes, leaping from the now 100-foot-high and rising stern. The ones that did not attempt to leave were those who could not swim and those who either chose to stay with others who could not leave, or who would not abandon their babies and infants. Turner waited as the sea sucked the hull of the great ship forward and down, and then he clambered up a ladder from the bridge towards the signal halyards as the water chased him up.

Now the immense stern of the liner had risen to well over 100 feet, her four giant screws still turning but very slowly. The bulk of her poised and then entering her dive while hundreds of passengers still clung to her railings, some still trying vainly to launch a few of the lifeboats. Shortly after she began to dive, her bow struck the seabed and she balanced precariously for one last moment before settling at the stern with a terrible roar. When the huge smokestack funnels went under there was a brief silence until a massive boiler exploded and where she had gone down the surface of the sea seemed to be boiling, a great circular pattern of wreckage and people, living and dead. From the moment the torpedo struck, until her dreadful end, slipping beneath the surface, just eighteen minutes had elapsed.

President Wilson wept when told of the sinking. Former President Theodore Roosevelt called it "piracy on a vaster scale of murder than any oldtime pirate ever practiced. It seems inconceivable that we can refrain from taking action. We owe it to humanity, to our own national self-respect." When the U.S. Ambassador to Britain, Walter Hines Page, reported to Wilson the next day, he said of British public opinion: "The unofficial feeling is that the United States must declare war or forfeit European respect. If the United States do come in, the moral and physical effect will be to bring peace quickly and to give the United States a great influence in ending the war and in so reorganising the world as to prevent its recurrence." In Germany there was some question as to whether the U-boat commander Schwieger had mistaken *Lusitania* for a troop transport.

1,198 people had died in the loss of the *Lusitania*. Of them, 785 were passengers, of whom ninety-four were children, including thirty-five infants. Of the passengers who died, 128 were Americans. Indignation in the United States, Britain, and much of the world grew into fury, but still, no declaration of war came out of Washington. The United States, Americans, and the president were seen in Britain as cowards. Wilson wrote in protest to the German government: "Unless the Imperial Government should now immediately declare and effect an abandonment of its present methods of submarine warfare against passenger and freight-carrying vessels, the Government of the United States can have no choice but to sever diplomatic relations with the German Empire altogether."

The *Lusitania* incident worked on the minds of Americans, contributing significantly to a growing anti-German sentiment which gradually moved them, and the president, away from their steadfast anti-war stance. The quiet fury in the United States was building.

The Germans seemed taken aback by the increasing virulent feeling among Americans towards Germany and Germans, and by how deeply and powerfully the Americans had been moved by the U-boat attack. In response to that reaction, the Kaiser called a halt to all U-boat action against large passenger ships and ordered the end of unrestricted U-boat war on merchant shipping in British waters.

The United States did go to war with Germany, on 6 April 1917. Having been a long-standing trading partner with most of the countries involved in World War I, in 1914 the U.S. began increasing the amounts of material aid it was sending to Britain and France. President Wilson, who was campaigning for re-election in 1916, was particularly sensitive to the intense anti-war attitude of most Americans at that time and was determined to keep the nation out of the European conflict. Circumstances, however, led to a sea change in the American position.

The sinking of the *Lusitania* by a German submarine in May 1915 had a profound effect on the American mindset. Nearly 1,200 innocent civilians had died in the loss of the liner, more than ten percent of them Americans. The German government intended to destroy all transport and cargo ships it suspected of bringing anything of aid to its enemies and was conducting unrestricted submarine warfare in the Atlantic and elsewhere to that end. Though the Germans had halted that practice following the *Lusitania* sinking and the hugely anti-German reaction to it in the U.S., they resumed the practice in 1917, and that, together with the Lusitania incident, changed Wilson's mind and led to the American declaration of war against Germany. Other considerations undoubtedly affected that decision too. The U.S. then had enormous economic investments in both Britain and France, which were at great risk should those countries lose the war to Germany. In that event, they would be unable to repay the debt to the U.S., leading to the likely collapse of the American economy. Additionally, France and Britain were largely financing their participation in the war through American loans and investments, and were buying huge quantities of arms from the U.S. on credit, and the U.S. wanted security about being repaid.

The First World War was the first large-scale demonstration of psychological warfare in a relatively sophisticated form. The powerful effects of propaganda as practiced by both sides in the conflict were obvious and considerable. President Wilson, though reluctant to take the nation into war, was moved both politically and ideologically away from his fundamental anti-war stance when former president Teddy Roosevelt decided to run for another term. That, and Wilson's desire to "make the world safe for democracy", as he would later articulate in his war address to the Congress, spurred him to shift his thinking and planning. He announced a new war preparedness programme and hinted that America might go to war after all. That eventual decision worked to place the U.S. in a new light and the world to see her as an emerging world power. In the context of all this, thinking in the U.S. had definitely shifted. Americans now generally perceived that Britain and France were the white hats, struggling for freedom against the evil of the German cause. American public opinion was now finally ready for the fight, nearly two years after the loss of *Lusitania*.

The U-boat attack on *Lusitania* had established the German submarine as a uniquely effective new weapon proven in the field. The
Germans now chose to divert many of their U-boats from Atlantic
and North Sea duty and base them in the Adriatic and the
Mediterranean areas in support of their allies in that region. The
action there involved striking at neutral and British merchant vessels carrying cargo from the far east and troop transports bringing
reinforcements to the Gallipoli front. The successes of the U-boats
against British battleships there soon led to the Admiralty withdrawing all its capital ships from their bombardment activity in the area.

The most remarkable achievement by a submariner ever was that
of the U-boat commander Kapitänleutnant Lothar von Arnauld de la
Periére, skipper of *U-35* operating in the Mediterranean. Between
26 July and 20 August 1916, he sank fifty-four enemy ships with a
total tonnage of 91,150. In the process, he fired approximately 900
gun rounds and launched only four torpedoes. His matter-of-fact
recollection of the patrol included: "My record cruise was quite
tame and humdrum. We stopped ships. The crews took to the boats.
We examined the ship's papers, gave sailing instructions to the nearest land and then sank the captured prize." His record of sinkings
for his entire period in command of *U-35* totalled 195 vessels—two
warships, five troopships, one armed merchant cruiser, 125 steamers, and sixty-two sailing ships. His total of tonnage sunk during the
war amounted to nearly half a million.

The German submarine *U-20* was built by Kaiserliche Werft at
Danzig and launched 18 December 1912. In her three years of war
service she attacked and sank thirty-six ships, including warships,
with a total tonnage of 144,000. Her most significant kill by far,
however, was that of *Lusitania*. By early November 1916, her hunting days were over. On the 4th she ran aground on the Danish coast.
The crew was unable to refloat her and they abandoned the sub, detonating the torpedoes in her tubes to prevent her use by enemy
forces. The wrecked U-boat was declared a navigational hazard by
the Danish authorities, who sold the wreck for salvage. In 1921 it was
resold to another owner who took what he wanted from it. In August
1925, divers put mines around the wreck and blew it apart. The
explosion failed to entirely destroy the boat, and additional salvage
attempts ensued. Following another effort in 1980, the remains of
the submarine's conning tower were displayed in a museum, the

Strandingsmuseum St George in Denmark. What is left of the wreck today still lies in fifteen feet of water where it was grounded.

Nearly a century after the sinking of *Lusitania*, evidence appears to have emerged exonerating the British, who over the years have been blamed by historians and others for the very high loss of life in the sinking, owing to their having illegally stowed high explosives on board, concealed as containers of beef or cheese and so listed on the liner's manifest. These explosives, it was claimed, had been the cause of the secondary blast that led to the rapid sinking of the ship, and were material destined for use on the Western Front. In 2012, however, new evidence based on a search of the wreck of *Lusitania*, laboratory tests, and a computer reconstruction of the sinking, have apparently debunked the theory about British involvement. These investigations found no evidence in support of the claims against the British, concluding that the second blast must have been one of the liner's boilers exploding.

Using a miniature submarine and other advanced equipment, the researchers made a series of dives on the wreck at its depth of 300 feet, which included the insertion of a camera for inspection of the cargo hold and blast damage. At the Lawrence Livermore National Laboratory in California, an American government-funded research facility heavily involved in studies relating to explosives, test and controlled explosions were conducted to explore various theories about the explosions on the liner—tests involving aluminium used in making landmines, and gun cotton, an artillery propellant. The testing results indicated that a gun cotton explosion could be ruled out as it would have been instantaneous, rather than delayed by fifteen to twenty seconds as reported by survivor witnesses. Ruled out too was the possibility that the second explosion was caused by the ignition of coal dust, as that would not have caused sufficient damage to sink the ship. The investigation did attribute the second explosion to the boiler but stated that that in itself did not cause significant damage, and that the torpedo strike did, in fact, sink the ship.

The original wartime investigations in the United States and Britain had been stifled by WWI secrecy and propaganda to direct all blame on Germany. The contentions about a cover-up and a secret cargo of war-related materials have never ceased since the sinking. German authorities then contended that the *Lusitania*—

which had been partially financed with a British government loan on the condition that the ship could be used by the Royal Navy in wartime—had been carrying "contraband of war", and that it had "large quantities of war materials in the cargo."

Prior to a hearing on the loss of *Lusitania*, the British government amended the Defence of the Realm Act, eliminating the possibility of any discussion about "war materials" having been on board the liner.

The British inquiry into the sinking of *Lusitania* was convened five weeks after the disaster. It lasted less than a week and produced a statement, as expected, laying the blame squarely on the German government: "The Court, having carefully enquired into the circumstances of the above mentioned disaster, finds that the loss of the said ship and lives was due to damage caused to the said ship by torpedoes fired by a submarine of German nationality whereby the ship sank. In the opinion of the Court the act was done not merely with the intention of sinking the ship, but also with the intention of destroying the lives of the people on board. The whole blame for the cruel destruction of life in this catastrophe must rest solely with those who plotted and with those who committed the crime."

Rescue vessels brought survivors and bodies from *Lusitania* to Queenstown harbour, Ireland, beginning in the evening of 7 May and throughout the following week. As an incentive to help in recovering the maximum number of victims in the sinking, a reward of £1 was offered for each body found. The American government paid an additional pound for each American victim body found. Alfred G. Vanderbilt's family offered a £200 reward for his body, but it was never found.

Over the years since the sinking of *Lusitania*, there has been considerable interest in recovering items from her, including some of the various treasures rumoured to have been lost with her, treasures that included great works of art and a £6 million horde of gold. Only days after the sinking, enquiries began arriving in the Cunard offices about the possibility of purchasing the wreck. The Leavitt Lusitania Salvage Company was formed in the 1920s to recover treasure from the wreck, but nothing came of it. In 1935 a diver for the Tritonia Corporation located, identified and dived on the wreck, and nothing more came of that effort. In 1960, an American diver, John Light, and his crew, completed a series of 130 dives on the site, beginning in July, photographing much of the wreck, which he later purchased for £1,000 from the British War Risks Commission. He hoped to pursue a salvage operation, but ran out of funds in 1967, ending his efforts. Light's exploration was followed in 1982 by that of a group called Oceaneering International, whose divers spent six weeks diving on the wreck until their support ship was forced to return to port due to severe weather. Problems then arose in the Irish courts over the ownership of the wreck. But various artifacts had been recovered from the ship, including the bell from the crow's nest.

Walter Storch, one of the survivors of the *Lusitania* sinking, sent money each year until his death, to the offices of the Cunard line in Queenstown, requesting that flowers be put on the three mass graves of the victims.

ATHENIA

1 September 1939. German troops invaded Poland. At 11:15 am on 3 September, British Prime Minister Neville Chamberlain broadcast to the people of Britain, announcing that the British ambassador to Berlin had given a final note to the German government stating that unless Germany announced plans by 11:00 today to withdraw from Poland, a state of war would exist between Britain and Germany. "I have to tell you now that no such undertaking has been received and consquently this country is at war with Germany."

The first major casualty of that declaration occurred at 7:40 that evening when the British ocean liner *Athenia*, a 13,460 gross ton vessel of the Anchor-Donaldson Line, was sunk by a torpedo fired by the crew of the U-boat *U-30* under the command of Kapitänleutnant Fritz-Julius Lemp. It was the first shot of the Battle of the Atlantic.

Athenia had been launched in 1923 at Govan, Scotland and most of her Atlantic crossings had been from Liverpool or Glasgow to Montreal or Quebec during summer and autumn months. She was operated as a cruise ship in the winters. Her passenger capacity numbered 516 in cabin class and a further 1,000 in third class. With twin propellers her steam turbine engines drove her at a top speed of fifteen knots.

The ship left Glasgow for Montreal, via Liverpool and Belfast, with 1,103 passengers, more than 300 of them Americans. She was manned by a crew of 315 and had left Liverpool at 1:00 pm on 2 September. She was sixty miles south of Rockall when a lookout aboard the German submarine *U-30*, sighted the liner at about 4:30 pm. The U-boat commander, Lemp, tracked the *Athenia* for three hours. He later stated that it was a "darkened ship" running a zig-zagging course well off normal shipping lanes, leading him to believe that she was either an armed merchant cruiser or a troop ship. At 7:40 Lemp had made his decision and as he closed on the *Athenia*, between Tory Island and Rockall, he ordered the firing of two torpedoes.

The second torpedo misfired, but the first exploded when it hit the liner, which rapidly began settling by the stern. 1,418 persons were on board *Athenia* when she was attacked. 98 passengers and 19 crew members were killed. Many fatalities occurred in the engine room and stair well areas where the torpedo struck. Several others resulted from accidents that happened during the evacuation from the liner.

The distress signal sent from *Athenia* summoned various ships to the immediate area, including HMS *Electra*, whose captain took charge of the rescue efforts. When a destroyer, HMS *Fame* arrived, he sent it on an anti-submarine sweep of the area. Other vessels arrived, a Norwegian tanker, the MS *Knute Nelson*, the destroyer HMS *Escort*, the freighter SS *City of Flint*, and the Swedish yacht *Southern Cross*, and, collectively they rescued 981 passengers and crew members. Fortunately for most of those aboard *Athenia*, the ship remained afloat for several hours after the attack. At 10:40 the following morning she sank.

A wide-spread furore arose the day after the attack on *Athenia* when dramatic headlines on newspapers around the world were headed with LINER ATHENIA TORPEDOED AND SUNK. In Berlin, Grossadmiral Erich Raeder, the head of the German Navy, learned of the sinking and, when he looked into it, was told that no German submarines had been within 75 miles of the location where the liner had been torpedoed. This he reported in good faith to Adolf Hitler and the German leader decided that, for political reasons, secrecy should surround the incident. Raeder chose not to court-martial Lemp, in the belief that the U-boat commander had made an understandable error. The logbook of the *U-30* was then altered to support the official denial of German responsibility. Some weeks later, *Voelkischer Beobachter*, the official newspaper of the Nazi Party, published an article blaming the loss of the *Athenia* on the British and accusing First Lord of the Admiralty, Winston Churchill, of sinking the liner in order to sway neutral public opinion against Nazi Germany. Skepticism was raised in the United States by some politicians and other prominent figures, about German responsibility for the sinking; in disbelief that the Germans would do something as clumsy, infuriating, and inflammatory. A poll there, however, showed that sixty percent of Americans thought the Germans were responsible for the sinking and only nine percent thought otherwise. There were even some who thought that Britain had reason to have make the attack—to infuriate the American people and bring the U.S. into the war against Germany.

With the end of the Second World War, the matter was finally aired publicly when Grossadmiral Karl Dönitz, read a statement at the Nuremberg War Crimes Trials, admitting that the U-boat *U-30* had indeed torpedoed *Athenia*, that there had been a cover-up, and that Kapitänleutnant Lemp had falsified the ship's log and sworn his crew to secrecy in the matter.

The question of legality in the matter of the sinking of *Athenia* is linked to violations of the Hague Conventions and the London Naval Treaty of 1930, enabling all warships and submarines to stop and search merchant vessels, and specifically forbade the capture as prize, or sinking of such a vessel, unless it was seen to be carrying contraband or engaged in military activity. Even if this was the case, and if it was decided to sink the ship, the passengers and crew must be first transferred to "a place of safety" as a priority. While Germany had not been a signatory of the 1930 Treaty, the 1936 German Prize Rules (Prisenordnung) incorporated most of the same rules and held German naval commanders to the restrictions. Clearly, *Athenia* was an unarmed passenger ship and Kapitän- leutnant Lemp obeyed none of the restrictions.

Lemp was the central figure in the *Athenia* incident and one of the key personalities in the Battle of the Atlantic. He commanded the submarines *U-28*, *U-30*, and *U-110*, and was a recipient of the Knight's Cross of the Iron Cross. On 9 May 1941, while in command of *U-110* south of Iceland, his submarine was located, depth-charged and shelled by the British destroyers HMS *Bulldog* and HMS *Broadway*, and the corvette HMS *Aubretia*, whose lookout had spotted the wake of the *U-110* periscope. *Bulldog* then tried to ram the sub. Lemp ordered his crew to abandon the damaged U-boat. Thirty-four survivors of the crew were picked up by the British vessels, but Lemp was not among them. Accounts of the incident vary from his being shot by the boarding party from *Bulldog*, to his drowning or being shot in the water while swimming back to the U-boat when he realized that it was not sinking as he had intended.

When Sub-Lieutenant David Balme and a party from HMS *Bulldog* went aboard *U-110*, they conducted a search, recovering one of the greatest prizes of the war, the submarine's complete, uns-abotaged Enigma code machine, together with the associated paperwork. The machine and related papers were taken to Station X, Bletchley Park in England where Alan Turing's code-breaking team went to work on the Enigma cipher. When the British broke the Enigma naval code, that access to German naval communications proved to be the turning point in the Battle of the Atlantic.

Among the passengers on board *Athenia* on her final voyage, Judith Evelyn, an American stage and movie actress, Professor John H. Lawrence, a pioneering nuclear medicine scientist and brother of Professor Ernest O. Lawrence, who invented the cyclotron and was a key figure in the Manhattan Project to develop the atomic bomb, Nicola Lubitsch, baby daughter of the German-American film director Ernst Lubitsch, Carmen Silvera, who starred as Edith in the acclaimed British television comedy series *'Allo 'Allo!*, and James Alexander Goodson, who would become a famous WW2 fighter pilot of the Royal Canadian Air Force and then the U.S. Army Air Force. Having survived the sinking of *Athenia*, he joined the RCAF and flew combat with 416 Squadron, 43 Squadron RAF, and 133 Eagle Squadron, before transferring to the 336th Fighter Squadron, 4th Fighter Group, USAAF, in which he was credited with thirty enemy aircraft destroyed. Eventually shot down and captured by the Germans, he was a prisoner of war at Stalag Luft III, Sagan, Silesia. Colonel Goodson described his experience aboard *Athenia*: "I have always liked the sea and started to work my way around the world. I got a job as a steward on the *Athenia* and crossed from the States to England on her. Then I went to France, but at Paris the United States consul sent me back. I booked a third class passage on the *Athenia* for the return trip.

"I had just mounted the staircase and was moving forward to the dining room when it struck. It was a powerful explosion quickly followed by a loud crack and whistle. The ship shuddered under the blow. The lights went out. There were women's screams. The movement of the ship changed strangely as she slewed to a stop. People were running in all directions, calling desperately to one another. We all knew the ship was mortally stricken; she was beginning to list.

"The emergency lights were turned on. I went back to the companionway I had just come up. I gazed down at a sort of Dante's Inferno; a gaping hole at the bottom of which was a churning mass of water on which were broken bits of wooden stairway, flooring and furniture. Terrified people were clinging to this flotsam, and to the wreckage of the rest of the stairway which was cascading down the side of the gaping hole. The blast must have come up through here from the engine room below, past the cabin decks, and the third class restaurant and galley. I clambered and slithered down to the level of the restaurant. I started by reaching for the outstretched arms and pulling the weeping, shaking, frightened women to safety; but I soon saw that the most urgent danger was to those who were floundering in the water, or clinging to the wreckage lower down. Many were screaming that they couldn't swim. Some were already close to drowning.

"I slithered down the shattered stairway, slipped off my jacket and shoes, and plunged into the surging water. One by one, I dragged them to the foot of the broken companionway, and left them to clamber up to the other rescuers above.

"When there were no more bodies floundering in the water, I turned to those who were cowering in the openings of the corridors which led from the cabins to what had been the landing at the foot of the stairs and was now a seething, lurching mass of water. I went first to the children. They left their mothers, put their small arms around my neck and clung to me. They clung as we slipped into the water, as I swam to the foot of the dangling steps, as I climbed the slippery wreckage, and as I prised their arms from around me and passed them to those at the top. These were members of the crew, a few stewards and stewardesses and even some seamen. They knew their jobs, they rose to the challenge, and above all, they kept their heads. One seaman had climbed halfway down to take the women and children from me and pass them on to those waiting above. With a strong Glasgow accent, he soothed and comforted the mothers and children, and shouted praise and encouragement to me.

" 'Bloody guid, mon! Keep 'em coming!'

"I looked up out of the water.

" 'I could do with some help down here.'

The seaman shook his head sadly.

" 'Ah wish the hell ah cuid, but ah canna swum!'

"I looked up at the others. They shook their heads too. It had never occurred to me that members of a ship's crew would not be able to swim. Finally, there were no more left either in the water, or waiting at the openings of the corridors. I was at the base of the broken stairs. Now the ship had listed much more.

"The crew members were waiting to help me up the wreckage, up past the smashed dining rooms to the upper decks.

" 'Thanks!' I said when we got to the top. The ship was listing quite a bit now. We headed up the sloping deck to the higher side.

We found them launching one of the last lifeboats. It was crowded. Members of the crew were holding back those for whom there was no more room and telling them to go to another boat. Meanwhile, the two seamen fore and aft in the boat were desperately trying to lower it. But as the heavy boat lurched down as the ropes slid unevenly through the pulleys of the davits, a problem arose which was apparently not foreseen by the designers of lifeboat launching systems. Because of the listing of the ship, when the lifeboat was lowered from its davits, and as it swayed with the slight rolling, it fouled the side. Although the seamen were playing out their ropes as evenly as possible, the forward part got caught against the side of the ship. The seaman continued to play out his rope. Suddenly it slid free and dropped. But the after rope hadn't played out as much as the one forward. The front of the boat dropped, but the rear was caught by its rope. Soon the boat was hanging by the after rope. The screaming passengers were tumbling out of the boat like rag dolls, and falling down to the surface of the sea far below.

"There was nothing we could do. I helped the crew to shepherd the remaining group of passengers to the other side of the ship. We made our way to what seemed to be the last lifeboat, at least on that deck. Here there was another problem caused by the same list and the same swell; the boat was hanging on its davits, but swinging in and out. On its outer swing, there was a yawning gap between the lifeboat and the ship. Most of the passengers were women or elderly, or both. The responsible crew members were trying to persuade them to make their leap into the boat when it was close to the ship, but many of them waited too long, and the boat swung out again. "We pushed our way through the waiting crowd to help. As I reached the boat, the seaman in the bow shouted to an elderly lady: 'Jump! Now!' But she hesitated. Perhaps she was pushed and the push badly timed. As the boat swung away, she lurched out towards it, the gap was already too wide. Her arms reached the gunwale, but her body fell through the space between the lifeboat and ship, wrenching her arms away from the boat and those who were trying to drag her into it.

"Finally the lifeboat could take no more passengers, and was lowered away, leaving a small group of us on the deserted, sloping deck. One of the ship's officers took command.

" 'That was the last of the boats, but the Captain's launch will be back for us soon; it's distributing the passengers evenly between the boats. Some of the ones that got away weren't quite full'

" 'Aye, but how much time do we have before she goes?'

" 'There's no immediate danger. There was only one torpedo which hit midships and blew up through that compartment. The watertight doors were closed before other compartments were flooded, so they should keep her afloat awhile.'

"Now that there was nothing to do, I felt depressed. Somehow I didn't feel like waiting for the Captain's launch.

"I went to the higher side of the ship and looked down the sloping side to the dark, rolling sea. There, just about 100 yards from the ship, I saw a lifeboat. Hanging from the davits, and making down the steel side of the ship were the ropes which had launched the boats.

"In the dark, I couldn't see if they reached all the way to the sea, but they went far enough for me. Soon I was going down a rope hand over hand, fending myself off the side with my feet as the ship rolled. It was further down than I had thought. Halfway down, my arms were aching. Long before I reached the bottom, I couldn't hold on any longer. As the rope slipped through my hands, I kicked away from the side and fell. It seemed a long time before I hit the water. I went in feet first. I started to struggle to the surface right away, but it seemed to take a long time. I thought I was a good under-water swimmer, but soon I desperately needed to breathe. In the darkness there was no sign of the surface. For the first time I wished I'd been able to get to my life-jacket. If I passed out, it would at least have brought me to the surface. I gasped for breath. The sea was choppy, and I got a mouthful of water. It was colder, rougher and more brutal than I had expected. I looked for the lifeboat I had seen from the deck. I could only see it when I was lifted by a wave, and it looked much further away now.

"I struck out in the direction of the boat, but it was a struggle. At times I felt I was making no headway at all. Eventually I got close enough to see one of the reasons. They had a few oars out, and were trying to row away from the ship. I knew that was in line with instructions, because of the danger of being sucked down with the ship when she sank; but, as I struggled to keep going, I did feel they could at least stop rowing until I caught up with them.

"Fortunately, their efforts were badly co-ordinated and I finally reached them, and grabbed the gunwale, I tried to pull myself up, expecting helping hands to lift me into the boat; instead a young man, screaming in a foreign language put his hand in my face to push me away. A frantic middle-aged woman was prising my fingers off the side of the boat and banging on my knuckles. Dimly I realised they were panicking because they felt the boat was already over-crowded. I heard the voice of the seaman in charge down in the stern yelling to them to stop, but help came from another direction, and it was much more effective. The diminutive figure of a girl appeared. In a flash, she had landed a sharp right to the face of the young man, and sent him sprawling back off his seat. In the next second, my other tormentor was hauled away, and the strong young arms were reaching down to me. Other hands helped to haul me over the gun-wale.

"I collapsed in a wet heap on the bottom of the boat and gasped my thanks to my rescuers.

"Amid peals of young female laughter I heard: 'Hey! You're an American!'

" 'So are you!' I mumbled in surprise.

" 'My God! You're half-drowned and freezing cold! Here!'

"A blanket was being wrapped around my shoulders. I struggled to sit up, and opened my eyes to look at my guardian angel. She was a small, slim brunette, about nineteen or twenty, with an elfin face, full of life and humour. She was wearing a bra and pants and nothing else. I realised she had been wrapped in the blanket she was now trying to put around me.

" 'No! No! You need it more than I do,' and I took it off my shoulders and put it around hers.

" 'Ok. We'll share it. That way we'll keep each other warm!'

" 'What happened to the rest of your clothes?' I asked.

" 'We were dressing for dinner when the torpedo struck. We grabbed what we could and ran.'

"I looked around and saw we were surrounded by young girls in various stages of undress. Some had borrowed sweaters and jackets from members of the crew. Others were huddled in blankets. At least most of them had life-jackets. As they snuggled together around us, I showed my surprise.

" 'Who are you?'

The little brunette laughed. 'We're college kids. We've been touring Europe after graduation. I guess our timing could have been better. I'm Jenny. This is Kay. That's Dodie.'

"They were a wonderful, cheery bunch, cracking jokes and singing songs. We were an oasis of fun in the lifeboat. Most of the others were frightened or seasick or both. Many were refugees, most-ly from Poland. Many were Jewish, but by no means all.

"I was surprised at how large the boat seemed, even as it rolled and pitched on the North Atlantic swells. Up in the bow was a member of the ship's crew, and another in the stern. In spite of the crowd in the boat, they had been able to get some of the oars out, and had got some of the men to start rowing. After getting warmed up, I felt guilty at not pulling my weight. I got up and picked my way careful-ly to within shouting distance of the seaman in the stern.

" 'Do you want me to help out on the oars?'

"He was surprised to find a volunteer. 'Aye! These two here are having a struggle. Maybe you could help them out. All we need to do is to keep away from the *Athenia* and head into the waves.

"After an hour or so on the oars I suggested that we could stop rowing. We were far enough from the ship to be out of danger, but shouldn't get too far from her, because the rescue ships would be heading for her last reported position.

"I went back to Jenny and my friendly college girls. Through the night, we clung together, chatted, sang and slept fitfully. At one point, I remember the Jews joining in singing that beautiful plaintiff dirge which became the hymn of the Jewish refugees, oppressed and martyred throughout the world.

"Occasionally we looked across to the stricken *Athenia*. We were amazed at how long she was staying afloat. She was sinking lower in the water, and listing further, but during most of the night, she was still there. It was about 1:30 am when everyone in our boat woke out of their fitful sleep and looked across at the dark hulk. There had probably been a noise of some kind; or perhaps a shift in her posi-tion, although I don't remember either. Anyway, we were all watch-ing when the stern began to sink lower. Soon it seemed to me that most of the near half of the ship was under water. Everything was in slow motion. Gradually, as the stern disappeared, the bow began to rise. Finally the entire forward half of the ship was towering above us. When it was absolutely vertical, it paused. Then she started her final dive; imperceptibly at first, but gaining in momentum until she plunged to her death. A column of water came up as she disap-peared, then there was only a great turbulence, and then nothing but the rolling sea and some floating debris. We felt lonelier and sadder. There was no singing now. We were tired and shivering with cold.

"It was 4:30 when I saw it looming up through the dark. It was a ship. It was even carrying lights. We were too numbed to cheer. There was just a stirring in the boat; a grateful murmuring. The rowers picked up their oars and started rowing slowly towards the ship.

"Other lifeboats were doing the same. Soon we found ourselves close to the big rescue ship, surrounded by five or six other boats. The big ship had stopped as soon as she was close to the boats. Rope ladders were dropped over the side near the stern of the ship. She was a tanker and must have been empty. She towered above us and we could see the blades of her big propeller as we came around to her stern. I looked up and saw her name and home port: *Knute Nelson*—Christiansand; a Norwegian tanker.

"As we came close, I called on the seaman on the tiller of our boat to keep us away from the menacing propeller. It was not moving, but I knew it could windmill, or the Captain might call for some weigh, unaware of the boats under his stern. One lifeboat was being tossed by the waves ever closer to the propeller. I yelled across to them, but apparently there were not enough rowers to stop the drift. Then the great propeller started to turn, churning up the water, and sucking the lifeboat in under the stern. As we watched, they were drawn into the whirlpool. We saw one big propeller blade slash through the boat; but as the shattered bow went down, the rest of the boat was lifted by the next blade coming up. The rearing, shattered boat spilled its human cargo into the churning water.

"I called to the man on our tiller and on the rowers to make for the spot where the survivors were floundering in the water. The screw was no longer turning, and the ship had moved forward slightly. Some of the strong swimmers were already making for the bottom of the rope and wooden ladder dangling down the side of the ship close to the stern; some were pulled into our boat; others clung to the gunwales or oars for the short distance to the ladder; but many just disappeared under the foaming water.

"We got the survivors from the broken lifeboat onto the ladder first. Then it was the turn of the weakest from our own boat. It wasn't easy. The boat was rising and falling on the waves, smashing against the steel sides of the tanker. Sometimes we got someone onto the ladder only to have them fall back into the boat as the ladder swung, or the boat dropped away too soon. We had to get them to get onto the ladder when the boat was at the top of its rise.

"Finally there was no one left in the boat but the two seamen, the American college girls and myself. One by one, the girls started up the twisting, writhing ladder. Even for the lithe, young, athletic teenagers, clambering up the tricky rope ladder required all their strength and concentration. There was no way they could keep the blankets wrapped around them; even those who had huddled into seamen's jackets which were far too big for them, wriggled out of them before attempting to scale the towering side of the tanker.

"When I finally reached the top of the ladder and was hauled over the rail by two large Norwegian sailors onto the deck, I saw the incredulous Captain of the *Knute Nelson* staring at a group of shivering girls, mostly dressed in pants and bras, and nothing else. He hurried them to a companionway.

" 'Go down! Down! Any door! Any room! Warm! You must have warm!

I followed them down the iron stairs until we came to a lower deck, and into the first door. The cabin was dark, but warm! It smelt cosily of human sleep; there was the sound of heavy breathing.

"The light came on. We saw a series of bunks, one above the other. In each bunk was a large Norwegian seaman. The girls had only one thing in mind: to get warm. They didn't hesitate. The seamen, who had been at sea for weeks, and didn't even know that war had been declared, awoke to find half-naked girls clambering into their bunks and snuggling up to their warm bodies under the rough blankets. I'll never forget the expressions on the faces of those big Norwegians. They knew they must be dreaming.

"When we had explained what had happened, to those who understood English, and they had translated it to the others, those magnificent gentle giants turned out of their bunks, made us coffee, served out hard-tack biscuits, lent us their sweaters, and blankets, showed us the way to the 'head', and made us feel that, in spite of what we had been through, life was good!

"We slept the sleep of the exhausted for many hours. When we came to, we learned that, as a ship of a neutral country, the *Knute Nelson* was taking us to the nearest neutral port: Galway on the west coast of Eire. We heard that other rescue ships, including British destroyers, had picked up other survivors."

SHELTERS

"Despite the most rigid checks by the Gestapo on the French ship-yard workers, underground agents actually wormed their way into the yards where the U-boats were readied for their next cruises. These seeming collaborators, ostensibly working for the Germans, slipped little bags of sugar into the lubricating oil tanks of U-boats. The sugar dissolved into the oil and those U-boats came limping back to Lorient with their engines in sad shape. The underground agents made sound-looking welds on pressure fittings that would give way when the boat went deep. Some skippers who didn't take their boats down to maximum depth on trial runs, are on the bottom of the ocean now with their whole crews because these welds gave way under attack.

"Workmen drilled small holes in the tops of fuel tanks and plugged the holes with stuff that was soluble in salt water. A few days after this boat went to sea, the plug would dissolve and the boat would leave a tell-tale oil streak behind her when she submerged.

"It was impossible to keep secrets in a base such as Lorient. The whole life of the town revolved around the operations of the U-boat fleet and everyone in town rubbed elbows with the U-boats one way or another. The shipyard workers, of course, got right down inside them. Tradesmen delivered food to the boats, and any fool could tell from their grocery orders when a boat was about to sail.

"A brass band met boats returning from a successful cruise and the boats came up the river proudly displaying pennants with the names of their victims printed on them for anyone to see. Bar tenders, waitresses, and gals of the evening took intimate parts in the continual round of arrival and departure binges. Anyone who kept his ears open after the first five or six rounds of drinks, could pick up many items of secret official information." —from *Twenty Million Tons Under The Sea* by Rear Admiral Daniel V. Gallery, USN

One of the dividends the Germans derived from the defeat of France in June 1940, was the use of many airfields, bases, and port facilities in western France and along the French Atlantic coast, stretching from Bordeaux in the south to Brest in the north. Admiral Karl Dönitz cashed in on this benefit, recognising the great advantage the locations of the Brittany ports afforded him in being much closer to the Atlantic killing grounds for his hunting submarines, than their former bases in Germany. The sites for Dönitz's new bases were Brest, Lorient, St. Nazaire, La Pallice, and Bordeaux. These ports were hundreds of miles nearer to the assigned patrol destinations of the U-boats, making it possible for the submarines to remain on station at sea for up to ten days longer than when they were based in Germany. Another plus was that by being based on the Brittany coast, they forced Allied merchant shipping heading for England to forego the Channel south coast ports of Southampton, Plymouth, and Portsmouth, and head for Glasgow and Liverpool instead.

Once the advantageous French sites were available to the admiral for basing his U-boat fleet, he had the problem of providing appropriate berths; shelters to protect the submarines from bombing attacks by the Royal Air Force. He discussed the matter with the Führer, and convinced Hitler of the urgent need for such protective structures. Adolf Hitler referred Dönitz to the Reich Minister of Construction, Doctor Fritz Todt, whose staff of German engineers and experts went right to work on the task. His outfit, Organisation Todt, was augmented with conscripted and volunteer French technicians and forced labourers. They began work with an initial project at a site near a small fishing port at Lorient. Early planning had called for development of a simple staging facility, to refuel, rearm, and resupply U-boats. It was intended that all flotilla headquarters and administration would continue to operate from Germany. But the Todt people designed and built something far more elaborate and extensive. The new, fully operational facility at Lorient was completed with nineteen submarine pen shelters, all connected by channels to the main harbour. There were complete facilities for main service, fuel stores, workshops, accommodation, dry docks, and all of it defended by batteries of anti-aircraft guns. It was basing on a grand scale, aspects of which would serve to inspire and be reflected in the design and construction of the other massive U-boat bunker facilities along the French coast. The Lorient facility became known within the Ubootwaffe as "the ace of bases". It served as home base to the Second and Tenth Flotillas, each of them having a complement of twenty-five U-boats, most of them being the longer-ranging Type IXC. The far more common Type VIIC submarines were operated mainly by the First and Ninth Flotillas based at Brest; the Third Flotilla at La Pallice; the Sixth and Seventh Flotillas at St. Nazaire; and the

Twelfth Flotilla at Bordeaux. Additionally, the Bordeaux facility supported twenty-three submarines of the Italian Navy, as well as an assortment of supply ships, refuelers, and mine-layers.

A civil engineer in road construction before the war, and a senior Nazi figure, Dr Todt was called on by Hitler in 1938 to plan construction of the so-called West Wall—referred to in Britain and the United States as the Siegfried Line—a collection of gun emplacements and anti-tank obstacles positioned along the western border of Germany. Rather than having any official military or ministerial status in the German government of the time, Organisation Todt was what today might likely be referred to as a Quango, or quasi-autonomous, non-governmental organisation. It employed fewer than 250,000 people before the war, growing to nearly 1.4 million by late 1944. Before the war, the organisation was responsible for a wide range of engineering / construction projects in Germany, and in the period between 1933-38, as the General Inspector of German Roadways, Todt supervised the construction of the Autobahn highway network, building more than1,900 miles of the roadway by 1938. It was then that his organisation began the substantial use of conscripted, compulsory labour through the Reich Labour Service. A new German law in June 1935 required all male Germans between the ages of eighteen and twenty-five to perform six months of state service, for which they would be compensated at a rate slightly greater than that of unemployment support. From 1940 through the war years, OT became increasingly reliant on a combination of civilian workers, guest workers, military internees, Eastern workers, and volunteer workers. Both the OT and the Labour Service adapted a paramilitary appearance, wearing armbands, chevrons, epaulettes, and other rank recognition insignia.

In 1938, Todt established the OT as a consortium of private companies to serve as subcontractors and as his primary source of expertise in technical engineering, with the Labour Service as his principal source of manpower. With the coming of the war, the continuing work on the autobahn system was de-emphasised in favour of greatly increased military project work, the first major example being the West Wall project.

In 1941, OT was given responsibility for a considerably larger effort, the design and construction of the Atlantic Wall, defences to be built on the coasts of German-occupied France, Belgium, and the

Netherlands, as well as the fortification of the British Channel Islands, which were occupied by Germany from June 1940 until the end of the European war in May 1945.

Todt was killed in a plane crash in February 1942, after which Albert Speer, the Reich Minister of Armaments and Munitions, absorbed the organisation into his department and expanded it to a total of 1.4 million workers, which by then included Germans rejected for military service, some concentration camp prisoners, prisoners of war, and forced labourers from German-occupied countries. There was speculation at the time of Todt's death that he had become convinced that Germany could not win the war and, in the belief that he was indispensable to the Reich, had discussed his view with Hitler, which may have resulted in Todt being covertly assassinated.

In addition to the continuing construction of the great U-boat pen facilities along the western coast of France, in Germany, and Norway, and that of the Atlantic Wall network, OT was assigned the construction of the V-weapon flying bomb and rocket launch platforms in northern France and, later, the construction of air raid shelters and bomb-damage repairs in German cities, as well as the design and construction of underground aircraft and armaments factories and refineries. All of this colossal effort took place in the context of the enormous Allied bombing campaign against Nazi Germany, and the consequent impact of the manpower and materials shortages on the German economy and war effort. Still, through it all, Speer increased war production by a considerable measure, undoubtedly due in large part to the dramatically greater use of forced labour by OT.

Four types of U-boat bunkers were built by the construction crews of OT. The first of these was the Covered Lock—a bunker built over an existing lock to provide some protection for a submarine when it was most vulnerable, such as when the lock was being emptied or filled; Second was the Construction Bunker—a facility used for the building of new submarines; Third was the Fitting-out Bunker—a protective structure in which many submarines were fitted out after being launched; Last was the Shelter for Operational Boats and Repairs—the most numerous bunker type. These utilised two designs; one built on dry land and the second over water. The land-based bunkers required the movement of U-boats on ramps, and the water-based bunkers enabled the boats to enter, shelter, and depart at will. Some facilities enabled certain pens to be pumped out and used as dry docks for total external repair access. Some bunkers were of sufficient size to allow the removal of aerials and periscopes.

U-bunker pens were built in Germany at Hamburg, Bremen, Heligoland, Kiel, and Wilhelmshaven; in Norway at Bergen and Trondheim; at IJmuiden in the Netherlands, and in France at Bordeaux, La Rochelle/La Pallice, Lorient, St. Nazaire, and Brest. Of these, the Lorient facility was the largest of the U-bunker sites and contained three structures called Keroman bunkers, two known as Dom bunkers, and one called the Scorff bunker. Keroman I was the only U-bunker facility requiring a submarine to be hauled from the water and moved on a large "buggy" into the bunker on a sliding-bridge system. The two Dom or 'cathedral' bunkers were built on the sides of a large turntable on which submarines were moved into the repair bays.

OT specialists preceded the engineers and building workers to the potential construction sites of the U-bunkers and support facilities in France and Norway. The design and planning of the bunkers had to provide spaces for much more than the U-boats. The sites, which required bunkers with extremely thick, bomb-resistant walls and roofs as well as armoured doors, had to accommodate offices, workshops, guard rooms, lavatories, ventilators, medical facilities, communications, accommodation for crewmen and key workers, radio test facilities, electrical facilities, water purification facilities, facilities for painters, carpenters and mechanical engineers, compressor reconditioning and motor rewinding shops, anti-aircraft gun emplacements, and substantial storage spaces for explosives, oil, ammunition, and spare parts. These sites were carefully surveyed and considered relative to the soil, and proximity to sources for sand, aggregate, cement, and building timber. Railway lines had to be constructed to transport building materials, cranes, pile-drivers, cement mixers, and the men and goods needed for the projects. In the period of construction at the Lorient-Keroman facility alone, more than 60,000 rail freight cars visited the site. In France, the procurement of the raw materials, machinery, and labour was certainly easier than it was in Norway, where the people were much more reluctant to assist the Germans. Most of the labour had to be brought in from outside the country. Another difficulty in Norway was the nature of the sites which were at the heads of a fjords, requiring the footings and foundations for the bunkers to be cut from granite, and the accumulation of several metres of silt also had to be dealt with.

In the Bergen and Trondheim, Norway bunker projects, OT had to contend with many interruptions in the construction due to Allied air raids. The raids destroyed machinery and harassed the workers, and hampered the delivery of materials.

A further requirement for OT was the development and construction of massive storage depots for the stockpiling of the immense quantities of materials needed for the projects. Preparation of the building sites involved the use of huge pumps to dry out the ground before the digging of foundations for the gigantic U-bunker buildings could begin. The actual pouring of concrete was a twenty-four-hour- a-day job, and, using enormous quantities of steel reinforcement rods, the work of gradually building up the thick walls and roofs of the bunkers continued through twelve-hour workdays, excepting Sundays, which were half-days.

The most technically demanding aspects of the U-bunker construction effort, as well as the repairs to the U-boats, required the expertise of German staff brought in from Germany. The combination of German technical personnel and the local French workers posed particular problems as many of the Germans did not speak French, nor did the majority of the French workers understand German. The work, especially the repair work on the boats, relied to a large extent, on the importing of spare parts from locations as far away as Kiel in northern Germany. Those in charge of boat repairs in the Brittany coast U-bunkers were at the mercy of a transport supply line that was constantly being interrupted by Allied air attacks on the railway lines as well as on the German production and manufacturing plants.

Consideration by the British government of bombing the U-boat pen shelters was debated. Even after Mr Churchill said in the Commons that "from being a powerful ally, France has been converted into an enemy", his Chiefs of Staff were persuaded by the Foreign Office that "R.A.F. bombers, in all humanity, could not strike the land and people of defeated France". Thus, while a truly decisive, destructive blow should have been delivered on the U-bunkers while they were under construction, that opportunity slipped away as the wisdom of Whitehall seemed to be that, while many French supported the ideals of the pro-Nazi Vichy government, many more did not, and no R.A.F. bombing raids were staged against the pens until they were mostly completed and it was too late to make a meaningful impression on them.

In time, however, the hawks prevailed and heavy bombing raids were mounted in 1942 and 1943 on the Brittany bunkers at Brest, Lorient, and St. Nazaire. The results, though, were not impressive. The R.A.F. flew by night and, with relatively imprecise bombsight capability, utilised saturation or area bombing and, while destroying much of the towns of St. Nazaire and Lorient, failed utterly to do any significant damage to the U-boat bunkers.

In an example of an American Eighth Air Force daylight raid against a U-boat pen facility on 23 November 1942, a force of fifty B-17s and eight B-24s took off to attack the St. Nazaire bunker. They were bringing a total of seventy-eight tons of mostly 2,000-pound general purpose bombs to their target that early afternoon. As the B-17s of one bomb group in the formation, the 306th, turned off the target and were leaving the St. Nazaire area, the last bomber in the group, *Banshee*, piloted by 1/Lt William Casey, was suddenly attacked by eight Focke Wulf Fw 190 fighters of JG 2. From the interrogation report on the incident: "13.28 hrs—Enemy aircraft attacked from below. As he passed, tail gunner fired, hitting the tail and as the Fw 190 turned, he got a spray of bullets in the nose. Heavy black smoke came out and the plane disintegrated. One wheel seen to fly through air and pilot to bale out. 13.34: E/a came in from below. Right waist gunner fired steadily from medium range. At 200 yards the Fw 190 fell out of control. It was seen to hit the sea. 13.35: Fw 190 attacked from the rear, coming up from below. Ball-turret gunner fired first, hitting three e/a at 100 yards. At 50 yards bullets entered the motor and the fighter burst into flame and broke to pieces. Crew doubts if pilot could have baled out. 13.36: E/a came in from above, attacking from 1 o'clock. Top-turret gunner fired hitting the e/a at long range. At 200 yards the plane peeled off in smoke and flames, then broke into pieces after tracer bullets were seen to enter the engine. 13.38: Fw 190 came in from 1 o'clock high, out of sun. Right-waist gunner fired at medium range. At 200 yards the plane was hit in the nose, began smoking heavily and pilot baled out. 13.39: E/a attacked from below, zooming up at the ball-gunner, who fired, seeing tracers go into the engine and through cockpit. The aircraft disintegrated and was seen to fall into the water. 13.40: E/a came in from 1 o'clock high. As it came over, left-waist gunner fired, hitting plane as it dived away. E/a fell out of control at about 1,000 yards and was seen by ball-turret gunner to hit the sea." Of the fifty-eight heavy bombers dispatched on the raid, thirty-six successfully bombed the target. There is no record of damage inflicted on the sub pens at St. Nazaire that day. Three B-17s and one B-24 failed to return from the raid. The crew casualties numbered three killed, sixteen wounded, and forty-three missing.

For the most part, the 2,000-pound general purpose bombs of the American 8AF merely bounced off the concrete roofs and walls of the great U-bunkers. The bombs then available to the R.A.F. and the U.S.A.A.F. were not designed to penetrate the reinforced concrete of the bunkers.

In terms of design and construction, using as an example the Valentin submarine pen at Bremen, the U-bunker is 1,400 feet long, 318 feet wide at its widest point, and eighty-nine feet high at its highest point. The ferrous concrete walls are fifteen feet thick and the roof, built using dozens of reinforced concrete arches, is also fifteen feet thick, with portions of it up to twenty-three feet thick.

The great U-boat pens attained priority status as bombing targets beginning in March 1941 when the Royal Air Force first attacked them. That priority was reinforced in late 1942 when the American Eighth Air Force joined in the effort. While the Lorient, Bordeaux and Brest sites were natural harbours, the La Pallice and St. Nazaire harbours were not, and they required lock-gates to maintain a constant water level. Still, the majority of the U-bunkers, and especially those in France used by the operational U-boats in the Atlantic, suffered relatively little damage in the many bombing raids of the Eighth and R.A.F. Bomber Command. Some examples of these attacks follow.

ST. NAZAIRE 3 January 1943—Of 101 8AF heavy bombers dispatched, seventy-six located the target and completed their bomb run. Seven of the planes were shot down, with forty-seven damaged. Most of the bombs struck the submarine pens.

WILHELMSHAVEN 27 January 1943—Ninety-one 8AF B-17 and B-24 heavy bombers attacked the U-boat construction yards. Due to poor weather conditions, only fifty-three of the bombers dropped their bombs on the targets. Three aircraft were shot down.

BREMEN 3/4 June 1943—170 bombers of the R.A.F., including Lancasters, Wellingtons, Halifaxes, Stirlings, and Manchesters attacked the Focke Wulf aircraft factory and the U-boat construction yards with minor results. Eleven of the bombers were lost.

KIEL 13 December 1943—In the largest 8AF raid of the war to date, 649 B-17 and B-24 bombers of 710 dispatched attacked the

Deutsche Werke submarine workshops, storage buildings and boat building facilities, as well as targets of opportunity in the Hamburg area, causing substantial damage.

KIEL 23/24 July 1944—The largest R.A.F. bombing raid of the war to date, in which 629 aircraft struck at the port area, but also doing considerable damage to all parts of the city. Harbour facilities and especially the U-boat yards of Deutsche Werke were heavily bombed.

LA PALLICE, BREST and BORDEAUX 12 August 1943—A force of sixty-eight Lancasters and two Mosquitos bombed the sub pens without loss. One U-boat is believed to have been hit at La Pallice.

BERGEN 28/29 October 1944—Seven Mosquitos and 237 Lancasters were dispatched to bomb the U-boat pens. Cloud cover obscured the target. Forty-seven Lancasters dropped their bombs before the raid was abandoned. Three bombers were lost.

IJMUIDEN 12 January 1945—Lancasters of 617 "Dam Busters" Squadron attacked the U-boat pens dropping Tallboy bombs. Smoke obscured the results.

"The U.S. VIII Bomber Command flew its first mission against the submarine bases on 21st October 1942, when it dispatched ninety bombers to attack the enemy base at Lorient-Keroman. The objective was a small fishing port, situated about one and one-half miles southwest of Lorient on the Brest peninsula, which the Germans had developed as a major submarine base. Prinicipal targets were the U-boat shelters: twelve completed ones and a block of seven pens then under construction. Typical of their kind, these shelters had been built on dry land, then connected with the harbor by channels, and provided with heavily reinforced concrete roofs. Immediately adjacent to the pens stood lighter and smaller buildings believed at that time to contain workshops, transformers, oil storage, offices and other installations directly connected with the servicing of U-boats. Lorient had not been attacked by the R.A.F. during 1942, nor had the British ever attacked the area of the submarine pens. In 1941 they had made thirty-three night raids, dropping 396.1 tons of bombs, mainly on the town. Although little major damage was done to the base itself, the (American) bombing made a great impression on both French and German opinion. For once, the French people appear to have compared an attack by U.S. forces favorably with those made by the British. They seem to have been greatly pleased with the whole affair, standing in the streets watching and smiling and applauding the accuracy with which the Americans dropped bombs on the German installations. It was, they felt, too bad that Frenchmen had also to be killed, but the victims had asked for their fate in accepting employment at the base for the sake of the high wages paid there. As for the Germans, they appear to have been taken completely by surprise. The alarm was not sounded, and the bombs had fallen before the anti-aircraft guns went into action.

"Looking back over this first phase of the effort against the U-boat bases, leaders chiefly concerned with its prosecution could come to few conclusions regarding its effectiveness; it was easy enough to compile and quote certain operational data; ground reports and aerial reconnaissance pointed to certain specific effects. But it was much more difficult to determine whether any significant number of months of U-boat operations had been denied the enemy through these operations or to what extent, if any, the American bombing attacks had affected the number of U-boats operating in the Atlantic. Information gained since the cessation of hostilities indicates that the U-boats active in the Atlantic were steadily increasing in number during the period in question." —from *The Army Air Forces in World War II* by Wesley F. Craven and James L. Cate

"We were in the low squadron of the lead group, and Braddock was flying the lead ship of the whole attack, with some freshman general from Eighth Bomber Command riding along as a tourist, and they were perhaps two hundred yards above us and ahead of us, the craft a glinting silver tube against a midday cat's-tail sky.

"We were coming home from Lorient. It had been an early mission: up at two forty-five, briefing at three thirty. Since we had been to Lorient on our very first mission, we had felt a blasé detachment about the assignment, and indeed, the morning had seemed to go easily. After sun-up the sky had been a pale semi-globe of sapphire, flawed only by a thin sheet of frosty cirrus over Europe. There had been no ground haze; no contrails had formed; the target had been visible from forty miles away. Enemy opposition had been relatively light and had concentrated on formations other than ours. The bombing had been fair. At the rally point Marrow had suddenly asked Haverstraw, in order to check up on Clint's alertness, what the bearing would have been to the secondary target. Haverstraw, apparent-

ly having thought his day's work virtually over, had been daydream-
ing and hadn't the faintest idea how to answer, and now Marrow had
just finished eating him out.

"Braddock's ship was named *Bull Run*. Braddock was Marrow's
good friend, but I scarcely knew him, except as a ton of prime meat,
a big, tall, fat man, about whom I had heard it said that he was
incredibly cool and steady in the air; his nervous system must have
been primitive, like a whale's. I had not even stopped to think who
else was in his ship besides the tourist: eight nobodies; to me, the
plane was simply Braddock's up there, *Bull Run*.

"We were going along all right. We had flown through some of
Handown's 'iron cumulus' over the target, but none of our Group had
been knocked down, and it was good, leaving the rally point, not to
have any fighters around, and to have such a clear sky, with home
and rest ahead, and we were all socked in close, a good formation,
and nobody was saying a word on VHF about fighters, though the
general, being new, was chattering a lot of nonsense. On the whole we
were comfortable, with another mission, *The Body*'s seventh, practically under our belts; it was really wonderful up in the sky streaking
for England.

"Then Marrow was pointing. Up there, Braddock's ship. And I
thought, Look out, Brad, look out, look out, you're smoking, number
two's smoking. I could not take my eyes off the thin telltale of smoke,
more than exhaust but less than peril as yet; it did not blow out.
Someone came up on VHF to tell Braddock he was burning, and at
that the whole Group was alert to his danger. Suddenly the smoke
went black, and there were visible flames, pale against the sky, and
it seemed to me that the ships of the formation edged in closer (it
was a fact that Marrow pushed up the manifold pressure) to watch,
like insects crowding a night light.

"Braddock pushed over from his position above us and began a
shallow power glide to try to blow the fire out, and just then Max
Brindt shouted on our interphone, 'Look out! What is that?'

What was it? What was it? Something had come off *Bull Run* and
went flipping past us. I realized it was the little rear hatch door; the
tail gunner must have kicked it out. No, it wouldn't be the tail gunner in the lead ship with a tourist aboard. It would be the co-pilot,
because under the circumstances he would be back there flying tail
gunner-observer, watching the formation and reporting everything
up to the general, so the general could make a fool of himself with a

full supply of information; it would have been myself back in that tail position if we had been leading the Wing. I had a moment's fantasy that it was I who had kicked out that small flipping plate; I was getting out. I remembered then with a shudder that Braddock's co-pilot was not I but Kozak, a pale fellow who never seemed to speak a word—an impression white, white skin with a heavy black stubble of beard, a face immobile and silent. There came a leg, and another, and Kozak was squeezing out like a creature being born, and I almost shouted on the radio, 'Look out, Kozy! Christ, there are over a hundred ships here, we're all coming at you.'

"Surely Kozak had thought of just that, or surely he would not have done what he did. He ripped his chute the moment he was out. He was too excited. His body, fresh from the speeding Fort, was going through the air at more than a hundred fifty miles per hour. I saw a flutter of shining nylon, flaglike at first, then what seemed to be a big loose bunch of feminine understuff, and we were all coming up at it—he'd been small before now, with the breaking parachute, he seemed massive; he was too excited. Then the snap. Every bone in his body must have broken, he just—his back— we were right close under him—when the chute filled, his back arched and flapped like a ribbon snapping out in a wind; it must have killed him on the instant, the way he—Kozy, he jumped to save himself but he was dead, because of the speed we were all going up there, and he didn't wait. He just snapped, mind and body. What he thought would happen, with all those ships, he must have thought someone would run into him, that was the way I judged it, and he bailed out and did not hold his count, he must have been afraid of all those props, because we were coming all around him, and he was going to drift back through the formation, and he must have thought that if he could just get his parachute open right away, we'd all see him and could evade; but that was the wrong idea in every respect.

"I cooly thought: I'd be alive. If I'd been the tail gunner-observer in the lead ship, Kozy, I'd have dropped and dropped, a delayed jump, clear down to those newly forming white fluffy clouds on the edge of this high-pressure area of sparkling blue, a long, long drop, more than fifteen thousand feet; way down. That's what I'd have tried to do. Arms against the sides. Knees up . . . But you're dead, Kozy, from trying too hard to be alive.

"I had thought it was easy to get out, no problem, just get out and wait and pull and float down; that's what I had thought. Maybe it wasn't so easy. I had never let myself think about that.

"Braddock's plane was quite far ahead and below, now, perhaps a thousand feet down, going very fast and pulling forward and down and away, but the smoke was worse than ever and flames were pouring back off the wing, not blowing out at all but fanning up, it seemed, glowing like coals in a camp stove blown on with a deep breath.

"Braddock started to climb. As he got halfway back up to our height I noticed that Buzz had begun to climb in key with him, and I looked out and saw that we were all climbing, we were all flying formation behind and above Braddock' black plumes. We're going up with you, Brad, don't worry, we're sticking with you. No, not like that, we can't climb like that. Hey. Hey. Don't climb that way. You're out of control, you're going right up to the top. What an impressive sight!—a big Fort shooting straight up, ahead of us in the sky. Your smoke. Such a clear day . . . No! No! No!

"He blew up. Right at the top, right in front of us, the whole thing. That smoke—why didn't you all jump?—that smoke—fire, it must have been your number two engine and a wing tank and then everything. Two or three flashes . . . He blew up.

"Buzz! Look out for all that crap.

"Twenty, thirty tons of bits, we're going to fly right into the stuff. Look at it. Look at that big piece of metal. Head down, cover eyes, don't look. Nothing's happening, we're diving. It's past us.

"Marrow, good work. Marrow.

"What an explosion that was! I even heard it, I think I heard it, and that would be unusual at altitude, in all one's gear, and that far away; it made such a big thud I think I heard it in the cockpit.

"Now it was quiet. A minute before everyone had been chattering on VHF, everybody making his big remark, we had been talking away and then everyone stopped. It was such an impressive sight. Now there wasn't a sound, and there were more than a hundred Forts around us, but not a word, they all had something to think about; no one was saying a word, not even an exclamation. Why didn't somebody speak? It was so quiet. I wished somebody would come up and talk. There. There it was. High squadron. 'Well, form on me. We'd better take over and do something.' There, that was better.

"Junior Sailen called in. He hadn't heard anything, you understand. Only Buzz and I and Lamb in the radio room could hear the VHF, and Buzz had only pointed at Braddock. Just that one remark of Max's. Sailen cut in on interphone from the ball turret down under the plane, asking, 'Say, what was all the junk that went past us?'

"Marrow answered. 'Braddock, that was Braddock.'

" 'Any chutes?' Junior said.

" 'Anybody see any chutes?' Marrow asked.

"Max Brindt in the nose said, 'One out of the tail. The guy ripped too soon.'

" 'That was Kozak,' I said. 'That pale guy.'

"Then little Junior Sailen, down in the close cocoon in which he flew, said in a low voice, icy dead cold, 'I knew it. I knew it. You can't get out of these God-damn crates.'

"It hit me Nobody had got out. Not one. They all died. Kozak died. Braddock died. That general. Ten men dead. I had always thought you could get out of a Fort, it was so big. Plenty of hatches. But maybe you wouldn't get out. You'd just sit there and get killed. You couldn't escape.

"I thought: I'm scared. Somebody's got to help me. Look at Marrow, maybe he'll help. Oh, Jesus, look at Buzz, he's smiling at me. He can see I'm scared. I see his eyes smiling behind his goggles to buck me up. He wants to tell me something, his eyes are bulging out as they do when he talks about getting a piece of tail, he's going to speak to me, he's pushing the interphone button on his wheel with his thumb, he's going to say something to all of us. 'It can't happen to this bucket, boys, not while I'm in it.'

—from *The War Lover* by John Hersey

From a news report by *The Daily Telegraph* (London) of Tuesday, 28 July 1942, subtitled HAVOC IN CHIEF U-BOAT BUILDING CENTRE: "In 35 minutes, bombers rained down more than 175,000 incendiaries on Hamburg, Hitler's chief U-boat building base and, therefore, one of the most important targets in all Germany. This was the start of a devastating R.A.F. attack carried out in cloudless moonlight on Sunday night. And following the incendiaries, the largest number ever dropped in a single raid, came a wave of bombers packed with high explosives.

"The damage is believed to be colossal. It was certainly one of the most outstandingly successful raids of the whole war.

"Confirmation of its success was forthcoming from the Germans themselves. Their communiqué stated: 'The civilian population suffered considerable casualties, many buildings were destroyed and

preceeding page: Kapitänleutnant Joachim Schepke and his executive officer relaxing on the "wintergarden" of *U-100*, a Type VIIB inbound to Lorient after a patrol in September 1940; top: Loading torpedoes aboard *U-48* at Kiel in February 1940; above left: A cook aboard a U-boat tasting his creation; above right: crew members "hot-bunking" aboard *U-103*, under command of Kapitüanleutnant Werner Winter in May 1942.

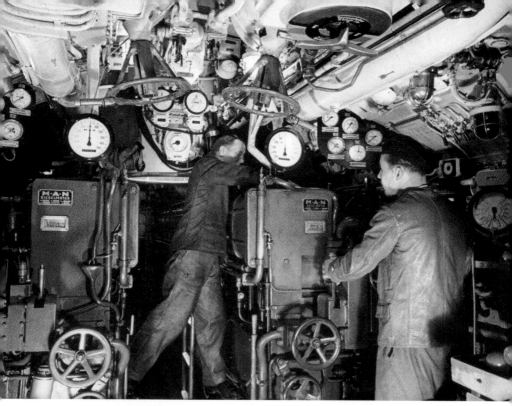

top: Engineers at work in the diesel room of *U-65*, commanded by Kapitänleutnant Hans-Gerrit von Stockhausen in September 1940; above: A "mixer" in the forward torpedo room of *U-103*.

above: An Allied convoy steaming on the North Atlantic in 1943; left: Admiral Sir Max Horton, commander-in-chief of the Western Approaches in the second half of World War II; top right: Oberleutnant zur See Paul-Karl Loeser (white hat) with members of his crew on the bridge of *U-373* in April 1942; bottom right: A Canadian corvette on convoy escort duty in the Second World War.

top left: Kapitänleutnant Herbert Kuppisch at his periscope during a war patrol; bottom left: An oil tanker broken in two by the torpedo of a U-boat on the North Atlantic run; at top: A lifeboat with survivors of a merchant ship sunk by a German submarine in World War II; above: Kapitän-leutnant Günther Krech, commander of *U-558*, which was sunk near Cape Ortegal, Spain, on July 20, 1943, by depth-charges from an R.A.F. Halifax bomber and a USAAF Liberator bomber.

top left: A Type VII and a Type IX U-boat sharing a berth at a U-bunker pen shelter on the Brittany coast of France in World War II; far ;eft: *U-566* returning to St Nazaire in April 1942; left: Captain Donald Macintyre, a famous U-boat killer; below: Kapitänleutnant Joachim Schepke celebrating his return from a patrol in September 1940.

left: A Short Sunderland flying boat patrol bomber operated by the R.A.F. to help counter the threat of German U-boats in the Second World War; above: An Allied warship on convoy escort duty, lays a pattern of depth-charges over a submerged U-boat in the North Atlantic, 1942.

Kapitänleutnant Helmut Möhlmann, his target vessel sinking in the distance, and a lifeboat with survivors from the ship, approaching the afterdeck of *U-571*; right: A crewman from a U-boat that has been sunk in an Allied aircraft attack.

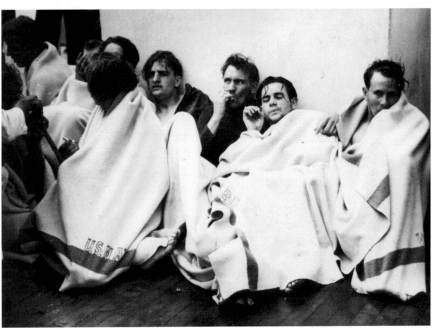

top: Crewmen and a boarding party from the U.S. Navy escort carrier *Guadalcanal* as the sub is captured intact. Years later the *U-505* was put on permanent display at the Chicago Museum of Science and Industry; above: Captured U-boat crewmen after the sinking of their vessel.

Kapitänleutnant Gerd Schreiber aboard *U-95* in St Nazaire, March 1941

Oberleutnant Erich Topp on patrol aboard *U-552*, April 1942.

damaged, almost exclusively in residential quarters,' phraseology they use only when there has been damage on a 1,000-plane-raid scale, or somewhere near it.

"And a military spokesman on the German-controlled Paris Radio last night said the raid 'may be considered a spectacular success for the British.'

"Berlin Radio warned German listeners of more heavy raids to come. Reprisal attacks on British towns were promised.

"Rome Radio said the raid 'was one of the heaviest so far experienced by Germany.' It added that damage to buildings was heavy, as were the casualty lists. Precise numbers of dead and injured would probably be announced today.

"From this attack, and also from raids on aerodromes in the Low Countries, 29 bombers are missing, not a heavy loss in proportion to the size of the 'extremely powerful force', the biggest since the 1,000-bomber attack on Bremen last month. Hamburg is acknowledged to be the best-defended city in the Reich. The moonlight made the task of the German night-fighters easier."

It was not until 1944, when the R.A.F. combined three 4,000-pound "cookies" into one armour-piercing "Tallboy" bomb, that the bunkers could be damaged at all. Of his attacks in early 1943, Air Chief Marshal Harris wrote: "The most we could hope to do was to cause universal devastation round the pens and in the town . . . we could also give U-boat crews on shore a disturbed night, if they were foolish enough to stay in the area, but of course they were not. The Admiralty may or may not have thought that this would exert a worthwhile influence on the Battle of the Atlantic . . . though before we began on it I protested repeatedly against this hopeless misuse of air power . . . The only effect [the attacks had] was to delay the opening of the Battle of the Ruhr and the main bomber offensive against Germany by nearly two months."

The great U-bunker bases on the Brittany coast of France were very well protected by German Air Force fighters as well as 88mm flak guns. During the many American and British bombing raids on the pen bases, more than a hundred bombers were shot down, more than half of them American. U.S. Army Air Force General Carl Spaatz shared Harris' misgivings about the bombing policy towards the pens. He wrote to General Hap Arnold, his commander-in-chief, in Washington: "Whether or not these operations will prove too cost-

ly for the results obtained remains to be seen. The concrete submarine pens are hard, maybe impossible nuts to crack." He accepted,
however, that the bombing of the surrounding installations should
seriously handicap the effective use of the bases, and he continued
sending Eighth Air Force bombers on eleven more raids to attack the
Brittany bases between October 1942 and April 1943, when both he
and Harris were assigned new priority targets.

"It was not until the end of 1943 that USAAF surveys of strategic
bombing results tended to confirm doubts hitherto hesitantly
expressed regarding the value of bombing submarine bases. By that
time the submarine had been defeated in the first round of the battle of supply, and it had become apparent that attack from the air
against the U-boat at sea had been the most effective single factor in
reducing the German submarine fleet, and that bombing of bases
had contributed relatively little in that direction. Grand Admiral
Karl Dönitz, who, as one-time commander of the U-boat fleet, was in
a unique position to know whereof he spoke, later confirmed this
opinion in an interview with Allied intelligence officers after his
capture in 1945. "Not only were the pens themselves impervious to
anything but the heaviest type of bomb," he asserted, "but they
housed virtually all necessary repair and maintenance facilities.
Bombing of surrounding installations did not therefore seriously
affect the rate of turn-around. What slowed turn-around most effectively", he claimed, "was the necessity for repairing the damage
done to hull structure by aerial-bomb and depth-charge attacks
delivered at sea." —from *The Army Air Forces In World War II*, by
Wesley F. Craven and James L. Cate

The haunting memory of a French woman, who had been five years
old at the time one particular bomber was shot down: "Our house in
Brest was destroyed, but a few days earlier we had fled to a remote
village. I was told that the 'Brestois' in their shelters prayed for the
RAF pilots while the bombs were falling. On 13th August 1943, an
aircraft fell in a field near our village. At the funeral of the crew,
German soldiers forbade the locals to enter the church. The silence
of what seemed to me a vast crowd was very impressive. When the
procession came out, the crowd moved forward but was stopped at the
gate of the cemetery. I broke through the row of soldiers and followed the procession. A German officer looked down at me but did-
n't say anything. Always, when we passed the cemetery, we prayed for

the British pilots, and when spring came we brought bouquets of primroses."

The British and American bombs, while making little impression on the U-bunkers in 1943, did, however, have a considerable impact on the environs. Local traffic and trade were largely halted, the streets of La Rochelle / La Pallice, Lorient, and St. Nazaire were littered with rubble, most buildings and homes were wrecked. So, too, was the fishing industry in these communities, where the deep-sea fishing boats remained moored or beached, most of the fishermen having no fuel, and those who did being frightened of putting out to sea in the mine-infested waters. All schools were shut; the children sent away to the countryside.

With the end of "the Happy Time" for the men of the U-bootwaffe, Allied fighter aircraft established air supremacy over the French Atlantic coast, and the U-boats attempting to approach and leave their bases were constantly under threat of air attack and having to dive to escape it. They had to be guided through the adjacent mine-fields by patrol boats and trawlers. They had to hide frequently among the inshore fishing boats and were safe only when they entered the shelter of the pens. One German recalled the scene in the Lorient pen: "A row of U-boats lay in water like a millpond, in a strange contrast with the ruins of the buildings in town. Some boats were standing in the dry dock and gangs of labourers were working on the hulls. There were the familiar smells of oil and seasalt and the reflections off the dark walls of welding torch flame. There were tired workers and tired submarine crewmen."

THE CAPTAIN

"A life of action and danger moderates the dread of death. It not only gives us fortitude to bear pain, but teaches us at every step the precarious tenure on which we hold our present being."
—from *On The Fear of Death* by William Hazlitt

". . . in the mess, the first round of drinks would loosen the captain's tongue: 'It's quite something—working on a convoy over a distance of seven hundred miles! And lousy weather all the way. At one point there was a destroyer coming straight for us. Narrowest silhouette you've ever seen. Once again we thought we'd had it. But it hadn't even noticed us. And then the gray nights up there. Faces the color of cheese, the way you look in the moonlight—only there wasn't any moon: those Northern Lights. Then we bagged a tanker sailing all alone. I was beginning to think we'd fired a dud—but then they started hollering on the bridge! The flames went up in a rush three hundred feet at least—every color from white to black-blood-red—one enormous mushroom! The ship looked like a slab of iron in a forge. It's pretty eerie when a ten-thousand-ton barge like that gets blown sky-high. It makes your blood run cold. God, I'd hate to be on board. But then perhaps it's better that way. At least it's all over in one go.' "
—from *U-Boat War* by Lothar-Günther Buchheim

When the commander of a U-boat returned to base from a patrol in the early half of the Second World War, the good years from the perspectives of those in the Ubootwaffe, he wore a beard, overalls, sea boots, often, a pea jacket, and almost always the white-covered cap that only U-boat commanders were authorised to wear. There was a thing called the jumping wire that stretched from the bow of the sub to the conning tower and from there to the stern. The boat had sharp cutters over the bow to cut through anti-submarine nets, and the jumping wire would then deflect the cut net over the hull to keep it from snagging on the conning tower, hand rails, etc. The forward wire also acted as a transmitting antenna for the high-frequency radio, while the pair of aft wires served as the receiving antenna. They served a further purpose on a boat returned from a successful patrol, displaying victory pennants, one for each vessel the crew had sunk, with the tonnage of the Allied vessels sunk. Often, in such homecomings, Dönitz himself would be there to greet the commander, as were attractive young women to present flowers and kisses to the feted captain, and a small band playing a stirring, upbeat tune.

Some U-boat commanders were *Korventtenkapitäns* (Lieutenant Commander), or *Fregattenkapitäns* (Commander), some were *Oberleutnants* (Lieutenant Junior Grade), but the rank of the great majority was *Kapitänleutnant* (Lieutenant). He was *Herr Kaleu* to the men of his crew and, in the early days at least, a genuine hero to the German people and to Dönitz.

"Since we have been at sea, the commander has changed: formerly gruff and unforthcoming, new he is cheerful, even engaging, whenever he makes an appearance on the bridge. He usually has a fat cigar between the forefinger and middle finger of his right hand, puffs ostentatious clouds of smoke and otherwise makes it plain how glad he is to be back at sea. I am probably not the only one to be grateful for this attitude of his: having confidence in your commander is more important aboard a submarine than on any other vessel. After all, during a periscope attack, he is the only one who can actually see the enemy and who has to know exactly how far he might dare go.

"The chief engineer is the commander's right hand. He is the absolute ruler of the engine rooms and responsible for precise depth control. He has to have something more than mere technical ability; as the man in charge of underwater steering he has to have a special sense which will enable him to anticipate the boat's every tendency to sink or to rise, because by the time these show up on the instruments, it is usually too late.

"The first and second watch officers are in charge of their respective watches. They are naval officers and the commander relies on them whenever he is not himself on the bridge. Apart from this, number one is in charge of the torpedoes, while number two is responsible for the machine guns and the artillery.

"Our crew is one of the most experienced. The engineers in charge of diesels and E-motors, the torpedo mechanics, the radio and hydrophone operators are all well trained, and so are the sailors.

"Apart from the bosun, the navigator, the stokers, and several petty officers, they are all exceedingly young.

"After the first few days, which were taken up with practice alarms, the commander withdraws from the regular activities on board. The curtains of his bunk are usually pulled shut. He sleeps with deliberation. His presence is felt rather than seen. His favorite maxim: 'You must have all the sleep you can get, so that your nerves will be in good shape when it matters.' The lesson he keeps drumming into his watch officers: Don't try too hard to second-guess your adversary; he's set in his ways and will usually do the obvious thing. And don't pay too much attention to the whispers of your so-called intuition.

"Years later, this is what the commander said: 'As a submarine commander, you were ultimately on your own. During an attack, you were usually being chased by destroyers, threatened by depth charges, and at that moment you held the sole responsibility for the entire crew that was stuck with you inside that iron coffin. And so, every hit you scored was a kind of vindication of yourself to the crew."
—from *U-boat War* by Lothar-Günther Buchheim

In 1936 Gross-Admiral Erich Raeder, head of the German Navy, appointed Karl Dönitz to run the U-boat force. His first significant act was to convert the Kiel Anti-Submarine School into a command training establishment for future U-boat officers. Among his earliest graduates were three commanders he considered perhaps the bravest, most able and competent in the service; the highly successful Otto Kretschmer, Joachim Schepke, and Günther Prien.

Kretschmer came from lower Silesia. He had excelled in both science and languages and had studied these subjects in Italy, France, and England, prior to becoming a naval cadet in 1930. His early "command" experience saw him in brief probing missions with the 250-ton *U-23* in northern British waters, trips that came to be referred to as "Kretschmer's Shetland Sorties." Nicknamed "Silent Otto", the inveterate cigar smoker was slim and hawk-nosed. He did not suffer fools but had a good humour. A fellow officer once described him as "a friend to no one, but popular with all".

A life-changing moment came for Kretschmer in April 1940 when Dönitz assigned him the command of *U-99*, a new ocean-going Type VIIC U-boat in which he was to achieve unusual success in the North Atlantic for nearly a full year.

"As *U-99* left the jetty, the dockyard superintendent and the staff came down to wave them good-bye. "She's a good ship, Captain," he cried out to Kretschmer on the conning tower. "Treat her well and

she'll sink the whole Royal Navy for you." "We will," shouted Kretschmer. "And I'll be seeing you when we take over Portsmouth dockyard."
—from *The Golden Horseshoe* by Terence Robertson

The fashion of personalising the U-boats with a symbolic decoration of some sort on the conning tower took hold during the period of Kretschmer's command of *U-99*. It would later become the norm to design and apply such artwork to the noses of the bombers and fighters of the American Eighth and Ninth Air Forces in England. Otto Kretschmer took it to be an omen when one of his crewmen happened to notice a pair of horseshoes hanging from their anchor and soon the conning tower of his boat was sporting the insignia of a pair of golden horseshoes.

Over the course of his command in *U-99*, Kretschmer accounted for the sinking of at least 200,000 tons of Allied shipping, and probably another 50,000 tons, including a destroyer and three armed merchantmen, for which he was not officially credited. He was considered the best torpedo marksman in the Kriegsmarine, and did not agree with the official navy position that the way to ensure a hit was to fire a fan of three or four torpedoes at the target. His approach to the kill was to stalk a convoy by day and attack it at night—from the dark side if there was bright moonlight and from the windward side on a moonless night. At periscope depth he would pass between the escorts and make his attacks from within the columns of the convoy.

Joachim Schepke was casual in his manner, tall and fair, popular with the ladies, he always wore his white cap at a rakish angle. Schepke also joined the German Navy in 1930, and the Ubootwaffe in 1934. Following command responsibilities in *U-3* and *U-19* at the start of the Second World War, he was given command of the Type VIIB U-100 in which he served through five patrols, attacking and sinking thirty-seven Allied ships for a total of nearly 156,000 gross tons, and damaging four more.

In Purnell's fine *History of the Second World War*, Lieutenant Commander Peter Kemp wrote: "Schepke took too many liberties with a convoy escort." A lookout on the bridge of the British destroyer HMS *Walker* sighted the wake of the *U-100* and Captain Donald Macintyre ordered his warship crew to chase the sub. The U-boat submerged and Macintyre dropped a pattern of depth-charges where Schepke had left the surface. There were no apparent hits by the

depth-charges, and the *Walker* was redirected to help pick up survivors from one of the freighters that had just been torpedoed by the
U-boats. HMS *Vanoc*, meanwhile, which was the sister ship of *Walker*,
employed its new radar and soon located the *U-100* which was
stopped on the surface as Schepke's crew inspected her damage from
the depth-charge attack. *Vanoc* now approached the crippled U-boat
and rammed her amidships, causing most of the submariners to end
up in the sea. In a ghastly result for Schepke, who was on the bridge
of his boat when it was hit by the destroyer, his legs were sheered off.
Along with forty-nine of his crew, the German commander was lost
with the wreckage of his boat.

Only moments later, the Asdic operators of both *Vanoc* and *Walker*
picked up a contact that turned out to be *U-99*, the submarine of
Otto Kretschmer, the Ubootwaffe ace of aces. Attacking Kretchmer's
boat with depth-charges, the destroyers inflicted significant damage
to the hull and both propellers. He was forced to take the boat down
to 700 feet and when he was finally able to resurface, *U-99* lay listing heavily to starboard, unable to manoeuvre, and out of torpedoes.
At that point it was Macintyre's intention to use his guns and force
the U-boat crew to abandon ship. The British captain planned to
capture it intact. Otto Kretschmer was equally determined that his
boat would not be taken by the enemy. He ordered his crew to scuttle the sub and signalled Macintyre: "Captain to captain, please
pick up my men in the water who are drifting towards you. I am sinking." Macintyre responded by readying a lifeboat to be lowered.
There was an interval in which the submarine remained on the surface, until Kretschmer's engineer asked permission to flood the ballast tanks. Then the boat went down, taking the engineer and two
other crewmembers with it. The crew of the *Walker* then lowered a
scrambling net from the destroyer's deck and the surviving crewmen
of *U-99* climbed aboard. The exhausted Kretschmer was rescued by
one of his own crew.

At his Lorient headquarters, Dönitz's men tried repeatedly to contact *U-99* and *U-100*. The following day, Captain Macintyre invited
Kretschmer to join him on the bridge of *Walker* as the destroyer continued its escort duties with the convoy. He then relieved
Kretschmer of his Zeiss binoculars, "You won't be needing these any
more."

The *Walker* returned to Liverpool and Kretschmer's crew members
were handed over to the British Army as prisoners of war. Otto

Kretschmer was taken to London for interrogation. There he was interviewed by Captain George Creasy who said of the U-boat commander: "He gave nothing away . . . I saw a young and obviously self-confident naval commander who bore himself, in the difficult circumstances of recent capture, with self-respect, modesty, and courtesy." He later learned from his captors that Dönitz had promoted him to Lieutenant Commander and added the Swords to the Oak Leaves of his Knight's Cross. Of Kretschmer, Donald Macintyre wrote: "Compared with his exhuberant fellow aces he seemed a sinister figure. Out in the wastes of the North Atlantic he and *U-99* were indeed a sinister and deadly menace."

Günther Prien came from Lübeck, near Hamburg. A love of the sea had caused him to join the merchant navy and spend nine years there before moving on to the Kriegsmarine. Somewhat stubborn, impetuous, but good-natured, Prien accumulated a total of more than 150,000 tons of Allied shipping sunk in his high-achieving Ubootwaffe career, which was marred only by an incident in June 1940 when he located, torpedoed and sank the 15,000-ton British liner *Arandora Star*. He learned then that the majority of the passengers had been German and Italian civilians being transported from England to Canada for internment there.

It was Prien who, as skipper of *U-47*, just after midnight on 13-14 October 1939, had guided the boat into Scapa Flow, the Royal Navy anchorage in the Orkney Islands, on a rising tide, and located the 29,000-ton Revenge-class battleship *Royal Oak*, which had first seen action at the Battle of Jutland in June 1916. Firing a salvo of four torpedoes at the battleship, Prien missed with the first three but hit with the fourth. He reloaded and fired four more torpedoes at the target. The attack was played against the striking backdrop of the Northern Lights and the old battleship went down in minutes, taking the lives of 833 officers and men of the 1,234-man crew. Prien's action shocked not only the Royal Navy but the British public who woke up to the news that the Germans were more than capable of bringing the naval war to Britain's home waters. Günther Prien was a new national hero in Germany. An irony of the attack was that Scapa Flow where it happened, was also the scene, at the end of World War I where the German Kaiser's captured naval fleet was scuttled by its crews while the Allies were pondering its disposal. During the run back to base in Germany, Prien's Executive Officer, Leutnant zur See Engelbert Endrass, who would become a future U-boat ace, designed and decorated the conning tower of *U-47* with a rendering of a red snorting bull, symbolic of their having charged, bull-like, into the British Navy's main anchorage and gored their famous battleship. Each boat in Prien's flotilla would later adopt the snorting bull insignia.

"No more striking measure of the strong sense of security against U-boats which dominated all minds at Scapa Flow can be found than in the fact that, after one torpedo from the first volley had actually struck the *Royal Oak* none of the vigilant and experienced officers conceived that it could be a torpedo. The danger from the air was the one first apprehended, and large numbers of the crew took up their air-raid stations under the armour, and were thereby doomed, while at the same time the captain and admiral were examining the alternative possibilities of an internal explosion. It was in these conditions that the second volley of torpedoes was discharged. Thus the forfeit has been claimed, and we mourn the loss of eight hundred gallant officers and men, and of a ship which, although very old, was of undoubted military value."

—from "the Loss of the *Royal Oak*" speech by Winston S. Churchill, 8 November 1939

In a recollection of his first patrol, Günther Prien, the leading U-boat commander of World War II, wrote: "At last, early in the morning of the fifth September, we sighted another plume of smoke. I happened to be on the bridge. A light mist lay over the waves and beyond, the sun rose, blood red. It was difficult to see clearly in the half-light. By the time we had sighted the smoke, the ship had already come over the horizon. She was steering a curious zig-zag course like a dragonfly flitting over a stream. Endrass remarked, 'She seems to have a bad conscience.'

"We dived. I stood at the periscope and watched the ship approach. She was a short and dumpy freighter painted in weird colours. The stack was flaming red, the superstructure black and the bottom grass green. On the bows *Bosnia* was painted in large letters.

"The English merchantman had obviously been warned and was prepared for the worst. It would have been a mistake to surface in front of her as she was possibly armed or might be tempted to ram us. So I let the ship go past and we surfaced a short distance astern and fired a shot over her. The ship altered course and turned stern to us and I noticed the foam of the propeller swirling up. She was trying to escape. We fired a second round, this time so close that the column of water splashed on deck. But she refused to stop. At the same time my signaller sang out; 'Signal to Commander: Enemy sending radio messages.'

"A runner came hurrying up the ladder. 'Here is the intercepted message, sir.' He gave me the slip of paper" Under attack and fire from German U-boat. Urgently require assistance. Here followed his position and the message ended with SOS, SOS.

"That settled it. I gave Endrass a sign. Swiftly and with precision the crew loaded the gun. Then Endrass barked 'Fire.' A sharp report and the *Bosnia* was hit amidships. A cloud of smoke rose up, but still the *Bosnia* continued her flight.

" 'Five rounds rapid fire,' I ordered.

"Again we could clearly see the second shell hit its target, then the third.

"At last the ship hove to and lay there like a wounded animal. From the hold heavy blue and yellow smoke belched up and formed a column over the ship like a pine tree swaying in the wind. The cargo must have included a large quantity of sulphur. We closed in on the *Bosnia*, as the crew rustled to the boats and launched them.

"Hansel sang out behind me, 'Column of smoke in sight.' I turned about. On the northwest horizon appeared a thick streak of smoke, heavy and black, like a mourning flag. Swiftly I considered my situation. It could be a destroyer coming to the aid of the freighter.

" 'Keep that ship well in sight,' I told Hansel, 'and report at once if you can see what her nationality is.'

"The crew of the *Bosnia* had been over hasty in their efforts to escape. One boat had filled with water and was foundering. It was pathetic to see the men drift helplessly away. Some of them shouted for help while others beckoned to us. We steered towards the sinking boat. Samann and Dittmer reached down to help the floating men aboard, leaning far overboard so that their hands nearly touched the water.

"By now the lifeboat of the *Bosnia* had filled with water and the sea swept over it. A few heads were floating close together, then a wave separated them. In the space of a few seconds only a handful were left.

"A few non-swimmers thrashed about with their arms. Others were swimming with long strokes towards a sea-worthy lifeboat of the *Bosnia*, which had turned towards the men in the water.

"Reaching out, Dittmer and Samann grabbed one of the men and heaved him on board. He was a small red-headed boy, probably the mess-boy. He sat up gasping, while water was running down his face and dripping from his clothes.

"Behind me Hansel reported. 'It is a Norwegian freighter, sir.' I turned round and took up the glasses. The ship was coming up from the sou'west lay high; apparently she had no cargo on board.

" 'OK Hansel,' I said, and heaved a sigh of relief. I would not have welcomed an encounter with a destroyer before I had sunk the *Bosnia*.

"In the meantime the boy recovered his breath, got up and stepped to the rail beside Dittmer. He was shivering with fright. I beckoned him to the bridge. 'Are you the mess-boy?' 'Yes, sir.' 'What was your cargo?' 'Sulphur, sir.' 'Where were you bound for?' He spoke in a cockney accent but his answers were completely unselfconscious. He was a boy from the London slums, a type of person who is impressed by no one and nothing.

" 'You are trembling. Are you afraid?' He shook his head. 'No, I'm only cold, sir.'

" 'You will have a spot of brandy later on,' I said. He nodded his head and added, perhaps to show his gratitude, 'Of course, we got a fright, sir. You can't imagine what it's like; you looks over the water and sees nothing, on'y sky and water and then suddenly a bloomin' big thing pops up beside yer, blowing like a walrus. I thought I was seein' the Loch Ness monster.'

"We approached the second boat of the *Bosnia*.

" 'Where is your Captain?' I called over the water.

"An officer stood up and pointed to the *Bosnia*. 'He is on board,' he said.

"I gazed at the ship which was wreathed in clouds of smoke and flaming like a volcano. 'What is he doing there?'

" 'He is burning his documents.'

"I understood. There was a man alone on the burning ship, hundreds of miles from land and without a lifeboat, destroying his ship's papers lest they fall into the hands of the enemy. I had to admire his courage.

" 'And who are you?' I asked the officer.

"He raised his hand to his cap, 'I am the First Officer of the *Bosnia*.

" 'Come aboard.'

"Dittmer helped him to climb on board. On the whole he did not look very much like a seaman; pale, fat and tired. When he stood on the deck he saluted again.

"In the meantime the little mess-boy had been taken on board the other lifeboat of the *Bosnia* and we steered towards the new arrival, the large Norwegian vessel which floated almost completely out of the water.

"On our way we came across one of the shipwrecked men and while we stopped Samann and Dittmer hauled him on board.

"I came down from the tower to have a look at the man they had brought up. He lay there lifeless, a small skinny man still fairly young in years, but worn out like an old horse. There were traces of coal dust on his clothes. He had probably been a stoker on board the *Bosnia*.

"Samann had removed his jacket and shirt; the fellow was painfully thin and his ribs showed up clearly like the bars of a cage. Dittmer grasped him by the arms and began artificial respiration.

"The First Officer of the *Bosnia* was standing beside me. Looking down at the man he said abruptly, 'You Germans are good-hearted people, sir.' I looked at him standing there, fat, well-fed and probably mighty satisfied with himself. I could not contain myself and said gruffily, 'It would have been better if you people had given that poor fellow something to eat in your ship.' Leaving him standing there I returned to the tower.

"The Norwegian vessel had now approached so close by that her large national flag flying from the fore-mast was clearly visible. I flagged her to a stop and she hove to, so close to our boat that the sides towered over us like a cliff.

"We signalled, 'Please take crew of English ship on board.'

"The Norwegian ship replied, 'Ready.' A boat was lowered and when it came alongside, the little stoker, still unconscious, was put aboard first, followed by the First Officer who saluted once more before he left.

"I talked with the officer in charge of the Norwegian lifeboat, and explained the situation to him. I pointed to the *Bosnia*'s lifeboat, with the *Bosnia* burning close beside. Just then a man on board the *Bosnia* jumped into the water, probably the captain who had managed to destroy his papers. I pointed towards him and said, 'You must save that man also.' The Norwegian officer nodded and cast off.

"We waited until they had finished the rescue work. It took quite a time, while our lookouts nervously scanned the horizon; the *Bosnia* had wirelessed for help and her cloud of smoke stood like a huge pillar over the burning ship, which must have been visible for hundreds of miles.

"At last the Norwegian vessel dipped her flag and steamed off.

"We were obliged to sacrifice a torpedo to finish off the *Bosnia*.

"It was our first torpedo release and everyone wanted to observe its effect. So, nearly the whole crew came on deck. We had, of course, seen from photographs from the First World War how the stricken steamer appears to rear up in the water and then swiftly slide to the bottom. But this was quite different, much less showy and all the more impressive because of that. There was a dull explosion and huge columns of water rose up high on the mast. And then the stricken ship simply broke in two pieces which, in a space of seconds, disappeared into the sea. A few bits of driftwood and the empty boats were all that was left.

"As we were doing our trim dive on the twelfth day, I was standing at the periscope and called over to Bohm, 'Gustav, your bloody periscope is covered in muck again.'

" 'But I've cleaned it, sir.'

"At the same instant I caught sight of a steamer. It was like an electric shock. 'Action stations,' I shouted. We rapidly approached the solitary tanker of about six thousand tons that was trying to evade us by zig-zagging wildly. We dived underneath him and came up close astern. 'Prepare guns for firing' I called.

"I happened to turn around and the blood froze in my veins. Over on the west horizon a forest of masts had appeared. It was a large convoy. We dived immediately.

"We had very nearly been caught in a U-boat trap, for the single vessel had been sent on alone as a decoy, but I decided to go for the convoy.

"For three hours we followed the convoy with the intention of cutting it off and coming to meet it. But it was hopeless, for underwater we were far too slow. When we surfaced again the forest of masts was floating far away on the horizon. Only a trawler was coming towards us with a foaming bow wave. We dived again and surfaced once more. This time a Sunderland came out of the clouds down at us so that we had to submerge quickly to take cover beneath the water.

"By this time the convoy had disappeared. I cursed our luck as I looked through the periscope, but suddenly I noticed a steamer was leisurely approaching us. It had apparently dropped out of the convoy. I estimated it at about six thousand tons.

"The deck was laden with huge crates and on the fo'c'sle I counted eight guns. We dived and sent him a torpedo which hit him amidships. Through the periscope I watched the crew take to the boats. Then the steamer slowly vanished in a foam. As we turned away we could still see the crates bobbing about in the water.

"I saw through the slats in the crates that they contained aeroplane parts, wings, propellers and so on. We watched them sink one by one. 'There goes a flock of birds that will never fly', said Meyer with satisfaction.

"Now I thought that the spell had been broken, but ill-luck stayed with us for the next seven days and we saw nothing but sky and water. The polar sickness on board assumed epidemic proportions. We couldn't stand the sight of each other any more and to see anyone eat or clean his teeth was enough to make one vomit.

"On the seventh day the watch on the tower sang out, 'Steamer in sight.' It was a convoy again. There were about thirty ships which appeared in a long line over the horizon.

"As we were lying in an unfavourable position I let the convoy pass, came up astern of it and circled it in a wide sweep. It was evening before we made contact again, but this time we were well placed.

"They made a lovely silhouette against the evening sky. I chose the three biggest ones, a tanker of twelve thousand tons, another of seven thousand tons and a third, a freighter of seven thousand tons. We approached them underwater. I glued myself to the periscope and watched while the First Officer relayed my commands. Tube one was discharged, followed by tube two and a few seconds later tube three should have fired also. But tube three did not fire. From forward came the sound of argument but just then I could not bother about it. I observed the effect of the explosion. The first hit the *Cadillac*, the twelve thousand tonner. There came the dull thud of the detonation, the up-spout of the water and behind it appeared the ship enveloped in yellow-brown smoke.

"The second hit. I could hardly believe my eyes. It was a steamer we had not aimed at. The *Gracia* of five thousand, six hundred tons. All three ships had been well and truly hit and not one of them could be saved.

"We pushed off as fast as we could, while behind us depth charges stirred up the sea in our wake.

"I sent for the torpedo man. 'What the hell happened just now?' He looked sheepish and said, 'I am sorry, sir. I slipped and fell on the hand-trigger and the torpedo went off too soon.' I had to laugh. 'Well, anyhow, at least you hit something with it, but still you did us out of fourteen hundred tons.' He was silent for a moment. Then he asked, 'How much was it all together, sir?' 'Twenty-four thousand tons,' I said.

"The news swept through the boat and faces shone like the sky after a long spell of rain. At last our luck had changed. Two nights later we spotted a blacked-out steamer loaded with wheat; about two thousand eight hundred tons. In order to conserve torpedoes I made the crew take to their boats and sank the vessel with shells. We were fairly far from land and I followed the lifeboats and gave them bread, sausages and rum.

"The following day brought us two ships. At the crack of dawn we got a four thousand tonner with a cargo of timber which we dispatched with a few shells below the waterline. In the late afternoon we met a Dutch tanker loaded with diesel oil. On his bridge he carried a huge barrier of sandbags.

"Finally, we aimed our gun at his engine room and at last the ship began to sink. The lifeboats and the crew were already some distance away when we spotted three men floating in the water. They were the Third and Fourth Engineers and the stoker. Their captain had not bothered about them but had left them to drown in the engine room. I picked them up and followed the lifeboats and handed them over. Then I addressed a short speech to this Christian captain beginning: 'You bloody bastard,' and ending in a similar strain.

"By now we had accounted for nearly forty thousand tons on this war patrol. Thirty nine thousand and eighty five tons to be precise. We were beginning to be pleased with ourselves. But then we received a radio message, 'German U-boat just returned from war patrol has sunk fifty four thousand tons.' Her commander had been trained by us. My men made long faces and Steinhagen, our sparks, gave expression to the general opinion. 'It is annoying to see these young upstarts leave us standing.' His chagrin struck me as rather childish but all the same I was glad to see the spirit of the crew under this provocation.

"I called for the First and Second Officers. The result of our discussion was devastating. We had only six rounds of high explosive and a few torpedoes left. The following night we shot one of the torpedoes into the blue. A steamer went past us in the distance at considerable speed and we had to shoot quickly if we were to get her at all. When the torpedo left the tube we began to count. First to fifty seconds . . . every second made a hit all the more improbable. One minute . . . one minute twenty . . . 'My beautiful torpedo,' moaned Barendorff between set lips. We took up the chase but the steamer eluded us and darkness swallowed it up.

"I was awakened with the news that the First Officer had spotted the *Empire Tucan*, a liner of seven thousand tons. Our boat was rolling heavily in the swell. 'We shall have to attack her with shells,' I said. 'I don't know whether we can hit her in this sea,' remarked the First Officer. I shrugged my shoulders. 'In any case we shall have to be even more sparing with our torpedoes.'

"The bo'sun Meyer was called to lay the gun. He refused to come. 'To shoot in this weather is mad,' he told the man who woke him. 'There is far too much swell to take proper aim.'

"We sent the runner a second time with a formal order from the bridge. Finally, he turned up, sleepy and annoyed. I gave him my instructions. 'Your first shot will be on the guns which you can see clearly on the quarterdeck and your second will hit the bridge so he can't radio.'

" 'Very good, sir,' he said, clicking his heels. But to judge by his expression he thought that we should economise with our shells as well. We stood on the bridge and observed the fire, for it was the last of our ammunition. The first shell hit the ship exactly between the guns and the second went into the fo'c'sle and the third into the stern. The fourth missed the target, the fifth was a dud and the sixth and last hit the bridge and was caught in the windsail. It was a weird sight. The pressure of the detonation within the sail pushed up what looked like a huge white ghost in the dawn and threw it right over the mast. In spite of the last hit, the radio was operating furiously and sent out its SOS. The crew manned the boats and drew away from the ship. Only the wireless operator remained behind and continued sending messages.

"There was nothing else we could do! We had to sacrifice a torpedo if we did not want to have the whole mob at our heels. The *Empire Tucan* was hit exactly amidships. The ship broke, dipped deep into the sea and then reared up again against the skyline. The operator was still at this station.

"Suddenly we saw a man run across the sloping deck. He grasped a red lamp in his hand and, holding it high above his head, he leaped from the sinking ship. As he struck the water the red light went out. We stopped at the place where he had disappeared but we could not find him. Then shadows appeared in the north, dark shapes of the dusk, probably destroyers. As we had only one useable torpedo left we decided to push off. Three minutes later Steinhagen brought me a radio message. It was the last message of the *Empire Tucan*. Torpedoed by U-boat. Sinking fast—SOS, and then a long dash. It was the operator's last signal.

"The next ship we encountered [was] two days later. It was a Greek freighter which we finished off with our last torpedo. It was only four thousand tons. Steinhagen put his head through the door. 'Have we got enough, sir?' he asked breathlessly. I had been counting already. 'No,' I said. 'We have fifty one thousand tons and the other U-boat has got three thousand tons more.' A wave of disappointment swept through the boat. We began our return journey with one defective torpedo left on board. I called the torpedoman. 'Have one more shot at getting the torpedo in order.'

"It was a clear and calm summer morning. We were steaming along in the vicinity of the coast in a calm sea. The lookout reported, 'A steamer on our starboard bow.' A huge vessel with two funnels approached us out of the sun in wild zig-zags. Against the light it was impossible to determine her colour, but by her silhouette I recognised that it was a ship of the *Ormonde* class; that meant over fifteen thousand tons. 'Fellows', I said, and I felt their excitement, 'cross your fingers and let's try and get it.' Then the command, 'Fire'.

"Then we waited, counting. Painfully slowly the seconds slipped by. The ship was a great distance away, too great a distance I feared. Then suddenly, right amidship a column of water rose up far beyond the mast and immediately after, we heard the crash of the detonation.

"The liner heeled to starboard. In great haste lifeboats were launched, many of them. In between them hundreds of heads were bobbing in the water. It was not possible to help them because the coast was too close and the ship still afloat. On her fo'c'sle a number of guns were clearly visible. We retreated underwater. When a few minutes later we surfaced only the lifeboats were visible on calm sea.

"I descended to my hole to make up the war diary. As I passed the control room I caught sight of a board which hung on the door. On it was written: 66,587 TONS. LEARN BY HEART."

It was all smiles, cheers, bouquets, kisses, a brass band, and the congratulations of both Admiral Dönitz and Gross-Admiral Raeder as Günther Prien and his crew made their triumphant way up the gangplank at Wilhelmshaven three days after the action against *Royal Oak* in Scapa Flow. Raeder personally presented the award of the Iron Cross 2nd Class to each member of the *U-47* crew. In the afternoon, Hitler's private plane arrived to fly the crew to Berlin and the adoring attentions of its citizens. An open car drove Prien through the Brandenburg Gate and, in the his Chancellery private office, Hitler awarded the U-boat commander the Knight's Cross, referring to Prien's accomplishment as "the proudest deed that a German U-boat could possibly carry out." Along with the decoration for Prien, came a promotion for Dönitz—to Vice Admiral, and a heightened regard by Hitler for the U-boat arm of his navy. The next to appear was Hitler's Minister of Propaganda and Public Enlightenment, Doctor Josef Göbbels whose subsequent handling of publicity over the *Royal Oak* incident was so overt that Prien was moved to complain, "I am an officer, not a film star."

Not film stars, but the stuff of legend. Prien, Schepke, and Kretschmer were celebrated by the German people and revered in much the same way as the ace fighter pilots of the Royal Air Force were for their achievements during the Battle of Britain. With postcards, books, pamphlets, interviews, Dr. Göbbels laid on the propaganda with a heavy hand. But nothing would persuade either Prien or Kretschmer to write about their achievements until the war was over. Unlike Schepke, neither man was a member of the Nazi Party.

By late March 1941, Schepke and Prien were dead; Kretschmer a prisoner of war. On 6 March, Prien, now a Korvettenkapitän, led a force of six U-boats, including Kretschmer's *U-99*, to sea on another hunt. Their objective was the westbound convoy OB-293 out of Liverpool and, within two days they had attacked four of the merchantmen, sinking two. But the response by the convoy's escorting warships was prompt and savage. One of the U-boats was badly damaged by depth-charges and was forced to withdraw and limp back to base at Lorient. A second damaged sub had to be abandoned and scuttled. Kretschmer weighed the odds in the engagement and elected to leave the scene. Not Prien. He carried on tracking the vessels of the convoy until the evening of the 8th. He had been using the cover of a dense rain squall to close on a target vessel when the showers stopped, revealing the U-boat's position to lookouts aboard the destroyer HMS *Wolverine*. Prien crash-dived *U-47* and suffered the depth-charges of both *Wolverine* and HMS *Verity*. When he tried to resurface an hour later, the submarine rose nearly to the surface, but then began to sink and in seconds exploded in an orange flash visible from the surface. None of the crew survived.

"At Dönitz's villa [in Kerneval near Lorient] there was a constant two-way stream of radio traffic, information coming in from all over the Atlantic and orders going out to the boats at sea. I am amazed at some of the things for which U-boats in operational areas broke radio silence and reported to headquarters. Dönitz took a 'calculated risk' on the incoming radio traffic and decided it was more important for him to get information than it was for his boats to keep radio silence at sea. Almost daily he arranged ocean rendezvous between U-boats to transfer spare parts for machinery, or to have homebound boats with extra fuel or torpedoes transfer the excess to boats remaining in the area, or to transfer a sick man to the nearest boat having a doctor aboard. He even held radio musters of his boats at times when he suspected trouble—ordering all boats to 'report position and successes.' It was by such a muster that he learned he had lost his three great aces, Prien, Schepke, and Kretschmer, early in March of 1941. When a boat in distress sent an SOS, Dönitz never failed to send nearby boats to her assistance. He was cold-blooded in his orders that they were not to jeopardize their own safety by rescuing Allied survivors, but he took long chances to save his own people. One effect of all this radio traffic was to make U-boat crews feel close to headquarters. They all knew that when and if they got in trouble an SOS to Dönitz would bring immediate help. This is important in an organization like a U-boat fleet, in which morale often affects results more than technical matters do."
—from *Twenty Million Tons Under The Sea* by Rear Admiral Daniel V. Gallery, USN

The admiral counted the cost of having lost three of his best and highest-achieving U-boat commanders in just ten days of operations. Still, the spirit and determination of the other experienced Ubootwaffe officers, and of those waiting in the pipeline to take command of their own boats, was undiminished. Erich Topp, a veteran of thirty-nine sinkings, including that of the U.S. destroyer *Reuben James*, over sixteen combat patrols; Günther Hessler, who had achieved fourteen sinkings in the course of a single patrol, for a Ubootwaffe record; as well as others who were soon to join the elité of the force, men like Werner Henke, Johannes Mohr, and Wolfgang Lüth, whose total of tonnage sunk was second only to Kretschmer's. Mohr would sink the cruiser HMS *Dunedin* on his second patrol, and add thirty-two merchant ships and an escort corvette to his account. Then there was Helmut Witte. His crew had exhausted their supply of torpedoes and shells when he ordered a boarding party onto a tanker to plant explosives and sink her, and who sailed on a 135-day patrol, the longest ever in the South Atlantic. As for high-achievers, Dönitz counted twelve of his boat commanders whose totals of authenticated claims of sinkings amounted to more than 150,000 tons.

By September 1944, Dönitz had appointed Wolfgang Lüth Commandant of the German Naval Training College at Flensburg, where the admiral would relocate what little remained of the German government near the end of the war in 1945. With nerves frayed and tensions high as the final days for the Third Reich ground on, it was just after midnight on 13 May 1945 when a young sentry on guard duty in the college grounds heard footsteps and challenged them shouting "who goes there?" With no response the guard repeated his call to the approaching darkened figure with head down. Still no response, and the guard fired what he intended to be a warning shot, but the round struck the intruder in the head. The sentry had killed his commandant, Wolfgang Lüth.

As for the fates of some of the other accomplished or promising U-boat commanders, Johannes Mohr perished in April 1943 in the sinking of *U-124* by convoy escorts. Engelbert Endrass was killed on 21 December 1941, when his boat, *U-567*, was rammed by a freighter. Erich Topp, Helmut Witte, and Günther Hessler survived the war, and Herbert Werner became an American citizen. Otto Kretschmer was released from captivity in 1947. Returning to peacetime duties in the German Navy, he rose to the rank of Konteradmiral and became Chief of Staff for the NATO Forces, Baltic Approaches. After the war he and Captain Donald Macintyre, his former captor, met in friendlier circumstances and Macintyre returned the Zeiss binoculars he had taken from Kretschmer in 1941.

". . . he wanted to prove he could attack by night on the surface

and carry out his personal principle of 'one torpedo, one ship.' Fans of torpedoes were, in his opinion, a waste of equipment and effort and allowed a U-boat commander to attack from a position of comparative safety in the hope of hitting something, instead of taking carefully calculated risks and by precision firing making every torpedo count. It was from this time that he became the first commander to attack convoys only by night and always on the surface. This attack was to set the pattern. At this stage of the war no other commanders followed Kretschmer's technique, considering it too dangerous, yet it was this method that led him to outstrip his colleagues in sinkings."
—from *The Golden Horseshoe* by Terence Robertson

"We were now battling our way through the February storms, the severest of the winter. The sea boiled and foamed and leaped continually under the lash of gales that chased one another across the Atlantic from west to east. *U-230* struggled through gurgling whirlpools, up and down mountainous seas; she was pitched into the air by one towering wave and caught by another and buried under tons of water by still another. The cruel winds whipped across the wild surface at speeds up to 150 miles an hour, whistling in the highest treble and snarling in the lowest bass. When we were on watch, the wind punished us with driving snow, sleet, hail, and frozen spray. It beat against our rubber diver's suits, cut our faces like a razor, and threatened to tear away our eye masks; only the steel belts around our waists secured us to boat and life. Below, inside the steel cockleshell, the boat's violent up-and-down motion drove us to the floorplates and hurled us straight up and threw us around like puppets. And yet we managed to survive the furious wind and water, and to arrive in our designated square in one piece."
—from *Iron Coffins* by Herbert A. Werner

"I have taught you my dear flock, for above thirty years how to live; and I will show you in a very short time how to die."
—Sandys

THE HUNTER BECOMES THE HUNTED

The North Atlantic shipping lanes were the most dangerous places to be for the Allied merchantmen of the convoys early in World War Two. Later, when Admiral Dönitz ordered the majority of his U-boats transferred to the Mediterranean, that sea, and the area off Gibraltar in particular, became the most dangerous place to be. Extremely heavy convoy traffic brought weapons and supplies from Africa to the men of the British Army in Egypt and other Allied merchant ships hauled raw materials in from the far east. It became the stage for a very important convoy battle and the laboratory in which new and improved tactics were developed for taking on the U-boats. It began in the afternoon of Sunday, 14 December 1941, when an Allied convoy, HG-76, made up of thirty-two merchant vessels, left Gibraltar in the care of several warship escorts, with Commander Frederick John 'Johnnie' Walker, whose reputation as a maverick had caused him to be passed over for promotion to Captain and compelled him to sail a desk through the first two years of the war. Walker, however, was an able tactician and had spent substantial time devising his own concepts for dealing with the U-boats.

Finally, in October 1941, Walker was given command of the *Bittern*-class sloop, HMS *Stork* and senior responsibility for a convoy escort force of *Stork* and seven corvettes. Walker's pet name for his wife was Buttercup, and that was the name he gave to the coordinated battle tactics he devised for use against the enemy subs. His intention was to use the maximum number of warships and the maximum amount of firepower against the U-boats and to do so in the darkness when attacks by the subs were most probable. He based his tactic on the belief, from experience, that when a U-boat made a successful torpedo attack, it would likely remain in the area of the wrecked target or attempt an escape on the surface at top speed to evade the convoy escorts. As he explained his idea: "Operation Buttercup is designed to force the U-boat to dive by plastering the area around the wreck with depth charges and by illuminating the most likely directions of his surface escape. Once submerged, the destruction of the submarine is considerably simplified."

At the start of the month, the little group of escort warships had guarded the convoy from Liverpool to Gibraltar without experiencing any U-boat attacks. Walker had, however, been receiving reports from the Submarine Tracking Room in London indicating that no such easy passage could be expected on the return voyage. In fact, it was known that a number of U-boats were heading towards the Gibraltar area and that others were being sent down as well from the Baltic on Hitler's personal orders. The scene was set for a spectacular battle.

To help counter the evident threat of the U-boats, nine additional warships that were then based in Gibraltar—two sloops, three destroyers, three corvettes and the escort carrier HMS *Audacity*—were assigned to augment Walker's protective force. Four days later, his force was dramatically reduced again when all the escort ships except the *Audacity* and the destroyer *Stanley* were required to return to Gibraltar. *Audacity* was a passenger ship that had been captured from the Germans and converted to the configuration of an escort carrier. It carried a small air complement of six Grumman Martlet (Wildcat) fighters.

Only two days at sea from Gibraltar, the officers of the convoy knew it had been spotted by the Germans when a long-range Kondor reconnaissance bomber appeared on the horizon. They realized the following day that the enemy was assembling a U-boat wolfpack when the German radio traffic began to increase substantially.

The Martlets from *Audacity* were flying local patrols and in the morning of 17 December one of them sighted a U-boat on the surface about twenty miles off the port side of the convoy. Commander Walker immediately sent five of his escort ships off to chase the sub. One of them, a corvette, was the first to approach the U-boat which by this time had submerged. The corvette crew laid a pattern of ten depth-charges which damaged the hull of the submarine, *U-131*, under the command of Korvettenkapitän Arend Baumann, forcing it to surface again. The five escort ships opened fire with their four-inch guns. The sub crew were far from beaten, and promptly shot down one of the Martlet fighters. Then, knowing that his vessel was finished, the commander of the U-boat ordered his crew to abandon it.

The next day lookouts aboard the *Stanley* sighted another U-boat. It was shadowing the convoy from a distance of six miles. The *Stanley* crew, and that of the destroyer *Blankney*, struck with depth-charges, bringing the *U-434*, commanded by Kapitänleutnant Wolfgang Heyda, up to the surface. Before the rest of the escorts could join the party north of Madiera, Portugal, the submarine and sank leaving forty-two surviving crewmen awaiting rescue. In the air over the action, the five remaining Martlet fighters encountered two Kondors that arrived to shadow the convoy. The Martlets quickly chased the German reconnaissance planes from the area.

During the long night the submarine *U-574*, commanded by Oberleutnant Dietrich Gengelbach, was tracking the convoy when, at just before 4 a.m., it was sighted by the *Stanley* lookouts who noted a pair of torpedoes "passing from astern." At that point, Walker in *Stork* diverted course to come to *Stanley's* assistance. As *Stork* approached there was a flash and a massive explosion as *Stanley* blew up. At least one torpedo of *U-574* had struck the old destroyer in the magazines, cracking her hull and turning her into a mass of flame. As the fires of *Stanley* faded, the night became like day when most of the convoy's merchant ships began firing their snowflake rockets, standard procedure when one of their number was torpedoed. With the suddenly improved visibility it became an easy matter for another of the U-boats to score a kill on one of the other merchant ships near the front of the assembly.

The furious Walker reached the spot where *Stanley* had taken the hit and instantly received an asdic contact. *Stork* spent the next few minutes laying two patterns of depth-charges and was about to begin a third run when the *U-574* suddenly emerged from under the surface a mere 200 yards off the bow of the sloop. The sub attempted to evade the attentions of the sloop by entering a very tight circle, but Walker and *Stork* advanced against the slightly slower submarine. As the sloop neared the sub, Walker's four-inch guns were firing until they were too close to be lowered any further. The *Stork* was within a few feet of the sub. In the next eleven minutes both submarine and sloop had turned through three circles and were beginning a fourth when the *Stork* caught and rammed *U-574*. The crew of *Stork* then finished off the partially submerged wreck of the sub with more depth-charges. Later that morning, Walker received a message from the Admiralty. He was warned that three additional U-boats were on the way to join the wolfpack against the convoy. It was known that one of the subs was commanded by Kapitänleutnant Engelbert Endrass, who had been First Officer on *U-47* under Korvettenkapitän Günther Prien at Scapa Flow during the attack on HMS *Royal Oak*. Endrass was then the highest-scoring boat commander in the Ubootwaffe.

A week later, 21 December, the eighth day of the convoy at sea, a Norwegian tanker was torpedoed and sunk and Walker's escort vessels embarked on another Buttercup U-boat search, sending up a flood of snowflake rockets to illuminate the area. About ten miles starboard of the convoy lay the carrier *Audacity* commanded by an officer who outranked Walker and who was determined to maintain the carrier in a position well outside the perimeter of the convoy. The carrier was steaming without escort as none of the corvettes could be spared for that task. It was then that an approaching U-boat happened to sight the carrier in the brightness of the snowflakes. Very soon a torpedo slammed into the engine room of *Audacity* causing major flooding and halting the carrier. *Audacity* lasted only ten more minutes as she received two additional torpedoes which quickly sank her.

Now it was the turn of Engelbert Endrass in *U-567*. Endrass had found his way inside the perimeter of the convoy northeast of the Azores, and was spotted by the crewmen of the sloop *Deptford*. The sloop hurried to the location of the U-boat which was already diving. The *Deptford* crew maintained asdic contact with the sub, though, and, together with the crew of Stork, and the assistance of the corvette HMS *Samphire*, started laying several depth-charge patterns over the position of the sub. The compounding effect of the depth-charges crushed the hull of the submarine, taking the lives of all forty-seven of the crew.

In the pitch darkness of the next night, the *Deptford* accidentally rammed *Stork*, causing substantial damage to both vessels.

By morning the action had ceased, or rather paused, as the wolf-pack boats had withdrawn to reload and await further instructions from Dönitz in Kerneval. The game then changed with the arrival of an R.A.F. Coastal Command B-24 Liberator bomber. The Lib had made an 800-mile flight from a base in England to fly a three-hour patrol over the convoy. In that period it met and chased off a Kondor reconnaissance aircraft, and attacked two U-boats that were recharging their batteries on the surface. Severe damage to one of the subs, which it had suffered during the action of the previous evening, now required her crew to abandon and scuttle her. While they were transferring to the other submarine, the Liberator attacked again with a rain of depth-charges.

In Kerneval, meanwhile, Admiral Dönitz was increasingly concerned by the combat reports he was receiving from wolfpack commanders in the area of the continuing battle with convoy HG-76. For more than a week the convoy had been under nearly constant attack by the admiral's submarines and had suffered the loss of only two merchant ships. Of the nine U-boats that Dönitz had assembled into a deadly wolfpack near the convoy, five had been lost thus far, including that of his ace, Endrass, the most experienced of his boat commanders. It was a difficult time for the admiral who decided it was necessary to order his commanders to abort the savage attack on the convoy. They had, in his view, simply been overwhelmed by the powerful combination of Walker's brilliant escort tactics and the new, more threatening form of air cover now being provided all the way from England to the mid-Atlantic. It had been a crushing defeat for the U-boats.

Soon, however, America was in the war. With the U.S. battleship fleet attacked in Pearl Harbor, Hawaii, on 7 December, she was now at war with Japan and its Axis partners, Germany and Italy. Looking for new and more promising hunting grounds than the Mediterranean and the North Atlantic, Dönitz determined to exploit the rich pickings of largely the unprotected merchant shipping traffic along the American eastern seaboard, from Nova Scotia down to South America. His boats sailed west.

RUSSIAN RUN

When the Soviet Union came into the Second World War, Lord Beaverbrook and W. Averell Harriman represented Britain and the United States respectively in an Anglo-American mission to Moscow in October 1941, to agree a series of unconditional munitions deliveries to their Russian allies. The most expeditious way of making these deliveries was by sea, around the North Cape and through the Arctic Ocean to the Russian ports of Archangel and Murmansk. In the agreement, the Soviets were to provide the cargo ships in which they would receive the supplies, equipment and war materiel transported from British and American ports. In practice, however, they were unable to spare sufficient vessels for the task, and the responsibility of providing the merchant ships fell mainly on the Western Allies, with most of the ships ultimately coming from the merchant fleets of Britain and America.

The defence of the Arctic convoys was the responsibility of the British Royal Navy, but the U.S. Navy's Fleet Admiral Ernest King then established Task Force 39, centred around the carrier USS *Wasp* and the battleship USS *Washington*, and assigned it to support the British convoy escort effort.

In August 1941, only two months after the Nazi invasion of the Soviet Union, the first Allied convoy bound for Russia sailed from Britain and an additional twelve such convoys had successfully made the voyage by the spring of 1942. Only one ship of the 103 in these convoys was lost to enemy action. After that, however, German opposition to the convoy operations increased dramatically as they brought into play every military resource at their disposal to halt the flow of war supplies to the Russians. Among the greatest threats the Germans imposed was the basing of their heavy capital ships in the Norwegian fiords, quite near the Arctic sea lanes on which the convoys had to travel. That concentration of naval surface firepower included moving the battleship *Tirpitz* to Trondheim where she was soon joined by the *Admiral Scheer* and the heavy cruiser *Admiral Hipper*. Until the availability of Allied escort carriers, the convoys of the Russian Run had to make their way through the icy reaches of that hazardous route without adequate protection against U-boat and aircraft attack.

The hard facts of the situation for the Allies were that the Germans intended to bring out their naval big guns in the form of their largest, most powerful warships, to strike at the Allied convoys en route to Russia. The German bases all along the coast of Norway positioned them well for such operations, and gave them the advantages of shore-based air reconnaissance and striking forces, as well as a screen of U-boats in the channels between Spitsbergen and Norway. The Allies' escort covering warships, on the other hand, were having to operate fully a thousand miles from their bases, without air support, and with their destroyers too short of fuel to shepherd a damaged vessel to harbour and safety.

"Through icy, fog-bound seas, their flanks exposed to the dive-bombers, surface raiders, and submarines moving out from the Nazi-held fiords of Norway the slow gray convoys moved—and kept moving. Nor was there sanctuary at their destination, for every hour on the hour, it was said, the black-crossed planes of the Luftwaffe blasted heart-breaking delays in the grim business of unloading the ships in the ice-cluttered harbor of Murmansk. Yet the cargoes were delivered."
—from the report by the American War Shipping Administration to President Harry S. Truman after the war

The hazards and hardships that the Allied convoys in World War II were exposed to challenged the capacity of the merchant seamen to endure even as it challenged the seaworthiness of their vessels. Of the various routes they sailed throughout that conflict, none was more arduous, demanding, and unforgiving than the horrendous north-east route to Russia. On the Russian Run the threat of enemy attack was virtually constant from departure to arrival. German Luftwaffe air power threatened the merchantmen from airfields along the coast of occupied Norway, hounding the Allied ships with Heinkel He 111 level bombers, Junkers Ju 87 Stuka dive-bombers, Junkers Ju 88 light bombers, and four-engined Focke Wulf Kondor reconnaissance bombers. The wolfpacks of Admiral Karl Dönitz's Ubootwaffe, many of them having been withdrawn from their Atlantic patrols, hunted now in the Barents and Norwegian Seas. And among the greatest threats to the merchant sailors were the big German warships, the formidably armed battleship *Tirpitz*, the cruiser *Admiral Hipper*, and the swift pocket battleships *Lützow* and

Admiral Scheer, lurking with all their attendant escort destroyers and corvettes in Norway's fiords.

"In the ice," said a convoy commander, "it's better to be loaded than light. When you are light, the propellers and rudder may be damaged by the ice; when you're loaded they are below it and safe." It is all so strange in the Arctic. In summer it is nearly always daylight; and in winter the weather is outrageous and the nights are interminable. In winter, all the details of a ship are crystalline and thick with milky-white ice. The perpetual salt spray of the sea freezes to every surface it touches, beautiful and deadly. And over it all, the spectacle of the incredible northern lights.

That was winter. In summer 1941, when conditions were better and things were generally easier for him, Adolf Hitler moved against his former ally, Josef Stalin, by ending the non-aggression pact they had signed. The falling out led in June of that year to Nazi Germany's Operation Barbarossa in which more than 160 divisions together with the might of the German air force attacked the republics of the Soviet Union along an entire 500-mile front. The move not only ended the supply of oil and grain that the Russians had been providing to Germany, it forged a new, if somewhat uneasy alliance between Great Britain and the Soviet Union, as unlikely a pairing of philosophical opposites as could be found anywhere.

Among the early benefits realised by the Soviets from the new alliance came when they signed the Anglo-Soviet Trade Agreement in August and were granted a five-year £10,000,000 credit at a 3.5 % interest rate. The first of many military aid convoys then assembled at Hvalfiordur on the west coast of Iceland and, on 21 August, sailed from the British Isles for Archangel on the Dvina River. The convoy comprised six old tramp steamers with cargoes of tin, rubber, and wool, along with fifteen Hawker Hurricane fighters shoe-horned into their holds. It was protected by an escort of three destroyers, three minesweepers and three anti-submarine trawlers. Other vessels of the British Home Fleet accompanied the assemblage as far as Bear Island to help ward off any interest on the part of German surface warships. Finally, there was the aircraft carrier HMS *Argus* which whose stately presence at the rear of the convoy brought twenty-four Hurricanes to be flown from her flight deck to the Russian airfield at Vaenga in the Kola Inlet.

The convoys of the Russian Run were all coded PQ and given a number. PQ was for the initials of the Admiralty planner Commander

Peter Quellyn Russell. All of the homeward-bound convoys from the Soviet Union were coded QP. But that first convoy was code-named Operation Dervish. For Britain, the alliance with the Soviets was one thing, but a far more genuine and meaningful alliance was nurtured in January 1942 following the Japanese surprise attack on the U.S. Fleet in Pearl Harbor, Hawaii, bringing America into the war on the side of the British against the Axis forces of Japan, Germany and Italy. President Franklin Roosevelt and Prime Minister Winston Churchill met in Washington that winter to agree that priority must be given to defeating Nazi Germany and, at all costs, the Russians must be maintained in the war. Now the United States would join Britain in the provision of military supplies and equipment by merchantman convoys.

The functional intent of the Anglo-Soviet Trade Agreement was that the supplies and equipment destined for the Soviets would be transported aboard Russian freighters, loaded and shipped from British (and later from American) ports. Such vessels were not forthcoming from the Russians, however, and the task and responsibility for both the transport and the escort protection became the burden of the British Admiralty. Early on a monthly quota of 400 tanks and 300 combat aircraft for the Russians was established. The convoys bringing this war materiel were to operate at a rate of approximately one every ten to fourteen days until the Allied victory had been won. The logistics gradually evolved to a point where, in the final months of operation, the ratio of escorting warships to merchantmen became one to one.

Off the Iceland coast on 20 March 1942, an Allied merchant convoy, PQ13, was assembled and sailed for Murmansk. It was composed of nineteen vessels of British, American, Polish, and Panamanian origin and it was being shepherded by two British battleships, three cruisers, eleven destroyers, and an aircraft carrier during the first stage of the voyage. The Admiralty was trying to tempt Germany's big warships from their hiding places in the Norwegian fiords, to emerge and fight and was using the convoy for bait. In close escort, the cruiser HMS *Trinidad* carried the flag of Rear-Admiral Stuart Bonham-Carter, the convoy escort commander. Additional close-in escort was being provided by two destroyers and three Norwegian whalers, the latter intended for delivery to the Russian Navy's minesweeper fleet.

Meanwhile, another well-escorted Allied convoy, QP9, was half-way through its return journey from Russia when it entered a treacherous storm system on 24 March. Convoy PQ13, moving in the opposite (eastbound) direction, entered the same storm but in more extreme conditions. Station-keeping for the vessels in the convoy formation proved impossible in the massive high seas, the gale-force winds and driving snow, and communications between the convoy commodore and the captains of the other merchantmen and escort ships broke down completely. The experience of the freezing, snow-blinded lookouts aboard the vessels was one of utter misery. And when the visibility did occasionally, if briefly, improve, Junkers Ju 88 multi-role aircraft from bases at Petsamo and Banak struck the convoy in a series of punishing attacks. As the situation for the convoy worsened, Captain Leslie Saunders of HMS *Trinidad* broke radio silence to inform the Admiralty and the Senior Naval Officer, North Russia, about it.

The chaos and violence of the storm had badly scattered the vessels of PQ13, and the *Trinidad* set out to round them up. In the freezing conditions later that evening, the British steam merchant ship HMS *Induna* was towing the armed trawler HMS *Silja*, which was nearly out of fuel. They were crawling through the ice floes when the tow rope broke. At 7:30 the next morning *Silja* was torpedoed in the number five hold just under a load of aviation spirit, causing a huge explosion and fire. Dozens of badly injured crewmen lay freezing in the lifeboats. In one of them fourteen men died over the next three days, after which a Soviet minesweeper appeared and rescued sixteen survivors, two of whom later died in a Murmansk hospital. As the lifeboats were rowed away from the *Silja*, another torpedo hit the ship, which then sank with some of the crew still aboard.

Between the North Cape and Murmansk lies the port town of Kirkenes, Norway, from which three German destroyers, *Z24*, *Z25* and *Z26*, sailed on 28 March to intercept convoy PQ13. The first vessels they discovered were lifeboats from the SS *Empire Ranger*, which had been sunk six days earlier in an attack by German aircraft. All but two of the thirty-eight men in the lifeboats had died. One of the two survivors was so badly frost-bitten that his arms and legs had to be amputated to save his life.

As the *Trinidad* continued to hunt for the scattered stragglers from the convoy on the 29th, her radar operator picked up a contact which turned out to be *Z26*, the German destroyer, and engaged her in an exchange of gunfire as she emerged from a snow squall less than 4,000 yards away. And as this action began, another of the German destroyers, the *Z24*, appeared and sent a spread of torpedoes at *Trinidad*. She evaded the torpedoes but took a big hit aft by a shell that started a fire, which was soon under control and the *Trinidad* continued to attack the *Z26*, severely damaging her. As *Trinidad* manoeuvred to finish off the destroyer, the low-temperature oil in her torpedo tubes had frozen, causing two of the three weapons to misfire. The third did launch, but a gyro malfunction made it circle back on the cruiser and blow a massive hole in the starboard side of the hull. The forward boiler rooms were flooded and an oil fire was ignited. Thirty-two seamen were killed. Now the German destroyers headed to the southwest, chased by the British destroyers *Eclipse* and *Fury*. They caught up with *Z26* and quickly sank her with gunfire. The crippled *Trinidad* was taken in tow until her propulsion could be partially restored. She later limped into Murmansk in the company of HMS *Fury*, and underwent repairs over the next month. In the voyage of convoy PQ13, five of its merchant vessels were sunk. From the day of its arrival at Murmansk, the seamen of the convoy experienced heavy bombing attacks every day for the next three weeks.

When the *Trinidad* was disabled, Rear-Admiral Bonham-Carter moved his flag to HMS *Edinburgh* which, on 27 April, lay off Vaenga in the Kola Inlet, waiting to take part in the escort of convoy QP11 back to Britain. As it waited, a lighter arrived and the crew then off-loaded a cargo of five tons of bullion, payment to the United States Treasury for American war supplies and equipment. QP11 sailed the next day and almost immediately got the attention of a U-boat wolf-pack.

The *Edinburgh* was steaming ahead of the thirteen merchant vessels of the convoy, when she was struck by two torpedoes from the *U-456* under the command of Kapitänleutnant Max-Martin Teichert, destroying her rudder, much of her stern and two inner screws. Teichert had been alerted to the presence of the convoy by German aerial reconnaissance. Of no further use to the convoy, *Edinburgh* was then escorted by four destroyers and two minesweepers as her skipper, Captain Faulkner, headed back to Murmansk. The next day she was well down by the stern and could no longer be steered. A tow was attempted by HMS *Foresight*, but three German destroyers then arrived and Bonham-Carter ended the effort. The crew continued firing on the enemy warships until *Edinburgh* was hit by a further pair of torpedoes and the Rear-Admiral told Faulkner to order her abandoned. The minesweepers *Harrier* and *Gossamer* then came alongside to rescue the crew. At that point, Faulkner recalled the backgammon games that he had had with Bonham-Carter during the rare quieter moments aboard *Edinburgh*, and told the rear-admiral that he was going back on board for something. "What the devil for?" asked Bonham-Carter. "For the tally. You now owe me thirty pounds!" The admiral replied "I'm afraid the tally goes down with the ship, along with the Russian gold."

When Bonham-Carter got to Murmansk he inspected HMS *Trinidad* and found that a naval raiding party had had to appropriate lengths of rail track to use as bracing for the welded deck plates. Only the aft boiler room was functional and able to provide steam for her turbines and she still needed significant repairs, but she was capable of the return voyage by May when he raised his flag from her once again. In company with an escort of four destroyers, the cruiser hurried to catch up with convoy QP11 in the Barents Sea. The convoy had left Murmansk on 28 April.

Having caught up with the convoy, *Trinidad* was attacked by a Ju 88 aircraft with a cluster of four bombs. Listing badly to starboard and down by the bow, her gunners fought back and downed the enemy plane, but with her fuel tanks burning furiously and the fire spreading, her captain ordered the crew to abandon ship. HMS *Foresight* arrived to take the crewmen and some survivors of ships sunk in convoy PQ13 aboard. Then the destroyer HMS *Matchless* was called on and used two torpedoes to send the wreck of *Trinidad* to the bottom.

Rear-Admiral Bonham-Carter had had five warships go down under him as an escort commander and later wrote: "We in the navy are paid to do this sort of job, but it is beginning to ask too much of the men in the Merchant Navy. We may be able to avoid bombs and torpedoes with our speed. A six or eight knot ship does not have this advantage."

They were not natural bedfellows, the British Merchant Navy and the Royal Navy, and their tenuous relationship became strained and nearly broken by the demands of the Arctic convoy operations. A growing notion among many merchant seamen was that the convoys were about more than simply bringing aid and materiel to the Soviets; that in reality they were also being run to lure the German capital ships out onto the high seas to be engaged in battle with the guns of Britain's Home Fleet. The view of many was, "Their Lordships in London don't give a toss for us, nor for the Russkis either, come to that."

In fact, the commander of the cruiser escort for convoy PQ17, Rear-Admiral Sir Louis Henry Keppel Hamilton, wrote in his operation order: "The primary object is to get PQ17 to Russia, but an object only slightly subsidiary is to provide an opportunity for the enemy's heavy ships to be brought to action." It was, perhaps not unreasonable that British naval officers would consider the potential sinking of the *Tirpitz*, or any other German battleship, more important, in the wider context of the war, than the protection of freighters and steamers bringing war materiel to Russia.

While an even greater quantity of such supplies was being transported to the Soviets via the Persian Gulf and from there by rail transport from Basra to the Caspian Sea, the items coming to them on the northern convoy route included 7,400 vitally needed aircraft (3,000 of them from America), 5,200 tanks (1,400 from Canada), 5,000 anti-tank and anti-aircraft guns, 4,000 rifles and machineguns, 1,800 radar sets, 4,000 radios, 2,000 sets of telephone equipment, fourteen minesweepers, nine motor torpedo boats, and four submarines. This material, together with huge amounts of ammunition, torpedoes, medical supplies and hospital equipment, food, wool, tin, rubber, and industrial plant, was of incalculable help to the Russian forces. It made it possible for them to foil and ultimately defeat the German invasion of the Soviet Union, to defeat the Germans in the massive tank battle on the plains of Kursk, and to switch from the defensive to the offensive, driving the Nazis back from their advances, all the way west to Berlin even before the other Allies reached the German capital in 1945.

The history of the Russian Run convoys in the Second World War shows some forty convoys of approximately twenty merchant ships each, sailing to Russia with goods essential to the Soviet war effort. Ten per cent of these ships were sunk en route by the Germans and a further nineteen were lost to accidents or act of God. These merchant vessels sailed under the flags of many nations and, from early 1942, were escorted by warships of the United States Navy as well as those of Britain and Canada. The primary responsibility, though, for the armed protection of the merchant ships in the convoys over the hazardous, deadly stretch of sea from North America to Iceland and on to Murmansk and Archangel was with the Royal Navy.

There was probably little satisfaction to the thousands of Allied seamen in the knowledge that the sailors of Germany's Kriegsmarine were experiencing the same brutal cold and threatening ice that they were enduring as they crept across the North Atlantic, between the North Cape and Bear Island, and through the Barents Sea towards Archangel and Murmansk. Additionally, the merchant seamen and the men of their escorts were subject to the attacks of U-boats, aircraft and surface warships.

The reception awaiting the Allied merchant sailor and navy men in the Soviet port cities was something less than welcoming. On arriving they found suspicion, ingratitude, waste, and often considerable delay in getting their cargoes off-loaded, their vessels having to lay at anchor awaiting their turn to tie up at a loading dock. Once in town, the visiting sailors ran into unfriendly guards at every turn, gate and doorway. The guards invariably found descrepancies in their passes and identity papers. Mail for the sailors was frequently interferred with or delayed. And the merchant sailors were often angered by the seemingly callous attitude of the Russians about many of the precious aircraft and other arms that the seamen had risked their lives to deliver, when the weaponry was carelessly or inefficiently off-loaded and then left standing uncovered and open to the elements because of laziness and inefficiency.

Certainly, conditions were tough for everyone in Russia then, but during their stays in the Soviet ports, the Allied seamen were required to subsist on a diet of barley and grass soup, black bread, and, due to local medical resources being overwhelmed by battle casualties from the front line a mere thirty miles away, medical treatment for the injured men of the convoys was, at best, primitive. Still, one stoker remarked: "There was only one redeeming feature, the vodka was cheap."

The British came in for a share of critcism in the convoy operation too. Stalin and officials in Murmansk charged that many cargoes loaded in Britain, as opposed to in America, were often damaged en route, arguably due to the British method of putting the heaviest items low in a ship which, the Russians claimed, tended to make the vessel laterally unstable and, as she rolled, to cause the lashing wires to penetrate the packaging and lacerate the goods.

"I don't know how we ever slept on the Russian run. We had no heating whatever down below, other than a coal-burning stove on the messdeck, which we could only use when the chimney could be erected, sticking up on the foredeck, if the weather permitted. The condensation from our breath built up into ice six inches thick inside the mess decks as, of course, the deck above had no wood, only bare steel. We spent the whole time wrapped up in anything we could find. At sea I was supposed to sleep in the wheelhouse outside the wireless office, so as to be on immediate call. I wore a one-piece Kapok zipped up suit which had an oilskin outer cover for working on the upper deck. I had also obtained a pair of wooden- soled fisherman's boots in Iceland, which were very efficient and, over my shoulders, as I could not wear it any other way, a duffle coat. The night before our return some of us were invited to attend a cinema show on board *Edinburgh* and the Russian sentries posted on every gangway annoyed us with their insistence on seeing our identity cards every time we passed them. Of course, at that time we knew nothing of the millions in gold bars being loaded on the *Edinburgh* and soon to spend many years at the bottom of the Barents Sea. Our original escort group sailed on 28th April again with the two Russian destroyers escorting QP11 and very quickly ice started to form again all over the ship, the upper deck crew keeping themselves warm by chipping off ice from the guns and depth charge throwers. Within two days the *Edinburgh* had been torpedoed by *U-456*, but did not sink. However, she could only go around in circles with the ship largely out of action. At this time six German destroyers moved in to finish off the *Edinburgh* and our destroyers *Amazon*, *Bulldog*, *Forester* and *Foresight* took them on in a classic line gun battle, helped by Edinburgh's guns. The leading German destroyer, the *Hermann Schoeman*, was blown out of the water, which discouraged the others, but by 1st May, *Edinburgh* had sunk with all the gold."
—Cyril Hatton, Leading Telegraphist, HMS *Snowflake*

Rudy Radmanovich was a member of the U.S. Merchant Marine in the Second World War. In the winter of 1944 he shipped out of New York as an oiler aboard the Liberty ship, SS *Stephen Leacock*. The ship was routed to Halifax, Nova Scotia, where they picked up an escort for the north of England. In the Hebrides they joined another convoy which set course north through the Norwegian Sea, the

Arctic Sea and finally, the White Sea north of Archangel. In navigating the North Cape, the convoy was caught between the Nazi submarines, planes, mines and surface warships. They went as close to the ice pack as they could, but were unable to evade the German attacks. Fourteen of the thirty-four merchant ships of Rudy's convoy managed to reach Russia. Twenty of the vessels were sunk in the ice-choked waters, and few of the crewmen survived. Rudy served on in the Merchant Marine through the end of the war. He was awarded the Merchant Marine Combat Bar, the Atlantic, Mediterranean, and Pacific War Zone medals, the Merchant Marine Victory medal and the Russian Medal of Commoration for the Murmansk Convoy Survivors.

"The *Schoharie* was berthed only a few streets from the Navy Yard and when we reboarded, her winches and booms were rolling cables in and out as cargo was hoisted aboard from the dock and lowered into the hatches for storage. Pallets of jerry cans filled with gasoline and crates of heavy duty ammo were being stored below. 'Goddamn, we're not a tanker' Lagola, the coxs'un yelled. Nevertheless, the loading of the jerry cans and the ammunition continued on for several days until finally the hatches were closed and secured with tarpaulin. Next came the deck cargo: locomotives, trucks, and huge wooden crates. The whole deck and hatches fore and aft were packed solid with deck cargo. We wondered whether the ship would sail or sink under such a load. And the locomotives were stencilled in white paint, lettering that didn't make sense: 0006095ARKHSU775698. Of course, this was the manufacturer's code or perhaps the shipping agent's. We figured it out later. The next evening a dozen cartons were delivered to the Navy crew and upon opening them, we found foul weather gear and athletic game equipment. The armed guard was well-equipped for the expected bitter cold of the Atlantic. We were issued cold weather, sea arctics, winter trousers (lined bibbed overalls), winter mittens, winter face masks, goggles, and heavy parka jackets, in addition to the standard sou'wester rain hat, oilskin coat and trousers. There surely was no secret where we were headed and many guessed we were going to Murmansk, Russia. The scuttlebutt gang were always speculating on every rumor and hunch that occurred to them. And so the guessing game began. But for the time being the only important thing was a last night of liberty. 'Button Your Lip' and 'Loose Lips Sink Ships', the signs we read as we

departed the ship. Fortunately, having a last night at home for the locals, and a good time in New York for the rest, probably did more to keep those lips closed. A few may have used 'We're shipping out soon' to gain an extra kiss or more from a worried young lady. We don't know that anyone used the guessing game of our destination, except, perhaps, 'It's gonna be damn cold wherever we're going'. But then it was late September and at sea cold weather comes early. The mystery letters we later realized were Arkangel, Soviet Union, a rather obvious message to anyone who cared to know."
—Thom Hendrickson, DEMS Signalman, USN

One notable irony of the Russian Run was that, on several occasions the heavy units of the opposing navies steamed in all their pomp across great stretches of the northern seas, the one under orders to destroy a convoy but, on no account, to get into a battle; the other directed to engage the enemy if possible but, on the other hand, to protect the convoy. Signals flashed through the ether from London and Berlin: Ultra decryptions were suggesting one thing, while B-dienst intercepts indicated another, and the big ships altered course accordingly. Consequently, it was only the aircrew, flying off the carriers or launched from the battleships, who got to fire a shot in anger.

In what was one of the most disastrous examples of the entire horrific Allied convoy operation of the Second World War, the bulk of the escorting warships for convoy PQ17 were withdrawn by the British Admiralty in order to counter what was in fact a non-existent threat from the German battleship *Tirpitz*. The act left the merchantmen of the convoy to struggle on, all but undefended, to their destination at Archangel. Unfortunately, too, PQ17 happened to be the first scheduled Anglo-American naval operation of the war under British command.

In terms of numbers, an assembly of thirty-five merchant vessels made up this convoy which sailed from Hvalfjordur, Iceland, at 4 pm on 27 June, 1942 on a northerly heading. The merchantmen were heavily loaded with cargoes that included 297 combat aircraft, 594 tanks, 4,246 trucks and gun carriers, as well as an additional 156,000 tons of war materiel. The initial escort force comprised four cruisers, three destroyers, two submarines and two tankers to refuel the vessels. Shortly after leaving Iceland, one of the merchantmen ran aground and, when refloated, was forced to return to port there.

On 29 June, the ships of the convoy encountered heavy ice and four of them were severely damaged, one so badly that it too had to return to port. Now the convoy contained just thirty-three ships, and three rescue ships.

Six destroyers guarded the convoy as a close escort force. They were HMS *Fury*, HMS *Keppel*, HMS *Leamington*, HMS *Ledbury*, HMS *Offa*, and HMS *Wilton*. They were supported by two anti-aircraft auxiliaries, HMS *Palomares* and HMS *Pozarica*, the corvettes HMS *Lotus*, HMS *Poppy*, and *La Malouine*, the minesweepers HMS *Halcyon*, HMS *Salamander*, HMS *Dianella*, HMS *Britomart*, and the anti-submarine trawlers HMT *Lord Middleton*, HMT *Lord Austin*, HMT *Ayrshire*, and HMT *Northern Gem*. Added protection was provided by the British cruisers HMS *London* and HMS *Norfolk*, and the American cruisers USS *Wichita*, USS *Tuscaloosa*, and four additional destroyers. Behind them all, and tracking the convoy about 200 miles back, was a force of British Home Fleet battleships. And added to all the above was the protection of a second heavy covering force which included the British aircraft carrier HMS *Victorious*, the battleship HMS *Duke of York*, the cruisers HMS *Cumberland* and HMS *Nigeria*, the American battleship USS *Washington* and nine destroyers.

On 1 July PQ17 was located by German forces and was, thereafter, continuously being shadowed and attacked. While observing the progress of the convoy, officials in the Admiralty received intelligence reports that German naval surface units were being fueled to sail and intercept the convoy. With that information, and fearing the presence of the great battleship *Tirpitz*, among others, the Admiralty ordered the vessels of PQ17 to scatter. Most of the close escort and covering cruiser escort ships then withdrew westward from the convoy, ostensibly to intercept the presumed German raiders, leaving the merchant ships with very little protection.

Essentially on their own, the ships of the convoy plodded on towards the Russian port of Archangel. On the journey they were repeatedly attacked by German naval and air units, with catastrophic losses. Only eleven of the original thirty-five merchantmen of the convoy arrived safely. Twenty-four of the cargo ships were sunk. 153 merchant seamen lost their lives. Of the cargo, 3,350 motor vehicles, 430 tanks, 210 aircraft, and just short of 100,000 tons of general war-related supplies and equipment were lost.

The convoy had already covered more than half its route and had experienced the loss of just three of its ships to the point when it was ordered to scatter. Spread over a wide area of sea, the merchant vessels were now without their previous mutual protection and were virtually without trained escort for the remainder of their treacherous journey. Only the relatively weak close escort force remained with the ships of the convoy. The opportunistic German navy now capitalised on the convoy's disarray after the escort had moved off to look for the supposedly threatening enemy surface force.

The ships of PQ17 that were lost were: the *Christopher Newport* (US) sunk by *U-457* under the command of Korvettenkapitän Karl Brandenburg, the *William Hopper* (US) sunk by *U-334* under the command of Kapitänleutnant Hilmar Siemon, the *Navarino* (UK) sunk by aircraft, the *Carlton* (US) sunk by *U-88* under the command of Kapitänleutnant Heino Bohmann, the *Fairfield City* (US) sunk by aircraft, the *Daniel Morgan* (US) sunk by U-88, the *Empire Byron* (UK) sunk by *U-703* under the command of Kapitänleutnant Heinz Bielfeld, the *River Afton* (UK) sunk by *U-703*, the *Earlston* sunk by *U-334*, the *Honomu* (US) sunk by *U-456* under the command of Kapitänleutnant Max-Martin Teichert, the *Peter Kerr* (US) sunk by aurcraft, the *Washington* (US) sunk by aircraft, the *Bolton Castle* (UK) sunk by aircraft, the *Zaafaran* (UK) sunk by aircraft, the *Pan Atlantic* (US) sunk by aircraft, the *John Witherspoon* (US) sunk by *U-255* under the command of Kapitänleutnant Reinhart Reche, the *Alcoa Ranger* (US) sunk by *U-255*, the *Pankraft* (US) sunk by aircraft, the *Aldersdale* (US) sunk by *U-457*, the *Hartlebury* (UK) sunk by *U-355* under the command of Korvettenkapitän Günter La Baume, the *Olopana* (US) sunk by *U-255*, the *El Capitan* (Panama) sunk by *U-251* under the command of Kapitänleutnant Heinrich Timm, the *Hoosier* (US) sunk by *U-376* under the command of Kapitänleutnant Friedrich-Karl Marks, and the *Paulus Potter* (Dutch) sunk by *U-255*.

When British Prime Minister Winston Churchill reflected aft the war on the losses suffered by the convoy PQ17, he referred to the event as "one of the most melancholy naval episodes in the whole of the war." At a post-convoy conference and review of the losses of PQ17, one Soviet Navy captain commented angrily "It's not enough . . . we want more tanks, more planes . . ." The Soviets simply refused to believe that so many ships could be lost from one convoy and openly accused the Western Allies of lying about the losses. Stalin himself found the order given by the Admiralty for the ships of the convoy to scatter inexplicable—that the escort warships should return, while the cargo ships should be dispersed and expected to make it to the Soviet ports one by one on their own with almost no protection. And the U.S. Admiral King, never a fan of the British military, was furious at what he perceived as the Admiralty's bungling. He withdrew Task Force 39 and reassigned it to the Pacific theater of operations. The German Navy's commander- in-chief Admiral Erich Raeder briefed Hitler in a conference about the Allied convoys and PQ17 in particular, "our submarines and aircraft, which totally destroyed the last convoy, have forced the enemy to give up this route temporarily . . ."

ROUTINE

"Shipboard routine had replaced the excitement of the chase and the battle. And it was a maddening routine. The small ship rolled and slapped, listed and shuddered endlessly. Utensils, spare parts, tools, and conserves showered down on us continually; porcelain cups and dishes shattered on the deck-plates and in the bilges as we ate our meals directly out of cans. The men, penned up together in the rocking, sweating drum, took the motion and the monotony with stoicism. Occasionally, someone's temper flared, but spirits remained high. We were all patient veterans. Everyone aboard looked alike, smelled alike, had adopted the same phrases and curses. We had learned to live together in a narrow tube no longer than two railroad cars. We tolerated each other's faults and became experts on each other's habits—how everyone laughed and snarled, talked and snored, sipped his coffee and caressed his beard. The pressure mounted with the passage of each uneventful day, but it could be relieved in an instant by the sight of a fat convoy."
—from *Iron Coffins* by Herbert A. Werner

Everyone aboard the boat had a particular job to do, and each man's day was divided into two parts. He was either on watch or off watch. How long a man was on his watch depended largely on the nature of his job. An ordinary seaman generally stood three watches a day of four hours each. Others might be required to do two watches of six hours each. The only exception among the crew was the cook because his job was to produce three meals a day for every man on every watch schedule, thus he was "on watch" constantly.

For the men whose role was mainly deck watch, their routine was normally four-hour watches, but in the most savage weather when the sea ran high washing the decks in great sheets of water and punishing horizontal rain blasted the bridge, these men stood half-watches at a time. In such conditions, the oilskin coats, sou'westers over their Balaclava helmets, leather trousers, heavy sweaters wrapped in towels, and two pair of socks inside their sea boots, all failed to keep them completely dry and warm and safe from feeling frozen only minutes after taking up their watch. On one such occasion, the men of the deck watch aboard the submarine *U-106* had not been properly secured to the bridge railing and were swept away when a monstrous wave struck their boat. Their loss was not discovered until another crew member from the control room happened to go up onto the bridge.

Among the officers of the boat, the First and Second Officers, the navigator and the Chief Petty Officer, stood their watches in turn. For all in the crew of a U-boat, the effect of the ordinary watch routine was mainly reassuring, as it enabled every man not only to know his job, but he always knew where he must be at any hour day or night. The other side of that coin, of course, was the sometimes maddeningly repetitive nature of his life in that situation. But he also knew that the "routine" included uneven and wholly unpredictable elements of tedium, fatigue, excitement, and stark terror. The mundane aspects meant seemingly endless hours of monitoring instruments and gauges, scanning the horizon in all directions, listening through headphones and watching radar detectors, cleaning, maintaining equipment, helping in food preparation, and emergency drills— attack drills, fire drills, escape drills, trim-test dives, simulated crash-dives, and gun practice. For the safety of the boat, the bridge watch lookouts had to maintain a careful, exacting scan of each sector of ocean, the horizon and the sky. The most taxing aspect of their search effort was scanning in the general direction of the sun, which was also the direction out of which an attacking aircraft was most likely to appear. Dönitz had decreed that his crews adhere to the wisdom of "he who sees first has won;" declaring that any and all sightings, no matter how apparently harmless and insignificant, must be thoroughly checked. Every lookout was charged with being able to accurately distinguish between a bit of cloud on the horizon and a smudge of smoke from the stacks of an approaching warship. With the aid of his excellent Zeiss binoculars he had to unfailingly make the distinction between a seagull and a Catalina flying boat in all weathers and every kind of sea condition.

Discipline had to be strictly maintained among the lookouts on watch. They would be harshly dealt with if found deviating from total concentration on their search role to gaze in awe at the spectacular Northern Lights, or the amazing sight of a violent electrical storm at sea, or the splendid display of constellations in their most perfect definition.

It was vital, in the truest sense, for the commander and crew of a submarine to have spatial awareness and know as much as possible about the boat's surroundings and who or what might be sharing them with it. Submerged, the sub was essentially blind, except for the sound waves coming from an array of microphones in the bow, in the headphones of the operators.

The internal atmosphere aboard the boat was hardly tailored to normal human requirements. The limited fresh water available was only for drinking and cooking; which was why no one in the crew shaved and the very occasional bath was sponging from a bucket— for up to three months at a time. Their clothes simply could not be kept clean and invariably stank from diesel oil and sweat. Mostly, the men wore gray shirts that made the filth a bit less obvious. A variety of lemon cologne was all that they had to use on their salty skin to cut the stench; sometimes supplemented by oily unguents. They commonly suffered constipation, gingivitis and problems with their teeth and gums due to lack of dental treatment. And when surfaced on a choppy sea, with the induction valves shut to keep the sea out and the diesels breathing inboard air, the temperature in the boat could rise to 120 degrees Fahrenheit.

Their was little relationship between the notion of the German public that the lives of the men in their Ubootwaffe were filled with the glamour of high adventure and great heroism. More accurately, their existence in the submarines was cramped, claustrophobic, unsanitary, strenuous and stressful. Normally, six bunks were stacked on each side of the relatively small bow compartment; a living space shared by twenty-five or more men and a lot of torpedoes and their associated equipment. The crew members, and their very limited personal possessions had to accommodate themselves around and between the bulky, sometimes greasy, apparatus of the boat. Sleeping had to be done in shifts and "hot bunking" was the norm, with exhausted crewmen crawling into bunks still warm from their mates who had just emerged to go on watch. The Type VIIC U-boat was furnished with two toilets or "heads" to serve the needs of roughly fifty men. When the boat departed its French west coast base on a patrol that would keep it at sea for several weeks, the need for storage space meant that one of the heads would become a temporary food storage locker. Even when both toilets were available, they would only function down to a depth of eighty feet. Below that, the pumps that flushed the toilets into the sea were unable to function against the water pressure on the hull.

"U-557 sailed out of the shipyard fully overhauled. She had

received a fresh coat of gray paint, and looked and smelled newly commissioned. We spent the day in the Bay making trim dives and other maneuvers, checking instruments and engines for proper function. I was amazed by the crew's high standards and the ship's great maneuverability. Although she displaced 770 tons and was 75 meters long and about six meters in diameter at the beam, she responded to the Chief's commands with speed and precision. *U-557* was ready to join her many sister ships in action.

"On May 8th we sailed to the arsenal, where we loaded the boat with 14 torpedoes. Most of them were of the newest design, electrically powered and equipped with magnetic detonators. After the last two torpedoes had been secured in their racks on the floor, wooden decks were fastened over the sleek metal fish, leaving just enough room for the men to crawl to their bunks and to the torpedo tubes.

"On May 9, *U-557* took on food and ammunition. Cans, barrels, and cartons were carefully sorted out and stowed away. While shells for our 8.8 cm. cannon and our 2 cm. anti-aircraft gun were lowered into special compartments, the provisions were distributed throughout the boat. I was astounded to see the food supply for eight weeks disappear between pipes and valves, ribs and machines, closets and ducts. Huge smoked hams were hung in the control room. Staples such as whipped cream, butter, coffee, and tea were locked up for distribution by the Captain. The fueling of *U-557* was accomplished on May 10. On May 12, we received loads of fresh vegetables, eggs, bread, and fresh water. We squeezed the crisp loaves into the last unoccupied crannies and filled three hammocks with the rest, letting them swing free in the bow and aft compartments.

"As these days of preparation ended, our carefree mood turned serious. Retiring to the cabin on the old steamer, I packed my surplus gear into suitcases, registered their contents, and labeled the luggage. In case I did not return my belongings would be sent back home. Then I wrote a last letter to my parents and another to Marianne. Now I was ready to face the unknown."
—from *Iron Coffins* by Herbert A. Werner

The requirement of recharging the batteries of the electric motors on a roughly twenty-four-hour basis, while leaving the surfaced sub entirely vulnerable to attack by aircraft and surface vessels, also afforded the crewmen a cherished chance to have a little time on deck, perhaps to soak up a bit of precious sunshine, breath real fresh air, enjoy a cigarette, and relieve themselves into the sea. All but the least generous boat commanders allowed the men to form a queue in the control room for a brief, much appreciated turn on deck.

As for the senses of a U-boat, when it was submerged it was virtually blind. It's crew was guided by sound waves in a hydrophone operator's headphones; sound waves originating from an array of fixed microphones in the bow. The sounds could warn of any ships within range, telling the sound man that ship's bearing and whether it was approaching the submarine or moving away from it. It worked within a range of twelve miles in general, and could even detect the sounds of a convoy at up to sixty miles. The sound man, and the chief engineer, were the highest priority crew members to the commander when the boat was submerged. The noise level in the boat varied, of course, but in the diesel room, with the engines roaring under power, it was utterly deafening. The men in there could only communicate with sign language. When the boat was operating on the surface, the radio telegraphist could send and receive shortwave transmissions and keep the sub in communication with BdU— U-boat Headquarters in France. His responsibilities included sending timely action reports of attacks and counter-attacks to BdU, as well as the position reports, fuel, torpedo, and ammunition status reports, and weather and sea conditions. The BdU sent deployment orders to the commander. The rest of the time the operator listened to radio signals from other U-boats and, when possible, he listened in on messages transmitted from merchant vessels.

Dining aboard the sub could vary in the pleasure it provided, depending heavily on the consideration of the boat commander. Kapitänleutnant Otto Kretschmer, for example, considerately made it habit to submerge for about two hours just before dawn at sea, both to take advantage of the hydrophone information that might be forthcoming, and, importantly, to partially offset the stress of the crew by giving them a chance in a relatively calm underwater environment (when the sea surface might be quite rough) to clean up a bit and have their breakfast in reasonable conditions. When trying to have a meal while the boat was on the surface and possibly in harsh weather, would usually result in an awful mess. Often, the food itself failed to successfully make the trip from the galley to the table. When the boat cruised underwater it normally moved smoothly and predictably. When running on the surface, though, it would sometimes pitch and toss with the odd and discomforting motions of the sea, rearing onto great wave crests and sliding into deep troughs, only to twist and roll in cross currents. On the surface the whining of the jumping wire on the fore-deck, the slapping of the waves against the hull, and the uneven, pounding throb of the diesels were unremitting.

The U-boat seaman's exposure to the occasional terror of Allied air and sea attack at least broke the punishing monotony of the morale-sapping routine. The proximity to his fellow sailors worked on his patience and tolerance to an extent that could easily become infuriating. Their often loathesome habits moved some men near to madness in that confined environment. From the disgusting personal tics of some, to the radio man who seemed to endlessly play the same annoying phonograph record, to the handful of pesky flies that had come along from France on the patrol—all such things combined to make their difficult, demanding life in the boat even more so. Tolerance of the conversation of one's mates after some time at sea could and did wear very thin and the intellectual level tended to drop as is so often true in military situations. Emphasis leaned heavily towards the obscene and ribald, and to one's real or imagined sexual triumphs as expressed again and again in all their lurid detail. It was a common game to single out such figures as Winston Churchill, the flotilla staff, and even Adolf Hitler for derision and creative verbal abuse. It was usual too, with the crewmen of a U-boat, as was true of any close-knit group, to frequently pepper the air with jesting insults which in the main were taken in the spirit in which they were intended.

Beginning early in 1943, U-boat crewmen were able to listen several times a week to radio broadcasts by a "Commander Robert Lee Norden", the nom de guerre of a German-speaking U.S. Navy officer who told them of appalling losses in the U-boat force, giving the names and numbers, and describing how ill-advisedly their campaign was being led, as well as mentioning disguting scandals within the Nazi Party hierarchy and declaring how well all would be but for Hitler's insane lust for conquest. All of this was seemingly backed up by solid evidence, and delivered soberly as though by a friend. The British had been waging a similar war of words, psychological warfare, with "Radio Atlantic", which purported to be coming from a resistance movement somewhere in the heart of Germany but, in fact, emanated from the Duke of Bedford's stately home, Woburn Abbey. Both of these propaganda efforts attracted a wide audience, in the manner of Lord Haw-Haw (William Joyce) broadcasting from Berlin and attracting many Britons to their wireless sets, mostly for amusement, but for some to say "Blimey, he's right, you know!"

A key role of the U-boat commander, and of all leaders in a military context, is that of establishing and maintaining motivation and morale among his personnel. Prime examples from history have included Winston Churchill, who plainly stated the public danger with "whatever is to come, we'll face it together, and in the end we'll win", and inspired the public confidence when it was needed most, with his famous "blood, toil, tears and sweat" speech. As has been frequently noted throughout history, the fighting man uses and enjoys humour, often the rougher and bawdier the more effective, to boost and stimulate his spirit and maintain his resolve. It has always been important to remind him that the target, whatever it may be, is attainable; that what is being asked of him is possible (though not necessarily reasonable), and that his life will not be spent in a hopeless cause. Then there is Shakespeare's Henry V, expressed as "a touch of Harry in the night", the words of the leader to show his men his consideration for them, reminding them that he knew many of them by name, was familiar with their families, and cared about them.

The more decent of the U-boat commanders saw to it that some consideration was given to the morale of the crewmen and would manifest that with the occasional ad hoc party in the fore-ends, perhaps with a cake, some cognac and beer, and some music, either that of phonograph records or someone's accordion or harmonica—simple human consideration from one whose authority and respect was essential to their success and survival.

"One of the regular jobs aboard is that of inspecting the torpedoes, which must be pulled from the their tubes and tested, 'regulated'. Every four or five days the bow compartment is transformed into a machine shop. Hoist rings are fixed to the carriage on the loading track and the floor breach of the torpedo tube is opened. The torpedo, thickly coated with grease, is extracted from its tube with the aid of a horizontal hawser and strung to the loading carriage. If the torpedo uses compressed air for propulsion the air tanks are refilled. The motor is checked to make certain that all its bearings and axles are functioning smoothly. Rudder and hydroplane controls are tested and the lubrication points filled with oil. It may sound pretty simple, but in the crowded confines of the bow compartment it is very hard work. Since there should always be three torpedoes in readiness, only one is inspected at a time.

"During the first phase of the war, the most common torpedoes were the G7A's, running on compressed air. Later on, they were largely replaced by G7E torpedoes driven by E-motors, which did away with the earlier model's revealing trail of bubbles. These torpedoes had a diameter of just over twenty inches and carried a load of approximately eight hundred pounds of high explosives. All in all, they weighed some three thousand pounds. Each one cost about 40,000 Reichsmarks to make (though such calculations of cost are probably meaningless when industry is on a war footing).

"The Torpedoes varied significantly with regard to their detonators. They were either conceived for concussion detonation or for magnetic detonation, activated by the target's magnetic field, while some were capable of both. These 'backbreakers' exploded directly beneath the target vessel. The famous 'Zaunkönig' model was 'an acoustic torpedo. Launched in the general direction of the enemy, it would home in on its target by making straight for the loudest noise in the vicinity. The ultimate refinement consisted of surface-scanning torpedoes, which were not aimed at a specific target, but directed at a whole herd of steamers in convoy; these torpedoes would follow a zigzag course through the convoy until eventually they either hit a vessel or simply foundered, having exhausted their reserves of energy.

"The routine ticks on, as regular as clockwork. Four-hour watches for the seamen, with six-hour watches in the engine rooms. The fuel reserves diminish, the filth just accumulates, and our beards grow longer. The word 'hygiene' is greeted by U-boat crews like a comedy routine. Fresh water is precious—to be saved for brushing one's teeth and an occasional mouthwash. Anyone determined to have a proper bath—for which there is no room in a submarine, and which is quite impossible when the seas are high—has to use saltwater softened with a special soap. Hardly anyone even thinks of shaving. Beards are tended with loving care; when the sub comes back to port their thickness will make the reception committee on the pier realize just how long the voyage has been. No matter how long the period at sea, no one is encouraged to change his underwear. The men have a preference for what they call 'whore's undies,' which are black, on the grounds that 'they don't get so dirty.'

"The entry in my diary says Thursday. Another new tack. Seas so high that no weapons practice is possible. The weather seems to be favoring the enemy, of whom there's not a trace to be seen. Friday: radio silence, apart from enemy reports. Apparently there are now a number of boats in our area. No sign, however, of the expected convoy. It looks as though we are fishing in a pond that has no fish in it at all. A light wind from the northwest. Stratocumulus clouds up high, but layers of haze close to the water. The goddam haze robs us of what little visibility we have. It shrinks our basin-size horizon to a thimble-size one. It would have to be a stroke of the most freakish good luck for a ship to drift across our tubes in godawful conditions like these.

"Our radio picks up the following message: 'Search quadrant XY. Reconnaissance plane in distress at sea.' We are all rather baffled. We had no idea that we still had any sea reconnaissance planes left. But in a matter of seconds the Old Man is at the chart table. And in no time he's begun to give rudder and engine orders. I can see it all in my mind's eye: poor devils, drifting somewhere in the sauce. How long can a plane hold out above water? God knows whether the fix on their position is really accurate.

"We charge full speed ahead toward the spot where they're supposed to be. The Old Man keeps asking what time it is. He's glued to the bridge. Now he's asking for the signal gun. I hand it up to him. Then I scramble topside myself. I am appalled to see how high the waves are. In seas like these the airmen cannot last long. The Old Man raises his arm and pulls the trigger. The cartridge bursts out hissing. A white light unfurls above our heads. We stare as though mesmerized into the floodlit water.

"Later on, when the search has been abandoned, depression sets in. Random talk about the dubious reliability of the machines in which we have to place our trust. The second watch officer says that he finds them frightening and thinks of them as creatures, treacherous and oppressive.

"One of our fellow submarines has signaled that it can no longer dive. Now it is merely an exceedingly vulnerable surface vessel, exposed to enemy discovery and attack, and practically defenseless. Not even someone lost in a desert could feel more abandoned than every man-jack on that boat deprived of its ability to dive. Probably it is just a matter of a leaking outboard valve—a mere nothing in so finely articulated a mechanism—but even such trivial damage is sufficient to rob a boat of its most precious asset, the protection of under-water invisibility.

"Four of us are sitting crouched together in the officer's mess. Nothing to report, is what the commander writes in his war log. A few bare figures which tell the uninitiated nothing at all, and one or two totally meaningless sentences. Taciturnity is the order of the day.

"Suddenly the Old Man puts his pen aside and says, to himself rather than to us: 'This is probably not the way most people imagine the submarine war—or us, for that matter! They probably never think of it as working for a haulage contractor. The bunkers were pretty full up when we left. Some boats are on their way to us, others on their way back or patrolling areas a long way from here. That leaves just a handful for these parts—perhaps about twenty.'

"And these twenty boats are expected to form a dragnet that can catch a convoy? It's a net with hundred-mile mesh. On a map, our range of vision is one single pinprick. So there's a pinprick right here and miles and miles away there's another one. There's enough room between the two for whole convoys to proceed unnoticed in stately progress—in ordered phalanx if they so chose. This kind of naval warfare is far too much a matter of chance. Everybody has stopped talking.

"At one point I wake up because the engine noise has stopped. The room is dimly lit by a single light bulb. Suddenly I can hear the waves beating against the sides of the boat.

"The alarm sounds in the middle of the night. Ragged snatches of thought race indistinctly through my brain like underexposed film. Below me, everything is one vast grumbling cursing surge toward the hatch. A voice rings out from the loudspeakers: 'Belay alarm! Belay alarm!' And then from the control room: 'That was our friend Mr. Rott, our good friend Seaman Rott!'

"The second watch officer is exasperated enough to be forthcoming: 'I put the fellow up in the tower as helmsman. The idiot hit the alarm by mistake!' Seaman Rott can thank his lucky stars that he's sitting topside in the tower. You could find one or two who'd gladly take him apart.

"I still have some residual sense of passing time. So do the others, apparently. A washbasin with water has been set up in the control room. One by one, they strip to the waist and wash, then they part their hair meticulously in front of a dull looking-glass hanging underneath the gyro-compass. It must be Sunday. Just like the para-military work battalions: the ablution never went beyond the waist-line there either. No drop of water ever reached those parts which were most in need.

"The cook has produced seven large Madiera cakes; he wants me to take a photograph of them. 'I can hardly move an inch in the gal-ley. There's no way I can stand back far enough. But the moment they're out on the mess table, I promise I'll take a picture.'

"At lunchtime we get strawberries and cream for dessert. 'Coffee and cake' is scheduled for 15:30. That's when I'll do it, just to keep the cook happy. 'If only we'd unloaded the eels!' I hear one of the seamen moan. The wish is all the more heartfelt in view of the cof-fee party to come. There's still no room to set up a mess table in the bow compartment. Up front you can only sit cross-legged, since the reserve torpedoes occupy the center passage beneath the floor boards: resting on wooden blocks, they cut another couple of feet off the headroom in the bow compartment, which is already as low as a gallery in a mineshaft on account of the hammocks suspended from the ceiling. Here in the bow, it is not uncommon for the men actual-ly to look forward to enemy action: at least it clears a space.

"The chief engineer has shaved his cheeks but left a goatee. He looks like the spitting image of Conrad Veidt as Rasputin.

"The first watch officer has to eat after everyone else, because he's on bridge duty. We sit there ostentatiously glued to his every move, which makes him quite jittery—a fair exchange because he tends to give us the jitters with his table manners. At breakfast he picks even the tiniest black specks from his porridge with a great display of dis-taste. We have to watch him at it all too often.

"The chief tells me to keep my knees to myself. His bitch is that if I keep pressing my knees against the lowered guard rail of the table, I'll soon force it off its hinges. The chief is not just obsessed about his diesels: he worries about every nut and bolt on board.

"What a tedious day. At daybreak I already had a hunch that it was going to be a dead loss.

"We've been assigned to patrol yet another new outpost. For all we know, the gentlemen of the Staff are throwing dice to decide which square on the map they want us to search next.

"A radio report informs us that German submarines have sunk an aircraft carrier in the Mediterranean. Wonder why the report says U-boats? At any rate, there's nothing doing in these parts.

"The commander comes shinning up the ladder, surveys water and sky with skepticism, and gives vent to his temper: nothing in sight. We seem to be looking for the proverbial needle in a haystack. *'Rien ne va plus'* grumbles the commander. 'Not a soul anywhere.' The entire ocean seems devoid of ships. He volunteers an explanation: 'They're no fools. Sometimes they'll opt for a course close to Greenland, and sometimes they head all the way south—as far down as Gibraltar. We've got nothing on our side but sheer luck. It would be lousy if they had a fix on our movements.' "
—from *U-boat War* by Lothar Günther-Buccheim

Eminent British naval historian Peter Padfield wrote an excellent description of the operation of a World War II diesel submarine in his fine book *War Beneath The Sea*: "A submarine was a thick-skinned steel cylinder tapering at both ends, designed to withstand enormous pressure at depth. Buoyancy chambers termed main ballast tanks, fitted in most cases as lozenge-shaped bulges outside the pressure hull on either side, kept the cylinder afloat. An outer steel casing liberally pierced with openings to let the sea flood in and out provided a sharp bow, a faired stern and a narrow deck atop the cylinder; only a few feet above the sea, this was washed in any weather like a half-tide rock. About midway along its length rose a low structure enclosing another small pressure chamber called the conning tower, accessible from the pressure hull via a circular hatch and allowing access to the bridge above it by another small, pressure-tight hatch.

"To submerge, the diesel engines which drove the craft on the surface, sucking air in through ducts from the tower structure, were shut down, and electric motors which took their power from massed batteries and consequently used no air were coupled to the propeller shafts. Buoyancy was destroyed by opening valves in the main ballast tanks, allowing the trapped air to be forced out by sea water rushing in; and horizontal fins, termed hydroplanes or just planes, projecting either side at bow and stern were angled against the water flow caused by the boat's progress to impel the bows down. Approaching the required depth as shown on a gauge in the control room below the conning tower, the diving officer attempted to balance the boat in a state of neutral buoyancy, 'catching a trim' in which they neither descended further nor rose. He did this by adjusting the volume of water in auxiliary tanks at bow and stern, and either side at mid-length, flooding or pumping out, aiming to poise the submarine so perfectly that she swam on an even keel, weighing precisely the same as the space of sea she occupied, completely at one with her element and floating firm and free as an air ship in the air. It was an art attained by minute attention to the detail of prior consumption of stores and fuel, and by much experience. Sea water is seldom homogenous; a boat passing into a layer of different temperature or salinity, and hence density, becomes suddenly less or more buoyant, dropping fast or refusing to descend through the layer until more tank spaces have been flooded; when going deep the pressure hull would be so squeezed between the ribs by the weight above that it occupied less space and the boat had to be lightened by pumping our tanks to compensate. Most vigilance was required at the extremes: going very deep the boat might plunge below the point at which the hull could withstand the pressure; near the surface at periscope depth she might porpoise up to break surface in sight of the enemy.

"Submerged, a submarine stole along at walking pace or less, either to conserve her batteries which could not be recharged by diesels until she surfaced again or, when hunted, to make as little engine and propeller noise as possible. With both sets of batteries 'grouped up' in parallel she might make twice a fast walking speed, 8 or 9 knots, but only for some two hours at most before the batteries ran dangerously low. This was her shortcoming: while she had great range and speed on the surface, once submerged she lost mobility by comparison even with the slowest tramp steamer. Against a battle squadron she could not hope to get within range for attack unless already lying in ambush very close to its track. For this reason the submarine was held to be a 'weapon of position and surprise'.

"Once her presence was detected and she became the hunted, her submerged endurance was limited by the amount of air within the pressure hull, which of course was all the crew had to breathe; as they exhaled it became progressively degraded with carbon dioxide; after twenty-four hours or so reaching dangerous and finally fatal levels. Headaches and dizzyness were common in operational submarines, but they were accepted among the other discomforts of an exacting life; remarkably little was known of the speed of deterioration of air. It was, for example, not appreciated that when the carbon dioxide content reaches 4 per cent thinking becomes difficult and decisions increasingly irrational; by 10 per cent extreme distress is felt, followed soon after by unconsciousness; at over 20 per cent the mixture is lethal. No doubt this was not realized, and air purifiers were not installed—although in the German service individual carbon dioxide filter masks with neck-straps were provided—since before the advent of radar a submarine could usually surface at night to renew her air while remaining invisible. That indeed was the usual operational routine: to lurk submerged on the lookout for targets by day, coming up after nightfall to recharge the batteries, refresh the air and perhaps cruise to another position.

"The submarine's main armament was provided by torpedoes, each a miniature submarine in itself with a fuel tank and motor driving contra-rotating propellers, a depth mechanism actuating the hydroplanes to maintain a set depth, and a gyro compass linked to a rudder to maintain a set course. At the forward end a warhead of high explosive was detonated by a mechanism firing on contact or when disturbed by the magnetic field of the target ship. These auto-piloted cylinders, known as fish or in the German service as eels, were housed in tubes projecting forward from the fore end of the pressure hull and often aft from the after end as well. In some classes two or more tubes were housed externally beneath the casing, but unlike the internal tubes from the pressure hull whose reloads were stowed in the fore and after compartments, external tubes could not be reloaded until a return to base.

"While devastating when they hit the soft underpart of a ship or exploded beneath her, torpedoes were neither as accurate as shells from guns, nor for several reasons could they be 'spotted' on to the target. They were launched from their tubes—after these had been opened to the sea—set to steer a collision course to a point ahead of the target ship, ideally at or near a right angle to her track. Whether they hit depended largely on whether the relative motion problem had been solved correctly, which before radar meant how accurately the target's course and speed had been estimated. The most certain data available was the target's bearing read from a graduated ring around the periscope. The range was obtained by reading the angle between the waterline and the masthead or bridge of the target, either from simple graduations of minutes of arc or by a split-image rangefinder built into the periscope optics. Using the height of the mast or whatever feature had been taken, the angle was converted into range by a sliding scale. Since in most cases the masthead heights had to be estimated from the assumed size or class of the target ship, usually a difficult judgement to make from quick periscope observations, and since there was a tendency to overestimate size, ranges were often exaggerated. In addition the observer made an estimate of the angle between the ship's heading and his own line of sight, known as 'the angle on the bow'; this too was often overestimated. Speed was deduced from a count of the propeller revolutions audible through the submarine's listening apparatus, the distance of the second bow wave from the stem, or simply from the type of vessel and experience. With this data a plot was started incorporating both the target's and the submarine's own movements; updated by subsequent observations as the attack developed, and the plot provided increasingly refined estimates which were fed into computing devices of greater or less mechanical ingenuity according to the nationality of the submarine.

"In British and Japanese navies the firing solution was expressed as an aim-off or director angle (DA) ahead of the target; in the U.S. and German navies as a torpedo course setting. Finally, a salvo of two or usually more torpedoes was fired with an interval of several seconds between each; this was to avoid upsetting the trim with such a sudden release of weight as would result from the simultaneous discharge of all tubes, and to allow for errors in the estimated data or the steering of the torpedoes themselves. In the British service, where it was assumed that at least three hits would be required to sink a modern capital ship, COs were trained to fire a 'massed salvo' of all torpedoes—usually six—at 5-second intervals, so spreading the salvo along the target and its track. In the German and American services particularly, where the torpedoes themselves could be set to run the desired course, 'spread' was often achieved by firing a 'fan' with a small angle between each torpedo.

"Few attacks were as straightforward as this description might imply: the target was generally steering a zigzag pattern; surface and air escorts were often present to force the submarine into evasive alterations during the approach. The periscope could be used only sparingly, the more so the calmer the sea, lest the feather of its wake were spotted by lookouts; and between observations the submarine CO had to retain a mental picture of the developing situation, continuously updating his calculations of time, speed and distance in his head as he attempted to manoeuvre into position to catch the DA at the optimum time when the torpedoes would run in on a broad angle to the enemy's tack. There were other situations when snap judgements had to be made on a single observation or while the submarine was turning with nothing but the commanding officer's experience and eye to guide him."

DEATH FROM ABOVE

"They had given us St. Nazaire, another of the U-boat bases on the Bay of Biscay, and after Bremen we were nervous without yet knowing enough to understand why.

"Getting a mission started—that was when Marrow was at his best in those early days, for the wait before the take-off was the bad time, with so much idleness. He kept us all busy; poured out a stream of chatter. 'All right, Boman, watch that number three. Is number three coming up all right?. . . Watch the cowl flaps.' Then taxiing: 'How are we on the right? O.K. on the right?' because if a wheel went off the hardstand into the mud the whole mission could be loused up. And he had similar jogs for all the others, keeping them on their toes.

"That was a rotten mission. There were low-flying clouds and spotty rain at the base. The —th Group, which was supposed to lead the strike, left the rendezvous ten minutes early, and our people had to fly with our throttles wide open twenty minutes to catch up. Five ships aborted.

"Over the continent we flew through a clearing, and below it was surprisingly hazeless so early, and we had reached base altitude, and looking down I could see a spread of France, flat, farm-textured, the far-away greens night-washed and yellowy under the morning sun. I saw a river that must have hated the sea, so much did it writhe in its reluctance to reach the coast. And there were towns, like splotches of grey fungus, here and there on the carpet of Brittany. Views like this from the upper sky made me feel, even in danger, a kind of calm that came from considering myself an insect, or a unit of virus, for the activities of men—I imagined a Breton farmer playing a game with greasy cards at a tavern table, wine at his elbow, a fat brute with pink skin, bloated and selfish, oblivious to war, his bloodshot eyes flashing as he raised a winning card and slapped it down on the table and bellowed his triumph—were reduced to a microscopic scale, so that a whole city of such activities was no more than a stain on the earth, and a whole province of them was only a splash of cartographer's green. It was comforting to think of men as being so small as to be invisible altogether, and therefore of the self, too, as utterly insignificant: a poor target.

"Yes, I had begun to watch my own reactions very closely, and I decided that there was not, in the mission, the sensation of personal danger I'd experienced in more intimate conflict, such as boxing, which I'd doggedly done in school. Flying at high altitude in extreme cold, unnaturally masked and strapped, depending on oxygen for survival, forced to communicate with my fellow creatures mechanically (I had to remember to press the button at one end of my half-moon wheel to make myself heard), above all seeing the earth so far below as a mere pattern, a palette, gave me a feeling of severance, of being cut off, of being, as I was in an English pub, foreign. I think I'd have been very surprised at the connection with humanity that would have been involved if *The Body* had been hit; and I guess I would have reacted automatically with a further disconnection—by bailing out. I decided that the battle on the ground between missions was much more hazardous than combat itself, and up there I felt a kind of numbness, an alienation. All that changed later."
—from *The War Lover* by John Hersey

Near the end of the Second World War, a Consolidated PBY Catalina flying boat of R.A.F. Coastal Command located and attacked the German submarine *U-320*, in a bombing that sank the U-boat. It was the 196th and last U-boat of the war to be sunk by an Allied aircraft. A twin-engined Bristol Blenheim bomber of No 82 Squadron, 2 Group, R.A.F. Bomber Command, piloted by Squadron Leader Miles 'Paddy' Delap, spotted and made a low-level bombing attack on the U-boat *U-31* in the Schillig Roads near Wilhelmshaven in the Heligoland Bight on 11 March 1940. The Type VIIA submarine, commanded by Kapitänleutnant Johannes Habekost, was the first U-boat to be sunk by an R.A.F. aircraft in the war. In the attack, Delap dropped four bombs on the target, two of which were direct hits. At his extremely low altitude, Delaps's plane was damaged by the force of the explosions, but he managed to return safely to his base at R.A.F. Watton in Norfolk. *U-31* sank with the loss of her entire crew. The Germans later raised her, repaired the damage and recommissioned her. Eight months later, she was encountered and attacked by the British destroyer HMS *Antelope*, and sunk again, the only U-boat ever to be sunk twice. When Squadron Leader Delap was in his nineties, his son Mick wrote a poem about him: "A keen-eyed country boy who flew up / from an Ulster parsonage / into Europe's warring skies— / and landed in this wheelchair, / all his life leading / to this unravelling. He's lost his bearings, touched down God knows where, / but still knows how to look about— / hungrily at the ground / for an odd shaped pebble, / sweet paper, dandelion; then towards the horizon / for a benchmark tree; / then up, up, to the birded, / liberating sky. / Oh yes, then, quizzically, / at me."

In 1942, the American heavy bomber crews of the Eighth Air Force joined those of R.A.F. Bomber Command in frequent bombing attacks on the U-boat bases and shipyards of Hamburg, Kiel, Wilhelmshaven and Bremen on the Baltic coast. These raids continued until the German surrender in the spring of 1945. Many thousands of mines had been laid in the approaches to the U-boat bases along the Brittany coast of France. The subs had to be carefully led by patrol boats and trawlers through the treacherous waters when setting out from or returning to their bases. By 1943, the U-boats at sea were increasingly harassed and attacked by planes of the Allied maritime commands.

The Fleet Air Arm of the Royal Air Force was transferred to the Royal Navy in 1938. While retaining ownership and administration of Coastal Command, the R.A.F. passed operational control of the FAA to the Admiralty, effective 1 April 1941. This decision of the R.A.F. leadership reflected a better understanding of the dynamics of inter-service working relations than that shown by German Reichsmarschall Hermann Göring, who operated under the principal: "Anything that flies belongs to me, and me alone."

Policy formatting was one thing, practice was another. Coastal Command C-inC Air Chief Marshal Sir Philip Joubert, referred to the arrangement with the navy as "a polite fiction". In autumn 1942, he called for "a single supreme control for the whole anti-U-boat campaign to co-ordinate the policies of the British, Canadian, and American naval and air authorities." When it came to implementation, however, though generally agreed advisable and strategically desirable—even essential—it was felt that such a supremo, almost certainly to be a British admiral, would not be acceptable to the American president and his people.

Coastal Command would be seen as a "Cinderella force" of the R.A.F. for the remainder of the war. The glamour boys were Fighter and Bomber Commands. That was where the bulk of the action was, and the aircraft and armaments industries' priorities. As such, the

roles for the crews of Coastal Command lay in the areas of reconnaissance—patrolling the shipping lanes and reporting sightings of
enemy vessels and submarines to the Navy for action.

With seventeen squadrons operating, Coastal Command had only
three that were equipped with the sort of aircraft suitable for and
capable of flying patrols far out in the Atlantic, locating and attacking enemy submarines. Armed with bombs and machine-guns, the
Short Sunderland flying boats and the American Lockheed Hudson
bombers were the only Coastal Command aircraft with the firepower
to be effective against the U-boats in the early years of the war. Most
of the other squadrons flew the slow, relatively short-range Avro
Anson, a nice aeroplane for ferrying personnel and other light duties,
but hardly appropriate for true anti-submarine warfare.

The big Sunderland attained the nickname "flying porcupine"
when one got into a fight with eight Junkers Ju 88 fighter-bombers
and its gunners shot down three of the Germans. And on 27 April
1941, a Hudson bomber of 269 Squadron flying a patrol from Iceland
found an enemy submarine, U-570, and attacked it savagely, causing
the U-boat commander, Kapitänleutnant Hans-Joachim Rahmlow, to
dive the boat in such a rush that the crew neglected to properly close
all the hatches and vents, flooding the batteries and sending a choking cloud of chlorine gas drifting through the boat, forcing the several
crewmen of the now resurfacing sub to struggle, gasping from the
conning tower. As recalled by the pilot of the Hudson: "We thought
at first they were making for their guns, so we kept our own guns
going hard. They didn't like that a bit, and tried to scramble back
again. The rest of the crew were trying to get out of the hatch, and
they sort of met in the middle and argued it out. It was a regular
shambles for a few minutes." As the bomber pilot flew low and tight
turns around the submarine, he saw one of the U-boat crewmembers
with a piece of white material, which turned out to be the commander's dress shirt, being waved in surrender. As the now short-of-fuel
Hudson circled the submarine, the bomber's wireless operator signalled for assistance, reporting: "Practically the whole crew [of the
submarine] seemed to be in the conning tower, packed in so tightly
they could hardly move. We were close enough to see their faces,
and a glummer-looking lot I have never seen in my life." From that
moment on, a relay of Allied aircraft maintained a watch over the
prize submarine until a Royal Navy destroyer arrived to escort the
U-boat into an Iceland port. She was the first U-boat to be captured

intact.

When the United States entered the Second World War, German submarines began operating along the U.S. east coast, and by early September 1942 they had sunk a total of 204 vessels in the area.

The leadership of the American Civil Air Patrol requested authority from the War Department to directly combat the U-boat threat. The request was initially opposed based on the inexperience of the CAP, but as the Allied shipping losses grew dramatically, the War Department relented and granted the permission. The CAP was authorised to fly a coastal patrol from fields at Atlantic City, New Jersey, and Rehoboth Beach, Delaware, and were given ninety days to prove their worth. Their performance in the trial period was deemed excellent and their operations were then authorised to be expanded in both territory and duration.

The CAP originated in the late 1930s when the security and interests of the United States and her allies began to be threatened by the Axis powers. As war clouds loomed, severe limitations and restrictions were being applied in countries around the world on civil aviation because of the threat of sabotage, and strict regulation of general aviation was being imposed. Fearing the imposition of similar measures in the U.S., many activist American aviators scrambled to persuade the federal government that civil aviation could be extremely useful and beneficial to an imminent war effort. In 1938, Gill Robb Wilson, then aviation editor of the *New York Herald Tribune*, happened to be on an assignment in Germany and was aware of the ominous intentions of the Nazi government, and that it had grounded all general aviation in Germany. On returning to the U.S., he planned the creation of a new organisation that would use the civil air fleet of New Jersey to aid in the pending war effort. With the support of the New Jersey governor, the Civil Aeronautics Authority, and Army Air Corps General Hap Arnold, the New Jersey Civil Air Defense Services was established. Other similar organisations were soon formed and related civilian pilot training programmes were begun with the aim of significantly increasing the pool of airmen who would be available for military service when war came. Additionally, the programme called for organising civilian fliers across America to be able to provide more manpower and flying experience for the nation in the seemingly inevitable coming war. This would lead to the launch of the Civil Air Patrol with Wilson as the new organisation's first executive officer. On 1 December 1941, prior to the Japanese surprise attack on the U.S. fleet in Pearl Harbor, Hawaii, the CAP was officially established. Following the attack, the fears of the American civil aviation community were realised as all civil aircraft, other than airliners, were grounded. Two days later the ban was lifted (except for the entire U.S. west coast). Membership in the Civil Air Patrol, meanwhile, was growing rapidly.

Like the Minutemen in the American War of Independence, civilian pilots stood ready at airports across the U.S. and especially on the east coast, to fly and serve the nation's defence. With the support of General Arnold, the pilots of the CAP were provided with aviation fuel by the Air Corps, and were paid $8. a day to cover the costs of their accommodation, food, uniforms, and servicing. With the war, their CAP membership was no exemption from the Selective Service draft, and most of the younger men in the CAP either enlisted in the armed forces or were drafted. The gaps they left in the CAP were soon filled, however, by older fliers.

From the *Salem News*, 13 December 2009: "One of the Civil Air Patrol's most famous World War II 'subchasers,' honored for heroism by President Franklin Delano Roosevelt, died on Saturday, Dec. 5, after a long illness. He was 96 years old.

"Col. Edmund I. 'Eddie' Edwards was widely known as the first Coastal Patrol (later Civil Air Patrol) pilot to spot a Nazi U-boat and radio its position to U.S. naval forces. The vessel crash-dived and headed farther out to sea, where it was less of a menace to U.S. shipping. This occurred on March 10, 1942, near the start of the war.

" 'He was probably one of the first subchasers to see the enemy,' said Roger Thiel, a senior member and independent historian with CAP.

"Based at Coastal Patrol Base 2 in Rehoboth Beach, Del., Edwards flew sub-hunting patrols offshore in Delaware and Maryland, safeguarding oil tankers headed for Delaware Bay. The Coastal Patrol flights, made from 21 bases along the East and Gulf shorelines of America, were instrumental in making CAP an auxilliary of the U.S. Air Force, which it is today.

"Despite his notoriety as one of the very first subchasers, Thiel said Edwards held 'celebrity status' within CAP as one of the first Coastal Patrol pilots awarded the Air Medal for heroism during World War II. He and his commanding officer, the late Maj. Hugh R. Sharp Jr., received the medal after Roosevelt heard of their daring rescue of a fellow airman downed in bitterly cold high seas off Maryland.

"Edwards, in an interview for the Civil Air Patrol Volunteer in 2006, clearly remembered the rescue of 1st Lt. Henry Cross that earned him the medal and subchaser fame.

" 'I got the call that one of our planes was down, and Maj. Sharp asked me to go with him,' said Edwards. 'We had no trouble finding the crash site. We spotted a body, so we made an emergency landing and fished him out. He was alive, but we never found the other guy.'

"The rescue on July 21, 1942, required that Edwards and Sharp land their aircraft a Sikorsky S-63 single-engine amphibian piloted by Sharp, in swells reaching 8- to 10-feet high and, in the process, they crushed the left pontoon. So, to get back to base 2, Edwards accomplished a daring feat by climbing onto the right wing and using his weight to level the plane. A half-frozen Edwards clung there through the night until the early morning hours of the next day before a Coast Guard boat water taxied the unflyable aircraft to shore.

"Roosevelt conferred the Air Medal to Edwards and Sharp in a White House ceremony in February of 1943. By that time, Edwards had joined the U.S. Navy, where he served as a flight instructor and later piloted Douglas SBD Dauntless dive bombers on patrols out of Hawaii. Though Edwards and Sharp were the first civilians to receive the Air Medal, they were soon joined by others from their own ranks. By the end of World War II, 800 Air Medals had been presented to CAP members."

Operationally, the CAP pilots, in their Taylorcrafts, Stinsons, Pipers and Wacos, patrolled the eastern seaboard in pairs at low altitudes and as far as sixty miles from the coast. Flying these patrols from dawn to dusk, they communicated on single-channel radios and wore "life-jackets" that were inner tubes from car tyres.

The Coastal Patrol of the CAP was intended to fly unarmed reconnaissance misions. When they sighted a U-boat their responsibility was to notify the Army Air Corps and the Navy of the sighting and position, and remain in the area until relieved. That policy would be reviewed, however, after an incident in May 1942, when a CAP crew, Thomas Manning—pilot and Marshall Rinker—observer, flying a coastal patrol off Cape Canaveral, Florida, sighted a U-boat. The aircraft of Manning and Rinker was also spotted by the lookouts of the submarine who did not realise the aircraft was unarmed. When the sub tried to escape, it became stuck on a sandbar and completely vulnerable to attack. Manning radioed to report their sighting to their base and continued circling the U-boat for the next half hour. But by the time Army Air Corps bombers arrived to destroy the sub, the Germans had dislodged it from the sandbar and fled to deep water. It was this incident which resulted in CAP aircraft being authorised to carry bombs and depth-charges and to employ them when sighting U-boats.

Their work flying the patrols, sighting and reporting the positions of U-boats, vessels in distress, and drifting lifeboats inspired major oil companies to grant a large cash contribution to the CAP, and the Army Air Corps responded further by providing 100-pound bombs and 350-pound depth-charges to be carried under the wings of CAP aircraft. Such an aircraft, a Grumman G-44 Widgeon carrying two depth-charges and flown by Captain Johnny Haggins and Major Wynant Farr, operating from Atlantic City in July 1942, became the first CAP aeroplane to attack and sink an enemy submarine off the New Jersey coast. They had been scrambled to the area of the sighting by another CAP aircraft crew who were running low on fuel and had to return to base. When they arrived in the area of the sighting, Farr saw the U-boat running beneath the surface. Farr and Haggins were unable to tell the depth at which the sub was cruising and they tracked it for the next three hours in the hope that it would surface or rise to periscope depth. Finally, when they were running low on fuel and were about to abandon the flight and return to base, the sub did come up to periscope depth. The CAP crew circled and aligned their plane on the enemy boat. They released one of their depth-charges and heavily damaged the sub, causing it to leave an oil slick. On their second run, they dropped the other depth-charge which sent the U-boat down permanently, leaving considerable debris at the spot marking the first U-boat kill by the CAP.

The coastal patrol of the CAP flew their anti-U-boat patrols for eighteen months until that role was taken over by the U.S. Navy, confining the CAP to search-and-rescue activity. In that eighteen months, CAP pilots had flown 86,685 sorties in over 244,600 mission hours and made 173 U-boat sightings. They had dropped eighty-two bombs or depth-charges and had claimed the destruction or damage of two U-boats. They had reported ninety-one vessels in distress and aided in the rescue of 363 survivors of U-boat attacks. They lost ninety aircraft and fifty-nine pilots.

Vessels of the Italian Navy, assigned to keep Feldmarschall Erwin Rommel's Afrika Korps in Libya supplied, were incurring heavy losses to Fleet Air Arm fighters from the carrier HMS *Ark Royal*, and other Royal Navy warships in the last months of 1941. To help his Italian ally, Hitler ordered Dönitz to shift the majority of his Atlantic U-boat force to the Straits of Gibraltar and the Mediterranean. Basing for the subs would be provided by Mussolini at La Spezia on the northwestern coast of Italy. It was a disturbing turn for the admiral, who was dismayed by the effect of the new deployment on his Atlantic campaign strategy. He knew, too, the added hazard his U-boats would be facing when operating in the clear blue waters of the Med which made spotting them relatively easy for Allied aircraft. It meant his boat commanders would be having to surface quickly, launch their torpedoes, and dive again rapidly if they were to avoid the highly likely aerial attacks.

The presence of the numerous U-boats in the region would be at great cost to Britain. In a month of activity there, Dönitz's charges produced frightening results.

U-331 tracked and torpedoed HMS *Barham*, the only battleship ever sunk on the high seas by the U-boat force. The Royal Navy cruiser HMS *Galatea* was sent down by *U-557*, and the great carrier HMS *Ark Royal* was attacked by torpedoes from *U-81*, sinking before she could be towed to Gibraltar. The principal effect of *Ark Royal*'s loss, and that of her air strike force against Rommel's supply lines, was a substantial blow to the British. By January 1942, Rommel's divisions were rolling eastward again, even as the Atlantic convoys were given a short and welcome respite from the freqent attentions of the U-boats.

Allied airmen flying anti-submarine patrols then were often frustrated by the difficulty in assessing their achievements. From Coastal Command published by His Majesty's Stationery Office in 1942: "The attack is so swift and the results, if any, so prompt that the surface of the sea has closed like a curtain too swiftly for them to be accurately perceived and recorded. Though great patches of oil have stained the sea, though bubbles have formed and burst upon it, the U-boat may not be stricken to death. It may still be able to limp back to one of the numerous bases at its disposal for a refuge between the north of Norway and the South-West of France. On the other hand, it is equally possible that the opposite may have occurred and that the bombs or depth-charges have accomplished their purpose and that the U-boat went down on the long slant to destruction, manned by a crew of choked and drowning men."

The arrival of the long-range Consolidated PBY Catalina flying boat and the Consolidated B-24 Liberator GR in the Battle of the Atlantic anti-submarine role for R.A.F. Coastal Command was a genuine game-changer. The PBYs were equipped with bomb racks and British radar and these new aircraft were supplemented by the addition to Coastal Command of Bristol Blenheims, Bristol Beaufighters, and Vickers Wellingtons for support work. The Catalinas and Liberators were now armed with the new 300-pound depth-charges, 600-pound bombs, low-level bombsights, and torpedoes with acoustic homers, all of which made them much more effective in the role than their Hudson and Sunderland predecessors.

Significantly, the long-ranging, twin-engined Wellingtons of Coastal Command were mostly equipped with centimetric radar, which enabled the operator in his "Wimpy" at 10,000 feet over the Atlantic to scan a 4,000-square mile area of sea. A blip painted on his radar screen displayed the range and bearing of its source—the target submarine. Suddenly, everything was different for the lookout on the bridge of his U-boat as he was shocked to see an enemy aircraft approaching his sub with unerring accuracy, frequently from heavy cloud cover. The U-boat crew also found that, contrary to the manufacturer's representation for the Metox radar warning detector, the device was largely ineffective against the short-wave transmissions of the new Allied search radars, causing several radio reports from U-boats at sea to BdU like: "Crash dive. Attack by aircraft. No radar warning."

The U-boats were not standing still technologically. Some were now equipped with improved anti-aircraft armament, and when a commander of such a boat was threatened with attack by an Allied plane, he sometimes elected to remain on the surface and slug it out with the aerial opponent. The pilot of the attacking aircraft then had the option of engaging in combat with the U-boat, or simply circling out of range and requesting the attendance of the nearest destroyer or corvette to deal with the sub. Observing the behaviour of the U-boat, the aircraft crew would note the disappearance of the first crewman from the bridge of the boat, indicating that it was about to submerge, and would know that the aircraft crew had about half a minute to execute their attack, whether with bombs, depth-charges or torpedoes. This was the most vulnerable moment for the submarine. For example, Sergeant Clifford Chatten was piloting a Whitley bomber about 500 miles off the French coast on 21 May 1943. Though still in training, Chatten spotted a surfaced U-boat and attacked it with four depth-charges. But the attack took too long and the sub dived and escaped. Three days later, Chatten found and depth-charged another U-boat, scoring at least one significant hit. The subsequent Command Routine Order on the incident stated: "It is certain that very severe damage was done. In all probability, the U-boat was sunk." In fact, the German sub, *U-523*, under the command of Kapitänleutnant Werner Pietzsch, managed to limp back to Lorient for repairs. There had been many very experienced Coastal Command pilots who flew hundreds of hours over the Atlantic and Biscay and never saw a U-boat, much less attacked one. The inexperienced but keen Chatten sighted and attacked two in four days.

Sgt. Chatten's outfit, No 10 Operational Training Unit, had been flying anti-submarine patrols for eleven months. In their 1,848 sorties, these rookie crews made ninety-one U-boat sightings and fifty-four attacks, resulting in one sinking, one probably damaged, and two probably slightly damaged. In the period, the OTU lost thirty-three aircraft, a seemingly heavy price for the return, but, in the words of the First Sea Lord in his message to Chatten's unit: ". . . this constant and strenuous endeavour has very materially added to the difficulties of the U-boat in passing the Bay [of Biscay], contributing to the subsequent U-boat sightings and sinkings."

To counter the now far more threatening actions of the Allied aircraft, U-boat commanders no longer spent much time on the surface during daylight hours, choosing to surface under cover of darkness to pursue their deadly attacks. This tactic was met by Allied warships that fired "Snowflake" rockets which illuminated the area. The "Leigh light" was another effective Allied counter-measure. Named for R.A.F. Squadron Leader Humphry de Verde Leigh who devised it, the Leigh light was a 22-million candle power, 24-inch searchlight that was mounted under the wings or fuselage of an anti-submarine aircraft. Beginning in June 1942, such aircraft, equipped with ASV radar and a Leigh light, were flying patrols over the Bay of Biscay, illuminating U-boat targets with no warning and having the added effect of changing the tactics of many U-boat commanders yet again. It seems they preferred to spend more daylight hours surfaced so they could see their attackers, even though doing so heightened the vulnerability of their boats. After widespread deployment of Leigh light-equipped aircraft, the shipping losses to U-boat attacks were reduced from roughly 600,000 tons per month to less than 200,000.

When the B-24s and PBYs joined the Allied anti-submarine effort, they too were equipped with Leigh lights. In practice, when the radar of these aircraft located a U-boat on the surface, the pilot would approach it in a shallow dive, switching on the Leigh light at 150 feet. The intense illumination temporarily blinded the lookouts on the bridge of the sub while the plane made its bomb run.

The history of refueling U-boats at sea on long-range patrols was not a favourite subject of Admiral Dönitz. By late 1941, nearly all of his surface tankers had been hunted down and sunk by the Royal Navy. The next year he launched ten of the larger, Type IX U-boats as specially-built vessels, which the British referred to as "Milk Cows." These 1,600-ton subs were designed to refuel, rearm, and resupply the other boats on the high seas, as well as providing medical stores and replacements for sick or wounded crewmen. With a ten-knot speed and a range of more than 12,000 miles, each of the milk cows could bring enough diesel oil to double the endurance of five Type VIIC boats. The idea was sound, but frought with problems. Managing the rendezvous of two such relatively small boats in a great ocean was a considerable navigational challenge. Worse still was the amount of time required of both boats on the surface for the transfer of fuel oil, supplies or weapons, leaving both vessels highly vulnerable to air attack. The missions of these U-tankers were promptly noted by the Allied air and naval forces, and all ten of the original milk cows were sunk. A second batch of ten such boats was cancelled when Dönitz realised that the rapidly increasing scope of the Allied anti-submarine campaign had turned the milk cow into a dead duck.

Air support for Dönitz's submarines was minimal. It amounted to a handful of Focke Wulf Fw 200 Kondor long-range reconnaissance-bombers based at Bordeaux. The Kondor was a converted civil transport aircraft, with neither the proper equipment nor the endurance for the support the admiral needed, and its crews lacked the experience to conduct such reconniassance operations effectively. The aircraft were being used for wide-circle patrols over the North Sea and the Atlantic, searching for Allied convoys and warships that could be reported for targetting by U-boats. They could carry a 2,000-pound bombload or naval mines for use against the shipping. But despite some success, from the summer of 1941, the Kondor crews were ordered to halt their attacks and avoid all combat so as to preserve their numbers. Dönitz complained to Hitler that: "It is wholly incomprehensible that the German Navy, in this twentieth century, the century of aircraft, is called upon to fight without an air arm and without air reconnaissance of its own." The admiral decided to call on Luftwaffe head Hermann Göring at the latter's hunting lodge in Germany to beg for more and better support for his U-boat crews. His plea did result in some temporary help in the form of two dozen Junker Ju 88 fighter-bombers to supplement the Kondors, but that would not be good enough.

The Americans of the U.S.A.A.F. played a large part in helping the British on anti-submarine patrol in the Bay of Biscay. The bay extends southward from the northwest coast of Brittany to Cape Finisterre on the northwest tip of Spain, roughly 300 miles from north to south and 120 miles from east to west. It was being patrolled as often and as extensively as possible by R.A.F. Coastal Command aircraft. To aid in the effort, the Americans assigned air groups in February 1943 and again in July of that year. Most of the aircraft operated by the 1st and 2nd Anti-Submarine Squadrons of the U.S.A.A.F. were B-24 Liberators stationed at St. Eval in Cornwall, equipped with microwave radar; undetectable by the Germans. These aircraft operated under the control of R.A.F. Coastal Command and flew their first anti-sub patrol on 1 November, well before attaining their full sixteen-plane complement. In a training mode, the Americans familiarised themselves with the R.A.F. ways of flight planning, patrol patterns, communications and administration, as they adapted to the new radar in the Liberators. And they adjusted quickly to the lengthy and tiring ten to twelve-hour patrols they were flying.

With the participation of the American crews, Coastal Command organised a nine-day February campaign against the U-boats that were returning to their Biscay bases from recent action among the North Atlantic convoys. Starting on 6 February, the combined force flew more than 300 missions over the bay area. Nineteen U-boats were sighted and eight attacks were made. Of these, the Americans accounted for fifteen sightings and five attacks. 10 February: A B-24 of the 2nd Anti-Submarine Squadron, *Tidewater Tillie*, piloted by 1st Lt. W.L. Sanford, spotted, attacked and sank the submarine *U-519*, commanded by Kapitänleutnant Günter Eppen, approximately 600

miles west of its Lorient base, for the first U-boat kill by the
U.S.A.A.F. in the theater of operations. In their four months of operations while at St. Eval, the two Liberator squadrons accumulated
1,966 flying hours in 218 missions. They sighted twenty U-boats and
attacked eleven, sinking one.

Reorganised and augmented with additional new aeroplanes, the
American crews which had been relocated from the St. Eval base to
Dunkeswell in Devon as the 479th Anti-Submarine Group, took off
on its first mission over Biscay on 13 July. Within one week, the B-
24 of 1st Lt. C.F. Gallmeir had found and bombed *U-558*, a submarine under the command of Kapitänleutnant Günther Krech, 150
miles north of Cape Finisterre. Hours later two U-boats combined to
shoot down an American Liberator. The entire crew was killed. It
was the only U.S.A.A.F. B-24 brought down by U-boat anti-aircraft
fire in the Biscay offensive. Two weeks later an American Liberator
near Cape Finisterre depth-charged and sank the sub *U-404*, commanded by Oberleutnant Adolf Schönberg. All the submarine crew
members were lost.

More and more Allied aircraft and warships were being released
from convoy patrol duties in the summer of 1943 and re-assigned to
the hunter-killer role in the Biscay area. Many U-boat sightings were
made by the air crews and when they attacked their foes without
success, they were sometimes able to save the day by radioing the
position of the submarine to Coastal Command HQ, which sent additional aircraft and / or warships to the position to finish the job.
Probably the best day for the Allied hunter-killers was 30 July, when
an American B-24 crew sighted three U-boats about 140 miles north
of Cape Finisterre. As the pilot was getting low on fuel, he radioed
for help and was soon joined shortly by another B-24, by a British
Sunderland flying boat, a U.S. Navy flying boat and two Halifax
bombers. The aircraft flew through a storm of anti-aircraft fire from
the three subs in their attack. A Halifax managed to hole the pressure tank of the sub *U-462* commanded by Leutnant Bruno Vowe,
sinking it. All but one of the sub crew survived. The Sunderland of
the Royal Australian Air Force bombed and sank *U-461* northwest
of Cape Ortegal, Spain, which was commanded by Korvettenkapitän
Wolf-Harro Stiebler. There were fifteen survivors and fifty-three
dead in the crew of the boat. A British task force of warships then
arrived on the scene, found and depth-charged the *U-504* which was
commanded by Korvettenkapitän Wilhelm Luis. The entire fifty-

three-man crew perished. The series of attacks, involving aircraft and warships of five Allied armed services that day, showed the effectiveness of joint tactical cooperation in anti-submarine warfare.

Three days after the events of 30 July, an American B-24 found, attacked and sank *U-706*, under the command of Korvettenkapitän Alexander von Zitzewitz. Of the crew, there were forty-two dead and four survivors. It was the final submarine kill by the U.S.A.A.F. in the Biscay campaign. With the improved and increased air support from Göring, Dönitz was able to threaten the Allies' air supremacy over the Bay of Biscay, forcing the American B-24 crews to spend all of August and September in action with German aircraft in the area. The Ju 88s provided by Göring took the fight to the American bombers and the other Allied aircraft of the Biscay campaign, shooting down twelve including two B-24s, but they were unable to halt the campaign. Between 13 July and 2 August, the aircrews of the 479th sighted twelve U-boats in the area, attacked seven and sank three. In the entire period of the campaign, the Allies located and sank twenty-eight U-boats and heavily damaged seventeen others. So thick was the air over Biscay with Allied anti-submarine aircraft that it was almost impossible for a U-boat to surface anywhere in the area without receiving the murderous intentions of these planes.

Only a few hours after the great Allied D-Day invasion landings at Normandy beaches on 6 June 1944, a B-24 Liberator bomber flying an anti-submarine patrol between the Scillie Islands and Ushant happened on a surfaced U-boat. The Lib pilot flew a perfect low-level attack with six depth-charges, putting three on each side of the sub's hull, sinking the enemy boat. Later that evening, the same bomber crew spotted another U-boat in the moonlit waters. Bomber and submarine both began firing at each other and continued firing as the B-24 crew made a depth-charge run on the sub, dropping four of the weapons on its port beam and two to starboard. The sub listed to starboard and began settling at the stern. Out of depth-charges, the bomber crew could only watch and wonder. "We were just going to send a message to base, hoping someone might come and finish the job, when the mid-upper gunner shouted 'She's going down. It's just like a Hollywood picture.' She was at an angle of seventy-five degrees, with her bow high in the air, sliding slowly into the sea. We hadn't needed the Leigh light for the attacks, but now we switched it on. It showed three dinghies, with the Germans in them, floating among the debris and oil. It all happened so quickly that the wireless operator, busy sending a report of the first attack to base, didn't realise what was going on, and he thought we were kidding him."

Oberleutnant zur See Herbert Werner commanded *U-415* from 17 April 1944 through 14 July 1944. Having joined the Kriegsmarine in 1939, he served as a watch officer in training aboard *U-557* under Korvettenkapitän Ottokar Arnold Paulssen for three patrols and ninety-three days at sea. In that time the sub sank five Allied ships. Werner left the boat in November 1941 for another training assignment. On 16 December, *U-557* was lost with all hands. From Werner's book *Iron Coffins*: "It was past 1700 when I returned to the bunker. The radios had been silenced. Instead, the huge vault-like structure resounded to the songs of our 800 crewmen, who remained eager to sail against the enemy even if it meant sailing straight to their deaths. At 2100, as night descended upon the Normandy battlefields, 15 U-boats slipped out into the Bay. The night was clear. The stars glittered faintly in a still light sky. Soon a full moon would rise and light up our way into the Atlantic.

"The moon had risen fully above the horizon in the southeast. Standing like a giant lantern in the sky, it illuminated the long row of U-boats and was sharply reflected in the calm sea. Contrary to common procedure, all the men had put on their yellow life jackets. The bridge had been stacked with piles of ammunition, the conning tower turned into an arsenal. The gunners hung at their automatics in tense expectation of the first enemy plane. I stood in my nook trying to keep my boat directly in the wake of *U-821*, and to hold the distance to a prearranged 300 meters.

"2310: The first radar impulses were picked up by our Bug and the Fly as the coast receded. The report from below—'Six radar impulses, all over forward sector, increasing in volume fast!'— alarmed every hand on the bridge. All ears turned into the wind, all eyes searched the quarters ahead. I kept my gaze circling above the armored superstructure, but the intense moonlight revealed no winged black monsters.

"2320: The head of our procession reached the open sea. With the escorts still in line, the eight boats sliced the silvery surface and drove ever deeper into the enemy's defense. The scream of high volume radar impulses and the stream of emergency messages from below never ceased.

"2340: Sudden fireworks flared up in the forward port quarter, five miles ahead. We had been warned that several of our destroyers were en route from Lorient to Brest, and we should not mistake them for the British. I focused my glasses on the disturbance and sighted seven destroyers in an athwart formation, fighting off a British air attack. Thousands of tracers were exchanged, and brilliant flares parachuted down upon our vessels, adding their white light to the yellow moonglow. The sound of gunfire and howling aircraft engines increased as we drew closer to the battling forces. The Tommies, noting our approach, halted their wild attacks to avoid being trapped in the crossfire between U-boats and destroyers. The destroyers raced eastward past our long file, and our trawlers, seizing the chance for protected trip home, swerved out of formation and fastened onto the destroyers' wake. Their sudden maneuver left eight U-boats at the mercy of the British. At that moment all eight U-boats acted in concert, and I ordered, 'Both engines three times full ahead. Shoot on sight.'

"June 7 At 0015, our long chain of boats was racing at top speed towards the Atlantic. The diesels hacked, the exhausts fumed, impulses haunted us all the way. I found myself glancing repeatedly at my watch as if it could tell me when the fatal blow would fall.

"0030: Radar impulses chirped all around the horizon, their volumes shifting rapidly from feeble moans to high-pitched screams. The Tommies were obviously flying at various distances around our absurd procession. They must have thought we had lost our minds. Sometimes I could hear aircraft engines at fairly close range, but could not spot a plane. The hands of my watch crept slowly ahead while the British waited for reinforcement; our eyes sharpened and our hearts beat heavy under our breasts.

"0112: The battle began. Our leading boats were suddenly attacked. Tracers spurted in various directions, then the sound of gunfire hit our ears. Fountains reached into the sky.

"One of the enemy airplanes caught fire. It flashed comet-like toward the head of our file, crossed over one of the boats, dropped four bombs, then plunged into the ocean. The bombs knocked out Sachse's *U-413*. With helm jammed hard aport, the boat swerved out of the column. She lost speed rapidly and sank below the surface.

"0125: The aircraft launched a new attack, again directed at the boats in the front. Three boats, brightly lighted by flares, concentrated their gunfire and held the planes at bay. A spectacular fireworks erupted, engulfing the U-boats and aircraft. Suddenly the Tommies retreated. Radar impulses indicated that they were circling our stubborn parade, regrouping for a fresh attack. I raised myself over the rim of the bridge, straining to see and sound out the roaming planes.

"0145: The boat at our stern, the last one in the column, became the target of a new British tactic. Trying to roll out the carpet of fire from the rear, a four-engined Liberator came roaring down on starboard, diving for the bow of *U-256*. Boddenberg's men opened fire. But the aircraft veered off in front of the boat, where her guns became ineffective. That was our chance. 'Open fire!' I screamed. Five barrels, all that we had available, blazed away at the Liberator as it dropped four depth charges ahead of *U-256* and roared past us. Four giant water columns leaped skyward behind the riddled aircraft as it tried to escape our fire. But some shells from our 37mm gun hit the plane broadside. It exploded in midair, then plunged into the sea. *U-256*, beaten and mutilated by the depth charges, lay stopped and helpless in our wake, slowly falling out of line. That was the last we saw of her. Realising that her demise left us the first target in any new attack from the rear, I called for more ammunition. Radar impulses increased rapidly. For a while, however, the British held back.

"0220: Impulses now from starboard. I presumed several planes were approaching. Suddenly, a Sunderland shot out of the night from starboard ahead. I yelled 'Aircraft—starboard forty—fire!' Short bursts from our two twin 20mm guns followed the sweep of the plane. It cleverly flew in from dead ahead, making our guns ineffective, and dropped four barrels in front of our bow. Simultaneously, a Liberator attacked from starboard bearing 90, firing from all its muzzles. An instant later, four detonations amidships. Four savage eruptions heaved U-415 out of the water and threw our men flat on the deck plates. Then she fell back, and the four collapsing geysers showered us with tons of water and sent cascades through the hatch. This was the end. Both diesels stopped, the rudder jammed hard-a-starboard. *U-415* swerved in an arc, gradually losing speed. Above on starboard floated a flare, its treacherous glare enveloping our dying boat. *U-415* lay crippled, bleeding oil from a ruptured tank, slowly coming to a full stop—now a target to be finished off with ease. Bewildered, I peered down through the tower hatch into the blackness of the hull. All life below seemed to have ceased. I feared the boat might sink at any moment and ordered, 'All hands on deck!

Make ready dinghies and lifebuoy.'

"Not a sound came from below. The men must have been knocked out by the blows. Interminable seconds passed. From the distance came the drone of planes regrouping for a new assault. It had to be fatal. Suddenly, some men came struggling up the ladder, shaken, mauled, groggy, reaching for air, tossing inflatable rubber floats to the bridge. As they jumped on deck and prepared the dinghies, the gunners raised their barrels toward the invisible airplanes circling their disabled prey. The speed of the attack and the resultant damages prevented us from sending a distress signal. This, I thought grimly, was the way many of my friends had died—the silent way, leaving no word.

"*U-415*, hopelessly damaged, lay waiting for the *coup de grace*. Since the boat did not seem to be sinking, I told my men to take cover behind the tower instead of lowering the dinghies into the water. I was determined to remain on board as long as the boat would float and to shoot as long as there was ammunition and men to handle the guns. It turned out, however, that we would not die unreported: the radio mate managed to patch up our emergency transmitter and sent Headquarters news of our destruction.

"0228: Increasing engine noise heralded a new attack, a fresh approach by Sunderland from starboard ahead, guns blazing. Zooming over our bridge, it dropped four canisters. Four deafening booms tossed the boat aloft. At that moment a Liberator attacked at low altitude from port ahead. Our men on two 20mm guns started firing at once and emptied their magazines into the plane's cockpit. The black monster swept across our bridge, dropped four charges, then zoomed away, blowing hot exhaust fumes into our faces. As the boat made four violent jumps to port and as four white mushrooms soared high alongside our starboard saddle tanks, the gunner at the 37mm automatic sent a full charge of explosive shells into the bomber's fuselage. The flaming aircraft plunged into the sea. Somewhere, the sound of the Sunderland's engines faded into the distance.

"Then all was very quiet. The flare still flickered on the surface next to our boat.

U-415 was near death, but still afloat. The Fly and the Bug had been shot away; we were without a warning device. The bridge was punctured by many projectiles. A gunner lay scalped by a shell. Other men had been hit by steel fragments. The Exec moaned in pain, his back badly lacerated by countless splinters. In the aftermath of battle, I felt hot. Assuming I was sweating, I wiped my burning eyes. But my hand came away red, and I realised that blood was streaming down my face. My white cap was punctured like a sieve, and the tiny fragments had torn my scalp.

"Then I heard the Chief's voice from below: 'Boat is taking heavy water through galley and bow hatches. Strong leak in radio room. I'll try to keep her afloat, if you keep the bees away.'

" 'Can you get her repaired for diving?' I shouted back.

" 'Can't promise. We have no power, no light. We'll do our best.'

"I lowered myself to the slippery deck. It was split in several places by the impact of depth charges which had hit the planks before falling into the water where they had exploded. One barrel had bounced off the starboard saddle tank and had left a deep dent. Far more serious, the starboard aft ballast tanks were split wide open. Diesel oil escaped in a thick stream, spreading rapidly over the surface.

"With each minute of truce, the danger of a new assault increased rapidly. The boat swung softly in the breathing ocean, paralyzed, seemingly dead. The next 20 or 30 minutes had to bring the finale. With every heartbeat we expected another attack or the boat to slip away from under us.

"Suddenly the Chief's creaking voice escaped the hull: 'Boat is ready for restricted dive. Twenty meters—no more. Only one motor good for eighty revolutions.'

" 'Can you hold her at twenty meters or will she go to the bottom?'

" 'I can't tell, we ought to try.'

"I tried. Quickly the men climbed up the bridge and dropped one by one through the round opening into their iron coffin. I watched the deck gradually sink below the surface. As the water crept up to the bridge I slammed the lid shut. Seconds later the floods engulfed the boat."

While the spectacular raids of R.A.F. Bomber and Fighter Commands grabbed most of the headlines in that time, the vital, demanding and dangerous operations of the Allies' maritime air commands and the naval air arm contributed greatly to the outcome of the Atlantic battle. Altogether, the Coastal Command air crews flew more than 800,000 hours over the water, making more than 1,300 anti-submarine attacks. Their losses amounted to more than 1,700 aircraft and

5,800 aircrew.

". . . we gave orders to the R.A.F. Coastal Command to dominate the outlets from the Mersey and Clyde and around Northern Ireland. Nothing must be spared from this task. It had supreme priority. The bombing of Germany took second place. All suitable machines, pilots, and material must be concentrated upon our counter-offensive, by fighters against the enemy bombers, and surface craft assisted by bombers against the U-boats in these narrow vital waters. Many other important projects were brushed aside, delayed, or mauled. At all costs one must breathe."
—from *The Second World War* by Winston S. Churchill

"By January 1943, two things about the anti-submarine bombing program had become clear. In the first place, earlier assumptions regarding the imperforability of the pens were now borne out by experience. Even with the use of heavier armor-piercing ammunition it was considered doubtful whether significant damage could be done to the pen blocks. Consequently, all that could be hoped for from bombing of bases would be disorganization of the turn-around and servicing schedule. Secondly, in order to paralyze the operating bases and so to deny them to the Germans, it would be necessary to employ much larger forces and to bomb much more frequently than had hitherto been feasible. In answer to a direct question from Washington, the headquarters of Eighth Air Force replied that to neutralize these five bases completely 250 sorties against each base would be required."
—from *The Army Air Forces in World War II* by Wesley F. Craven and James L. Cate

SIT THERE AND TAKE IT

Caught in a place where he shouldn't be, the commander quickly assesses the situation and concludes that, unable to outrun the threatening enemy destroyer, his only option is to dive and sit out the depth-charge attack that inevitably will come. His sound man has been reporting the enemy vessel contact, propeller noise, for the past eight hours. The contact has been definitely identified as an American destroyer, escorting the convoy of merchant ships and clearly back-lit in the orange glow of a burning freighter in one of the outer lanes of the convoy. The commander considers launching a torpedo attack against the destroyer, but now the destroyer has altered course and is heading directly for the U-boat.

With no other option available to him, the commander yells "Alarm! Dive! Dive!" Obviously, the submarine has been spotted by someone on the destroyer.

In seconds the submarine has knifed through the choppy surface waters and has entered a steep and rapid dive attitude. Effectively blind now, except for the contact noises being picked up by the sound man, the commander and his control room crewmen are diving to try and elude the tenacious enemy warship, an effort at which they will not succeed. Seconds before reaching the depth at which he intended to wait out the savage attentions of the enemy above, the commander and his executive officer and the others in the control room are shocked by the intensity of four powerful, nearly simultaneous explosions. Immediately after the explosions the hull is rocked and pounded, and right after that the entire crew of the U-boat hear the sound of the destroyer's screws passing overhead. And then the screw noise stops as the captain of the enemy warship, certain he has cornered his prey, brings the destroyer to a halt to let his sonar man take stock of the situation.

Some intense listening is also taking place through hydrophones in the radio shack of the submarine and the commander waits impatiently near the chart table for an indication of the destroyer's next move.

The next series of explosions come and rock the boat with a greater ferocity than the initial lot, and the continuing reports of the sound man are partially overwhelmed by the noise and vibration of the depth-charge blasts. When they come, the explosions bring new, previously unheard rattles and torqueing creaks as the entire submarine seems to shake itself like a dog after an unplanned dunking. In the twisting action, items not perfectly secured are shaken, with a few of them hitting the deck-plates, along with many flakes of gray paint. In the awkward shaking motion set up by the second series of explosions, the long narrow drum of the sub shudders through a lengthy convulsion before starting to sway as if it were being knocked off its non-existent rails. And then the lights go out. The darkness intensifies the level of fear and foreboding among the crew until, in a moment or so, it is replaced by the illumination of the auxiliary lighting system.

Now the commander reevaluates his options. Hampered by the crawling speed of his vessel underwater, there is virtually no possibility of making a run for it to elude the pursuing destroyer. The crew of the submarine will just have to sit there and take it for as long as the enemy warship chooses to persist with the attack.

The force of the continuing depth-charge blasts slam against the hull of the sub, yanking and jerking it back and forth like a toy boat in the hands of a toddler in a tub.

U-230, under the command of Kapitänleutnant Paul Siegmann was slowly returning to her base at Brest following a long and arduous battle with a convoy in March 1943. Thus far the return journey had been uneventful, the deck awash and the Metox warning device tuned to pick up any enemy contacts in the area. The only activity had come when, on three separate occasions, radar contacts with aircraft had resulted in Siegmann crash-diving the boat just in time to avoid three separate clusters of bombs dropped on him. Then on 26 March, a bridge lookout shouted "Aircraft!" and Siegmann again ordered the dive, following his men down from the bridge even as the sea lapped at the hatch. The sub descended at a fifty-degree angle and a four-bomb pattern struck the spot where the boat had just been, narrowly missing its starboard aft ballast tanks, but still causing the stern of the boat to be briefly lifted above the surface again. To be safe, the commander kept the sub submerged for half an hour, having been surprised by the aircraft which had not been picked up on the sub's radar.

Surfacing again, their stay in the fresh air was abruptly ended once again by the appearance of a twin-engined aircraft. It too had arrived unannounced on radar. Yet another crash-dive followed. Half an hour later, having resurfaced, another such incident occurred, with no radar warning. The pattern repeated twice more in the next two hours, the last occasion when a big four-engined Sunderland flying boat came low over the submarine, which was twisting to manouevre away from the approaching plane. The Sunderland dropped four bombs which did no damage to *U-230*.

In a prudent move, the commander chose to limit the surface travel of the boat to nighttime hours only and to run submerged during the day. Clearly, the Royal Air Force had established a very effective air cover in the area of the Bay of Biscay and it made no sense to continue risking the safety of the boat and crew as they had been doing. Operating at night on the surface would require the British to use their radar to find the U-boat, which is not to say that by changing their running schedule they would necessarily avoid and evade the enemy warships—and they did not. Siegmann was still obliged to crash-dive the sub three more times to escape twelve more bombs.

The next day the commander kept *U-230* submerged all day, floating at only three knots speed. The sound man continued his vigil listening to the propeller noises of the British hunter-killer warships patrolling nearby and the reverberating booms of distant depth-charge explosions in the huge bay.

The decision to travel on the surface only in darkness, while a sound one, did not achieve the level of protection that Siegmann had anticipated. During the next night the boat was forced to do six more crash-dives and in each of them, the crew had to endure the experience of a four depth-charge pattern attack. Still, escape they did each time, to surface again and proceed. Throughout the following day they sailed submerged at a sixty-metre depth, though still experiencing the occasional inexplicable explosion which rocked the boat and reminded the crew again and again of how it felt to be the hunted. Surfacing again just after dark, they sailed without harassment until midnight when they moved into the mass of a large fleet of French fishing trawlers out for sardines. Their presence spared *U-230* further attack.

The submarine was scheduled to rendezvous with another U-boat, *U-665*, under the command of Oberleutnant Hans-Jürgen Haupt, after daybreak, but soon learned that the other sub had been attacked and sunk by an R.A.F. Whitley bomber only hours before they were to meet. *U-665* had been assigned to escort *U-230* on to Brest. All hands aboard *U-665* were lost.

Six hours later, Siegmann's sub was met by a Coast Guard vessel, an escort for the final run into port. He allowed the exhausted, battle-weary crew of the sub to refresh themselves with the cool, clean air while requiring some of them to ready the deck guns for more possible action. At last the pale purple of the French coast hove into view, followed shortly by the white-painted walls and red roofs of the seaside houses. The commander managed to bring his boat into the harbour without further combat. As the sub drifted slowly into the basin of the U-bunker, Siegmann treated himself to his favourite cigar. The men, now assembled as smartly as was possible for such a dog-tired, dishevelled lot, on the after deck, blinking in the bright sunlight. They were somewhat surprised but pleased by the reception awaiting them. It had been their first war patrol and now a small band played, and a crowd had gathered to cheer and greet them at the end of a punishing eight-week encounter with the weather and the enemy. Rising dramatically over them, the massive concrete structure of the submarines pens, shelter for more than forty of Admiral Dönitz's grey wolves, received them as the helmsman nosed *U-230* into one of the berths. "Both half astern. Both full stop. Fasten all lines." The girls of the Ubootwaffe administration were present to deliver flowers and kisses all around.

What Siegmann and the crew of the sub wanted was to shower and shave. What they got was a seemingly endless round of receptions and celebrations lasting well into the night. They were totally caught up in the revelry. Executive officer Herbert Werner: "We overdid everything. We gorged ourselves on the plentiful food of Brittany; we drank too much French wine; we sang and joked and laughed with loud abandon. No one objected to our excesses. It was comforting to know that others understood our needs after our weeks of anguish."

In March 1943, nearly 250 U-boats were in action, in training in the Baltic, in port for refitting, and in shipyards nearing completion. But, with the increasingly larger convoys, and the coordination of the British and American naval units in improving their convoy defences, the successes of the Ubootwaffe were becoming far more difficult to achieve. Now the U-boats had to contend with newer and more effective convoy escort vessels which increased the hazards of U-boat attacks. The greatest threat to the submarines of Germany though, was the great and everpresent one from the sky. Ever more enemy aircraft were now able to range much farther out to sea and bomb the U-boats there and on their outbound and homeward runs with considerably greater accuracy. The cumulative effect of the rapidly growing war production and supply capability coming from the United States was reinvigorating the Allied war effort. The task of the U-boats was to prevent American food, ammunition, and aeroplanes from reaching the British ports and those of Murmansk and Archangel. They were charged with denying the British and the Americans the ability to amass the materiel and manpower to mount an invasion of Europe.

24 April, 1943. Herbert Werner, executive officer, "*U-230* lay in the shadow of her concrete berth, lines removed from the pillars. Her company stood in closed ranks on the aft deck, facing the farewell party on the pier. The men had flowers fastened at their caps or in the buttonholes of their olive-green fatigues. Beneath them, the oily water was beaten up by our screws, which turned silently in reverse. *U-230* detached herself gently from the concrete wall and sailed, stern first, out of the shadowy darkness of the protective bunker into the blazing sun. At the same time a second boat, *U-456*, separated from another pier and followed in our wake. Her orders were the same as ours. Then our boat rapidly increased the distance to land and friends. Once we passed the center of the Bay, everything on board was at war: the actions, the spoken words, and the thoughts. It was as if there had never been a port, never a leave, never a jovial moment at the Casino Bar, never a night in the arms of a woman."

Monitoring the radar detection gear, the bridge watch of *U-230* were alert as the boat raced at seventeen knots through the smooth sea surface. During her recent refit in Brest, she had been re-equipped with an improved version of the Metox. Its small antenna was permanently welded to the rim of the bridge structure, unlike the bulky earlier version which had to be removed and stowed down in the control room before the boat could be submerged, an especially annoying and inefficient chore in an emergency crash-dive situation. Since leaving the U-bunker, the Metox had been picking up only occasional weak impulses. As the two submarines progressed across the Bay of Biscay the impulses grew in both frequency and volume. The boats then submerged and lost contact with each other.

With the coming of night Kapitänleutnant Siegmann took the boat up to the surface again, determined to travel for as long as possible at speed. The efficient diesels were recharging the sub's batteries.

Werner, the executive officer thought of the large, phosphorescent whirlpool the boat was creating and what a superb target they were offering to any enemy aircraft in the vicinity. He checked his watch to see how many minutes they had been cruising on the surface. The Metox impulse suddenly came at top volume and Siegmann had to order a crash-dive. Werner: "The nights became our days and the days became our nights. The hours inside the hull were spent in darkness lit by a few dim bulbs, and the nights on the bridge were as black as tar. We continued our advance with our ears tuned to the enemy above and our eyes glued to the black sea, always ready to duck the bombs that came hurtling down from the sky with alarming frequency. And during daytime we floated at a depth of 40 meters, listening to the distant but intimate sounds of propellers, Asdic pings, and detonating depth charges and bombs."

In early May the boat reached what the crew referred to as the "Black Pit" area; a region that, as far as they knew, had not yet been achieved by enemy planes. The bright spring sun shone on them and the Metox impulses had gradually declined and then stopped completely. Siegmann elected to continue sailing on the surface. The exec, mindful of the hellish week of aerial attacks and the resulting crash-dives they had recently come through, now counted on the combination of the Metox warning system and the excellent visibility in the clear, sunny weather to afford them ample time to respond, should another attack from the sky occur.

Passing the 15th Longitude West, Siegmann signaled BdU headquarters in France that the boat had safely crossed the Bay of Biscay. Within a few hours the radio operator reported a response: PROCEED INTO GRID SQUARE BD95. EXPECT EASTBOUND CONVOY. In the improved weather, and more southerly search area, the boat commander anticipated better operating conditions and a more successful hunt.

The sub continued in calm seas and brilliant sunshine toward her search square. On 5 May the radio man intercepted a signal that would suddenly dampen the morale on board. It came from the submarine U-638: DESTROYER. ATTACKED. SINKING. U-638. It was the final message from the sub. Two hours later, the radio man intercepted another message: ATTACKED BY DESTROYERS. DEPTH CHARGES. LEAVE BOAT. U-531. The bad news continued the next day with yet another intercepted signal: ATTACKED BY CORVETTE. SINKING. U-438. And later in the day, another: AIR-

CRAFT. BOMBS. RAMMED BY DESTROYER. SINKING.
U-125. At this point the anger of the U-230 crew became shock. The following evening, as the boat sailed under a clear, starry sky, still another message of distress was picked up the radio operator: AIR ATTACK. SINKING. 47N 05W. U-663. Another day came and went and with it, the loss of yet another U-boat to aircraft attack, *U-528*. Shock on board *U-230* now turned to dismay.

On 11 May Kapitänleutnant Siegmann received new orders from BdU: ALL U-BOATS IN GRID SQUARE BD INTERCEPT EAST-BOUND CONVOY IN BD91. ATTACK WITHOUT FURTHER ORDERS. The commander changed course and ordered full speed ahead. The exec ordered all hands to prepare for action and had all torpedoes readied. At 06:20 the next morning *U-230* arrived on the convoy's calculated mean track. The exec ordered the boat slowed and turned westward towards the convoy.

Werner: "The sun shot like a fireball out of the ocean. At that spectacular moment, I spotted a smear over the southwesterly hori-zon—the convoy! I called Siegmann to the bridge and said as he arrived, 'I have a present for you, sir.' We watched the smudge grow bigger and wider. Soon the Captain turned the stern of the boat toward the gray and black fumes. Three mastheads crept over the sharp horizon in the west and mounted higher. Emerging fully, the three ships were seen to be escorts, the sweepers in front of the con-voy. They zigzagged closer, moving jerkily like puppets on an empty stage. We proceeded slowly eastward, maintaining a safe distance, to determine the convoy's exact course."

Now many more mastheads began appearing across the horizon, followed by the funnels. These were the merchantmen the U-boat was hunting. Siegmann sent the boat ahead of the parade of cargo ships, positioning it for attack. He estimated he would be set to launch torpedoes in about an hour. Twenty minutes later he ordered "Clear the bridge. On diving stations." In five more minutes the boat was submerged just below the surface and had been properly trimmed. From the periscope, he informed the crew "We have sight-ed an extremely large convoy, probably over one hundred vessels. We shall attack submerged. I need not remind you that this is no hol-iday cruise. I expect your utmost effort to make this attack a suc-cess."

At 07:16 the sound man reported that the convoy had apparently changed course. This news would alter the commander's plan to attack submerged. He was plainly irritated. "Damn dirty trick" he growled, raising the periscope higher to watch the massed vessels. As he did so, the pounding noises of the many merchant ships began to reach the U-boat, along with the high-pitched churning of the escort propellers.

Zigzagging, the giant convoy began steaming away from the track the U-boat had taken up. The boat was still undetected near the outer defence of the convoy, but Siegmann was unwilling to commence his attack until *U-230* had successfully passed through the cordon of destroyers and other escort vessels. It was then the exec's turn to peer through the periscope. Werner: "I swung into the seat. Seven miles on port I saw an amazing panorama. The entire horizon, as far and wide as I could see, was covered with vessels, their funnels and masts as thick as a forest. At least a dozen fast destroyers cut the choppy green sea with elegance. As many as two dozen corvettes flitted around the edges of the convoy. 'Quite a display of power, sir. It's probably the largest convoy ever.' Siegmann agreed and allowed that, once they were close to that wall of ships, their torpedoes could not miss.

The challenge for Siegmann now was to sail diagonally away from the convoy in order to reposition the boat for an effective attack. At 09:15 the commander ordered the boat to the surface. With the decks still awash he mounted the bridge accompanied by the exec, who scanned the horizon and focused on the masts and funnels of the convoy far to the northeast. Paralleling the convoy now, the commander aimed to arrive at a particular firing position before the coming nightfall. His radio man signalled headquarters and the other U-boats in the area: CONVOY BD92 COURSE NORTHEAST ELEVEN KNOTS. STRONG DEFENSE. REMAIN SURFACED FOR ATTACK. U-230.

It was then that one of the bridge lookouts shouted "Flugzeug!" and the exec spotted the twin-engined plane coming at them from out of the sun. "Alarrrmmm!" Almost as one, all the men on the bridge dropped through the hatch and into the conning tower as *U-230* plunged below the surface once again. The submarine was at her most vulnerable.

The massive reverberations of four explosions slammed through the sea immediately above the boat which was now descending in a sixty-degree dive angle. The hull trembled and the deck plates appeared to flex, as the ribs of the structure creaked. Once again the interior was in darkness. When, seconds later, the emergency lighting came on, everyone seemed astonished, disbelieving that the relatively small aircraft had the range to seek them out and attack them. It simply could not fly a round-trip from the nearest point of land to the middle of the Atlantic and back. The only possibility any of the crew could imagine was that this mighty convoy must include at least one aircraft carrier which was launching and recovering its own anti-submarine planes. It that was true it would be a devastating development for the U-boats and their whole approach to warfare and mean that they could no longer attack with the element of surprise without receiving a swift reprisal.

Siegmann and the crew of *U-230* continued the hunt on the surface. Shortly after 11:00, executive officer Werner spotted the metallic glint of a small aircraft diving towards them from between the clouds. "Alarrrmmm!" With amazing accuracy the plane delivered a clutch of four bombs near enough for the resultant shock waves to jar the sub, knocking her out of trim and stunning the crew. She descended to 180 metres before the helmsman was able to bring her back into balance and then back up to periscope depth. A few minutes later the commander had the boat surfaced again and in close contact with the convoy. Now he and the men in the control room and on the bridge drove the boat with renewed determination and in defiance of the very real threat from enemy aircraft. 11:42: "Aircraft. Alarrmmm!" Another crash-dive followed instantaneously by the no-longer surprising stick of four bombs whose blasts savagely rocked the submarine. Again, all the crew could do was wait for the threat to depart the area.

At precisely midday Siegmann resurfaced into a much more choppy sea and found that they had made good headway on the Allied convoy. The exec mounted the bridge and, scanning with his Zeiss binoculars, noted the positions of the convoy escort vessels, but was far more concerned with the now frequent attacks from the air. Eight minutes later the radio man reported to the commander about a signal he had just received: ATTACKED BY AIRCRAFT. SINKING. U-89. One common thought was circulating aboard *U-230*—how long before it is our turn?

Nine minutes more and another cry: "Aircraft dead astern. Alarrrmmm!" The now familiar pattern repeated, with four stunning blasts chasing them as they rapidly dived for safety. 12:30. Surfaced again.

Forty-five minutes later a twin-engined aircraft materialised from the low cloud cover at a distance of just 800 metres astern of the submarine. There was no warning and no time to dive and elude the attacker. The commander yelled, "Right full rudder!" The exec and the mate—the only other man on the bridge—manned the two anti-aircraft guns as the plane raced in to strafe the open rear "winter-garden" at the aft end of the bridge. The helmsman did his best to bring the boat around hard starboard. To their frustration, the guns of both the mate and exec were jammed and would not fire. In a few seconds four towering fountains of sea water erupted alongside the boat as the bombs from the plane exploded along the starboard saddle tanks. The attack was over; the enemy aircraft gone. The sub was still intact.

Less than an hour later another urgent radio signal came in: ATTACKED BY AIRCRAFT. UNABLE TO DIVE. SINKING. 45 NORTH 25 WEST. HELP. U-456. This was the boat that had accompanied *U-230* on this convoy patrol. Siegmann decided to try to rescue the crew of *U-456*, which was only twelve miles ahead of his own boat. The commander altered course and raced towards the stricken sub. When they approached the other U-boat, Siegmann and the exec saw that the bow was poking from the rough water, several crew members were clinging to the deck and the jumping wire, and an aircraft was circling slowly overhead. Another impediment to Siegmann's rescue effort was the ominous appearance of an escort corvette running in from astern of the boat. The potential rescue was hopeless. *U-230* turned away and headed towards the convoy again.

Moments later yet another aircraft, a single-engined type, approached at very low height right up the wake of the boat. Working furiously, the exec managed to clear the jam in his gun and quickly exhausted the magazine in the general direction of the attacker. Running hard to starboard, the turning sub spoiled the aim of the plane's pilot. The pilot then circled and came at the sub from dead ahead in another attacking run. But as it neared, its engine quit and it cartwheeled into the sea very near the U-boat. In the crash, the pilot was thrown from the cockpit and was floundering and waving for help. Then, as the commander and the exec watched, the bombs of the aircraft exploded, killing the pilot and sending violent shocks into the hull of the sub. Siegmann estimated they would intersect the convoy's track within the next hour.

At 15:45 a radio report was received: DEPTH CHARGES BY

THREE DESTROYERS. SINKING. U-186. It was the eleventh
U-boat lost to enemy action since the patrol of *U-230* began. Clearly,
a sea change in the fortunes of the Ubootwaffe had occurred.

Fifteen minutes later, the track of *U-230* met that of the convoy
and Siegmann sighted four columns of merchant ships coming over
the horizon and heading in the general direction of the U-boat.
Three minutes after that, a lookout shouted: "Aircraft, bearing
three-two-oh." Plunging down, the boat was again jarred by explosions nearby, followed shortly by a second series of blasts. Defiantly,
the commander took the boat up to periscope depth and was angered
to discover that the aircraft had dropped a yellow dye marker on the
spot where the sub had dived, to aid the convoy escorts in an attack on
Siegmann's boat. He intended to attack the convoy before any
escorts could arrive to depth-charge him.

The commander ordered tubes one to five to stand ready. Then he
suddenly ordered the chief to take the boat down, a destroyer was
lined up in ramming position, "Take her down to two hundred
meters, for God's sake!" The crew of the sub were engulfed in the
sound of the destroyer's engines and screws. Seconds later six depth-
charge blasts hit the hull so violently that the boat was lifted out of
the water and, after what seemed to the crew an eternity, the boat
finally descended from the surface and began to sink again. Now she
was diving at a sixty-degree angle, dropping to 250 metres before
the helmsman managed to stabilise her and get her level at 230
metres, where the threat of hull-crushing pressure was mounting. The
men of the submarine had to sit there and take it.

The British warships had cornered the sub and would persist with
their intensive depth-charge attacks, dropping spread after spread of
the terrifying weapons, shaking and destabilising the boat again and
again. Small leaks opened around the interior and soon the aft bilge
filled with sea water. Mostly minor damage was incurred, with water
invading different parts of the boat, loosening the periscope pack-
ings, sloshing into the engine room. The new weight of the water in the
hull drove the boat deeper.

Werner: "The uproar was at its peak. A sudden splash told us that
we had 10 or 15 seconds to brace against another barrage. The
charges went off just beyond lethal range. While the ocean reverber-
ated under the blasts, the bulk of the convoy slowly passed the spot
of our slow execution. I pictured the freighters making a detour
around the escorts massed above to end our existence. Perhaps we

should risk going deeper. I did not know where our limit was, where the hull would finally crack. No one knew. Those who had found out took their knowledge into the depths. For hours we suffered the punishment and sank gradually deeper. In a constant pattern, spreads of 24 charges battered our boat every 20 minutes. At one time we thought we had won. That was when the escorts departed and rushed to take their positions in the convoy. But our hope was short-lived. The hunters had only left the coup de grace to the killer group following in the wake of the armada."

265 metres beneath the surface, and that killer group, the crew of the submarine, grown nearly rigid with stress, fear, and cold, sat helpless. The two toilets were locked. Flushing, while under the tremendous pressure at that depth, would have been catastrophic. Instead, the men passed cans around so they could relieve themselves. Now the atmosphere inside the narrow drum contained the eye-watering stench of urine, sweat, oil, and battery gases. The many leaks increased the humidity condensing on the cold steel and the dampness soaked the men's clothing. They waited. The air was becoming much less breathable and the commander ordered the distribution of potash cartridges to supplement breathing. The bulky apparatus consisted of a rather large metal box attached to the chest, a rubber tube from it to the mouth, and a clamp on the nose.

By 01:00 more than two hundred explosives had been detonated above and around the submarine. Siegmann twice tried to bluff the enemy warships into believing that the sub had been sunk, by releasing clouds of air bubbles, but the clever enemy escorts never left the sight of the U-boat's descent entirely unguarded, preventing any possibility of the sub sneaking away. The only course remaining to Siegmann and his crew was to sit tight, conserve their air, power, and oxygen.

Through the morning hours the situation worsened for the sub and crew. There was no let-up in the enemy attacks. The leaks and leaking in the boat increased with water sloshing over the deck plates. The bilge pumps didn't work at their depth and the chief was continually having to release measured amounts of compressed air to maintain the sub's buoyancy. The down-angle of the bow had increased and they were running out of compressed air at a dangerous rate. The fragile hull creaked and contracted frighteningly.

Midnight. Having descended further to a depth of 280 metres, the commander and his executive believed that the boat had probably reached its crush-depth limit, and it was still sinking. Many of the men lay resting, trying to conserve what little breathable air and oxygen that remained within the hull. The exec roamed the aisle coaxing any who might be falling asleep to remain awake. By 03:10 the occasional barrages of depth-charges subsided and it seemed that the enemy warships might be withdrawing from the area, as the sounds of their engines and propellers were fading. No one in the boat dared believe that the British had given up the hunt. Siegmann decided to try and surface. The chief used the last of the available compressed air and battery power to slowly raise the boat until it finally surfaced. The commander and the exec rejoiced in their survival. Siegmann: "Both diesels half ahead. Steer one-eighty. Ventilate boat. Secure from action stations."

With the diesels powered up again, the electric batteries began to recharge, the foul air was expelled, the water drained away and the accumulated mess removed. The new day seemed promising. At 07:10 the first mate sighted smoke on the horizon to the southwest. A second convoy. The sight caused the exec to reason that the escorts depth-charging them through the past few days had probably withdrawn on the basis that the destroyers escorting this next convoy would take up the attack on *U-230*. The exhausted, sleepless crew went back to work. The commander and the exec took to the bridge and found that the new convoy had been on a zigzagging course that was now taking it away from the U-boat. They would have to chase it. Thirty-two minutes later: "Aircraft from the sun!"

Their crash-dive provided a relatively easy escape this time and the boat was soon floating at periscope depth. Surfacing again, an air attack was repeated twenty-three minutes later. When they resurfaced this time, a signal awaited the commander: AIR ATTACK. SINKING. U-657. At 10:05: "Alarrrmmm!" Another aeroplane appeared, forcing the submarine to dive desperately once again. The pattern was repeated several times throughout the day. By the late afternoon the effects of the attacks on the boat had her ribs bent, bolts cracked, hull dented, and rivets burst, but she still responded to commands and was still battle ready. Then, yet again, the sub faced the threatened attack of three convoy escorts and Siegmann had to order another emergency crash-dive.

Werner: "A thick layer of depth charges exploded in an enormous eruption that dwarfed all previous barrages. Darkness followed the terrible quake. I pulled myself up the steel ropes of the scope, aimed the beam of my flashlight at the depth gauge, saw with horror its needle swinging rapidly, saw the two planesmen dangling at their wheels in confusion, listened to the chief's desperate commands, and heard the shocking sound of splashing water. This was how the curtain went up for another long siege, an exact duplicate of the persecution we had just endured. As dusk settled upon the hunters above, the wind faded with the day and the sea smoothed; and as a result their bombardment increased in violence. The fierce salvoes made the ocean roar and rumble. We shivered and sweated; we were both hot and cold as we neared the limits of human endurance. As the night wore on, deadly fumes escaped from our batteries; we were half poisoned and nearly unconscious. And then when the sun rose for our assailants, they renewed their bombardment with over 300 charges by actual count. It was all in vain. *U-230* stayed afloat some 280 meters below."

They were nearly out of air by the afternoon and would soon have to decide whether to die or surrender. To buy a bit more time, the chief released a small amount of compressed air into the midship buoyancy tank, to raise the boat. That act brought a fury of additional depth-charges down on the boat, halting her rise and sending her down again. The crew felt that they were finished this time. Somehow, though, the boat leveled near 300 meters depth. They were drawing hot air through their potash cartridge breathing devices now and coughing violently. The series of blasts was followed eight minutes later by another barrage, and then nothing for more than an hour. Again, the chief tried to bring the boat slowly to the surface.

When they reached the surface, the pressure inside the boat was such that the commander and the exec were virtually sucked up onto the bridge when they opened the hatch. The day was clear and sunny, the air fresh and wonderful, and no vessels of any kind were visible in any direction. As they began inspecting the boat for damage from the attacks, they found a huge break in the starboard aft oil bunker, which had left a long trail of irridescent diesel oil in their wake, undoubtedly the reason for the enemy warships having broken off their attack in the belief that a direct hit by one or more their depth-charges had sunk the U-boat. They also found that two other tanks were ruptured, the starboard shaft was bent, and many other items of varying significance damaged, and worst of all, they had lost most of their remaining fuel. Whether they would make it back to base in France was problematic; there was no question of their continuing the mission against the convoy.

A rendezvous was arranged with a milch cow U-boat to refuel *U-230* at sea and on 21 May the two boats converged and *U-230* took on fifteen tons of diesel oil over the next two hours in which the boats were at their most vulnerable to air attack. 23 May. Werner: "*U-230* crossed the 15th Longitude West, the door to Biscay Bay—and purgatory. We intercepted more bad news. A signal from *U-91* told us that they had seen *U-752* attacked and destroyed by aircraft; there were no survivors. At 10:40 we crash-dived before a Sunderland airplane. No radar impulses. Quite obviously it must have attacked on sight. It announced the start of a six-day nightmare. Under cover of darkness, *U-230* made her dash at a pitiful top speed of only 12 knots. We crash-dived seven times and shook off 28 attacks by bombs or depth charges. By sunrise, we were stunned, deaf, and exhausted. 24 May. Apparently the British were aware that two U-boats were running for port; their aircraft seemed to be looking for us, including the land-based four-engined bombers. During that night we crash-dived nine times and survived a total of 36 bombing runs.

"25 May. Three hours after daybreak we floated into the deadly range of a hunter-killer group. Running submerged in absolute silence, we managed to slip by the endless, cruel, ravenous pings. One hour before midnight, we surfaced into the inevitable air assaults. On the first attack, four ferocious detonations rocked the boat as she surged into the deep. Suddenly there was a flash in the rear of the control room. A stream of sparks shot across the narrow space and enveloped us in choking smoke. The boat was afire. It seemed impossible to bring her to surface before we died. The round doors of the two bulkheads were slammed shut, the compartments sealed. Several men fought the fire with extinguishers. *U-230* rose sharply toward the surface where only seconds before the aircraft had dropped its diabolic calling card. Thick fumes choked us. Fire leaped from wall to wall. I pressed my handkerchief against my mouth and nose and followed the Captain into the tower. The boat leveled off, she had surfaced. We hastened to the bridge. Somebody threw ammunition magazines on deck. The port diesel began to mutter. Red light and fumes escaped the hatch. We drove like a torch through the blackest night until the men below managed to kill the fire. That night we outmaneuvered seven attacks and outlasted 28 bombs."

For the next four days and nights the boat crawled towards its French base, under the power of only one of her twin diesels, the other having been damaged in the many depth-charge attacks. After additional bombing attacks by aircraft during the long journey, the commander finally conceded to the exec, "There were no radar impulses. Our Metox seems to be in perfect order. The British must have invented a new kind of radar. It's the only explanation I can think of."

Squadron Leader Leslie Clark, who died 29 July 2012, aged 91, flew anti-submarine patrols at the height of the Battle of the Atlantic. He was credited with having destroyed a U-boat and seriously damaging two others during his tour with No 206 Squadron, R.A.F. Coastal Command.

As the command pilot of a Boeing B-17 Flying Fortress bomber on 19 March 1943, Clark was patrolling from a base in the Outer Hebrides in the area of a convoy of twenty-four merchant ships bound for England from Halifax, Nova Scotia. He was conducting a search beneath a rain squall near the rear of the convoy when he detected a U-boat. He flew a nearly perfect low-level bombing run on the sub and straddled it with four depth-charges. A massive explosion resulted in a thick, black oil slick rising to the surface. Clark had sunk *U-384* on her second patrol, under the command of Oberleutnant Hans-Achim von Rosenberg-Gruszcynski. All forty-seven crew members were lost.

Previously, on 15 January, Squadron Leader Clark had been patrolling in the mid-Atlantic and sighted a surfaced U-boat which he attacked with four depth-charges, severely damaging the submarine. Circling the area, the gunner's in Clark's B-17 fired some three hundred .50 calibre machine-gun rounds into the sub and watched as it slowly slipped backwards, its bow rising from the surface. *U-632*, commanded by Korvettenkapitän Hans Karpf, managed to limp back to its French base.

On 17 June, Clark's crew encountered a third U-boat. Now based on an airfield in Cornwall, he was on a patrol over the Bay of Biscay near the coast of Spain when one of his crewmen spotted the sur-faced sub. By this time, Admiral Dönitz had ordered his U-boat commanders to respond to attacks of enemy aircraft by remaining on the surface and using their anti-aircraft guns to fight it out with the attackers. In the incident, Clark's B-17 was slightly damaged, but he and his crew maintained the attack, badly damaging the submarine, *U-338* under command of Kapitänleutnant Manfred Kinzel, which was forced to return to its base at St. Nazaire. For the action, Clark was awarded the Distinguished Flying Cross.

From FLEET AIR ARM: THE ADMIRALTY ACCOUNT OF NAVAL AIR OPERATIONS, "Carriers have been escorting merchant shipping since the beginning of the war. In December 1939, HMS *Furious* escorted the first great convoy carrying Canadian troops to Great Britain, She was the flagship, and although it was an anxious passage, with 500 miles through thick white fog and the pocket battleship *Deutschland* at large, she brought the convoy safely through.

"The *Eagle* escorted the first Australian convoy to Aden, and at one time or another during the war every aircraft carrier in the Fleet has been employed on trade protection, usually in company with at least one capital ship. The combination of battleship, cruiser and carrier, with a destroyer screen, makes an ideal covering force. The carrier can send her reconnaissance aircraft into the sky to give warning of hostile movement or to detect submarines, while her fighters intercept shadowers and attack enemy formations; the destroyers hunt the submarines which the aircraft have sighted, the cruiser can make contact with surface vessels, and the big guns of the battleship can deal with a sortie by the enemy fleet, or put a barrage over the Force and the convoy.

"For many months the *Ark Royal* operated in this way in the Eastern Atlantic or the Western Mediterranean while in company with Force H, and at the same time the *Eagle*, and later the *Illustrious* and the *Formidable*, were working with the Mediterranean Fleet. The carriers did even more than give protection from the air, for, as part of a convoy themselves, they have ferried over 800 R.A.F. aircraft to places overseas, including Norway and Malta.

"In no part of the world have convoys met with opposition so fierce as on the passage to Malta. As that opposition increased it became necessary to strengthen the convoy's protection from the air. This was possible only by employment of more than one carrier to deal with the weight of the air attack, and on 9th August 1942, three carriers passed through the straights of Gibraltar to escort a great convoy for the relief of Malta: the *Victorious*, the Indomitable, and the *Eagle*. The carriers had a combined strength of some seventy fighters, including Sea Hurricanes, Martlets and Fulmars. The *Furious*, which was ferrying aircraft for Malta, was part of the convoy. The *Argus* remained at Gibraltar with replacements. Vice-Admiral E.N. Syfret, flying his flag in HMS *Nelson*, commanded the covering force (Force F). Rear-Admiral H.M. Burrough, C.B., was in command of the escort.

"Day One passed quietly. There was a hot sun in a clear blue sky as the convoy steamed steadily to the eastward. The fighters were ranged in readiness on the flight-decks. The crews of the Albacores had been told off to the ships' guns. It was a new role for them. The fighter pilots begged them to confine their attentions to hostile aircraft.

"By next morning the convoy had come within range of the enemy snoopers. A fighter patrol flew off at first light and a standing force of four was kept over the convoy throughout the day.

"Halfway through the forenoon a shadower was detected: the first certain intimation that the convoy had been sighted. Fighters from the *Indomitable* drove it off with one engine on fire, shakily losing height.

"As the morning wore on, several more shadowers appeared. Carriers follow the sound naval custom of telling the ship's company below decks what is happening in an operation. From time to time the loudspeakers sounded.

"D'ye hear there! A small group of aircraft, presumed hostile, is approaching the convoy from the north-east. Our fighters have been sent to intercept.

"As yet there had been no air attack. But at sea there are dangers other than from the air. At 1:16 a series of explosions shook the *Victorious* and *Indomitable*.

" 'God!' said someone. '*Eagle*! Look at the *Eagle*!'

"Smoke was pouring from her. The great flight-deck was already listing to port. Her sister ships increased speed, zig-zagging violently as they took avoiding action. A pandemonium of underwater explosions broke out. The loudspeakers spoke again: 'The *Eagle* has been hit by a number of torpedoes fired by a submarine and she is sinking. The explosions you can hear are depth-charge attacks being made by the destroyers. The air raid that was approaching the convoy has been turned away by our fighters and at least one enemy aircraft has been shot down.'

"The *Eagle* sank within ten minutes of being struck. Sixty-seven officers, including Captain Mackintosh, and 862 ratings were saved.

Many of her aircraft sank with her. Those of her pilots who were in the air at the time of the attack landed on the *Victorious* and the *Indomitable*.

"One of these pilots, who had made an emergency landing signal, circled the ship until his companions and the returning patrol from the *Victorious* had landed. His windscreen was covered with oil and his petrol was almost exhausted, but fearing that he might crash on landing he waited, lest by encumbering the deck he should prevent others from following him until the wreckage had been cleared away.

"A few minutes after the *Eagle* had gone a torpedo track crossed the bow of the *Victorious*. No less than six U-boats were sighted during the afternoon. The ships continued on their zig-zag course. The destroyers dropped more depth-charges. The *Furious* flew off her Spitfires for Malta and returned to Gibraltar, her mission fulfilled.

"For a while there was an ominous lull. The dog watches dragged on and only small groups of enemy aircraft approached. They did not wait to fight and were driven off. Dusk darkened sea and sky. The carriers waited for the attack they knew must come.

"The scene in the *Victorious* may be described by one of the officers on board: 'The stand-by squadron was all set on deck, the pilots in their cockpits gazing upwards and perhaps munching a biscuit. Men stood by the lanyards which secured the wing-tips; men lay by their chocks, men sat astride their starter motors. The deck officers fiddled with their flags and Commander Flying nursed his flight-deck microphone. They were all waiting: waiting for those vital 17 seconds which would follow the Boatswain's Mate's call 'Fighters stand-to.' The eighteenth second should see the ship returning to her station and the fighters airborne over the sea.'

Suddenly the call came. The Fulmar squadron flew off and merged into the gathering darkness. The *Indomitable*'s Hurricanes were already engaging the raiders—35 Ju 88s. Some they drove off, but the failing light made combat difficult. Two of the bandits broke through.

" 'Salvoes! Salvoes!' went the warning signal for the fighters to haul off and keep clear of the guns coming into action. The carrier's 4.5s, the multiple pom-poms and the Oerlikons, poured a barrage into the twilight sky as the great ships twisted and turned to avoid the bombs. Two fell close to the *Victorious*; the bombers which dropped them, silhouetted against the sunset, fell to the guns of the ship. One crashed blazing into the sea 'like a torch of fire in a sheaf.'

The remainder dropped their bombs in desperation to escape the fighters waiting for them outside the barrage.

"When the attack was over there was haste to land the fighters which had been longest in the sky. A Hurricane from the carrier *Indomitable*, out of petrol, had to land on the *Victorious* while the ship was still out of wind and under wheel. Coming on while the flight-deck was still slewing to starboard, it hit another aircraft stowed abaft the island and burst into flames. The pilot escaped unhurt. Led by the Air Technical Officer a party dashed in to extract the unexpended ammunition before it exploded, while one of the Albacore pilots from a nearby Oerlikon played a hose on them all. The crash was cleared within six minutes, freeing the flight-deck for the remaining fighters to scramble on.

"Six were found to be missing from the *Victorious*. The ship turned back upon her course to rejoin the convoy. At length tiny blue lights signalled from the Indomitable that the missing aircraft were safe. One of the pilots is said to have sat spinning yarns for 20 minutes before he discovered that he was not in his own ship.

"That was the end of Day Two. No ship in the convoy had been damaged. The night that followed was one of vigilance for those on deck, and in the crowded hangars and workshops one of preparation for the morrow, as the maintenance ratings sweated and strained to get every possible aircraft fit for service by daylight. One Hurricane had to have a complete tail unit and its airscrew changed, and a serious leak in the hydraulic system repaired: work which might have taken 48 hours in a yard ashore.

"The operational problem of convoying merchant ships to Malta is not dissimilar from that of convoying them to Murmansk or Archangel. As in the Mediterranean, the route through the Barents Sea lies within reach of the enemy heavy bombers but beyond the range of British shore-based fighters, so that once again the only means of giving effective air cover is by carrier. The passage of the Malta convoys had shown that it was possible to give fighter protection from carriers in the Mediterranean. In September 1942, similar protection was given in the Arctic to the largest and most valuable convoy ever sent to Russia up to that time.

"The composition of the two escort forces was, however, very different, and only a single carrier was employed. Before the convoy sailed it was known that the Luftwaffe had strengthened the Fifth Air Fleet, based on Norway, by the transfer of Heinkel 111s (which carry two torpedoes), Ju 88 dive-bombers, Focke Wulf Kuriers, and Me 109F fighters. This gave an operational strength of 300 bombers alone.

"Shadowers and U-boats sighted the convoy on 9th September, but the enemy attack did not begin until the 12th, when the ships were to the northward of Narvik. The Hurricanes shot down a Heinkel 111, but unfortunately they expended their energy in chasing the heavily-armoured Blohm and Voss 138 shadowers under cloud conditions, so that when the main attack came they were unprepared, and a formation of 37 torpedo aircraft broke through and sank several ships in the convoy.

"Next day the Hurricane pilots profited by that experience, conserved their strength, and concentrated their power. The enemy tried to throw the escort and convoy into confusion by dropping mines from aircraft and by high level bombing attacks before sending in the torpedo-carriers. The Heinkels swept into action in line abreast, flying in close formation only a few feet above the sea, fanning out as they approached. High above the Junkers and Heinkels flew a fighter escort of Messerschmitts.

" 'You could see them coming in layers, like a wedding cake,' said one of the carrier's pilots, 'and as we took off, it looked as though we had about three aircraft to every layer of Jerries. Our squadrons had to split up to tackle various bunches of Huns, and eventually I found myself with my section mate—a Petty Officer, who was a wizard pilot and a grand fighter—tackling 14 Ju 88s flying in diamond formation, a pretty hard nut to crack, for if they can keep formation, their cross fire keeps every plane covered. However, I made a quarter attack on the leading plane, then swung away straight at one of the planes on the side of the diamond. At the last second I flicked underneath him; he got the wind up and pulled the nose of his plane hard up, and the Petty Officer, flying just on my starboard wing, gave him a lovely burst which put paid to his account. The formation broke up, and there was a lovely scrap all over the sky. That sort of thing went on all day. As soon as we were out of ammunition or petrol, we dived down to the carrier, landed, re-armed and re-fuelled and took off again. My lunch was a gulp of cold tea. Our squadron made seventeen sorties that day.
I saw two Heinkels, having launched their torpedoes, flying along the side of the carrier dead level with the bridge. The gunners waited till they were only a few yards away, opened up—and the sky and sea were full of bits of Heinkel, an amazing sight.'

"During the afternoon of the 14th, the enemy decided to strike at the root of the fighter opposition by attacking the carrier with a force of Heinkels and Junkers which aimed seventeen torpedoes at her and a shower of bombs. But the fighters attacked the Heinkels and spoilt their aim. The Commanding Officer, who had had considerable experience as a torpedo pilot, handled his ship so superbly that she came through unscathed. Later she made a signal to the flagship that she had 'the honour of being the sole object of the attack' and claimed four enemy aircraft destroyed and three probables.

"Next day the enemy abandoned torpedo attacks, but kept up high and low level bombing on the escort and convoy for three hours. No warships were sunk during the passage and although the ranks of the merchantmen were thinned, they had come through with relatively fewer losses than any previous convoy, thanks not only to the terrific barrage the whole force was able to produce, accounting for 35 German aircraft, but also to the carrier's Hurricanes.

" 'I shall never forget the reckless gallantry of the naval pilots in their determination to get in among the enemy despite the solid mass of our defence fire,' wrote Rear-Admiral R.L. Burnett.

"They destroyed five German aircraft, with three probables, and damaged 14 for the loss of four Hurricanes, three of whose pilots were saved. Throughout the passage the Swordfish had carried out anti-submarine patrols, sometimes flying in icing conditions at 500 feet. They sighted a number of U-boats, kept them down with depth-charges and guided the destroyers to them; at least once this co-operation led to a kill.

"The carrier returned with Rear-Admiral Burnett's escort force and a homeward-bound convoy. Before sailing the Commanding Officer spared no effort to render every aircraft in the ship fit to fly again. Rear-Admiral Burnett made a signal congratulating him on being such a good father to his children. 'The nursery door is now definitely closed' was the reply. So decisive had been the victory over the Luftwaffe, however, that on the return passage there were no attacks from the air.

"Such was the Fleet Air Arm's answer to those who said that carriers cannot operate within range of enemy shore-based aircraft."

"DO NOT REPORT TOO MUCH BAD NEWS, SO AS NOT TO DEPRESS THE OTHER BOATS."
—signal from Admiral Dönitz to all U-boats, 5 August 1943

"The only thing that ever really frightened me during the war was the U-boat peril. Invasion, I thought, even before the air battle, would fail. After the air victory it was a good battle for us. We could down and kill this horrible foe in circumstances favourable to us, and, as he evidently realised, bad for him. It was the kind of battle which, in the cruel conditions of war, one ought to be content to fight. But now our life-line, even across the broad oceans and especially in the entrances to the island, was endangered. I was even more anxious about this battle than I had been about the glorious air fight called the Battle of Britain."

—from *The Second World War: Their Finest Hour* by Winston S. Churchill

THE END

"The Englishman, be it noted, seldom resorts to violence; when he is sufficiently goaded he simply opens up, like the oyster, and devours his adversary."
—from *The Wisdom of the Heart* by Henry Miller

"At the end of the war, all German naval vessels and submarines still afloat were divided among the four so-called great powers. Britain, Russia, the United States, and France, each got a dozen or so U-boats under an agreement whereby all these craft would be sunk in deep water or scrapped within two years. As the two year limit approached, we got ready to carry out our agreement and word reached me that the *U-505* was not included in the Four Power Agreement, which applied only to U-boats surrendered at the end of the war. The *U-505* had not surrendered, she was captured in battle on the high seas. She was therefore, U.S. property with no strings attached and we could keep her as long as we wanted. I had no immediate plans in mind for the sub at this time, but my boys had gone to a lot of trouble to prevent that U-boat from sinking off the coast of Africa, and I took a dim view of scuttling her now. Government bureaucrats always like to have some precedent or a piece of paper to justify what they are doing and there were no precedents for this case. But I raised such a fuss that the Navy Department finally changed its mind rather dubiously and vetoed the scuttling order."
—from *Twenty Million Tons Under The Sea* by Rear Admiral Daniel V. Gallery, USN

Many would agree that no single factor contributed more to the Allied victory in the Second World War—or was more important—than the long, hard-fought, extraordinarily punishing campaign to keep the oceans open to the vital shipping traffic, without which Britain could not have survived and the Russian allies could not have successfully prosecuted the war from the East. Without that challenging and desperate campaign, Britain could not have provided the springboard for the Normandy invasion.

The real heroes of the campaign were the largely unheralded, mostly forgotten seamen of the British Merchant Navy, the American Merchant Marine, and the Canadian Merchant Navy. Their astonishing courage and unparalleled devotion to their duty in the most outrageous and intolerable of conditions, and under nearly constant menace by enemy submarines, aircraft and surface warships, is to their everlasting credit. That is, of course, not to take away from the performance of the gallant escort crews, both naval and air, who, for much of the conflict were often super-human in their performance and achievements.

It is important, too, to note the invaluable and wide-ranging aid provided to Britain from both the United States and Canada in the form of the "Cash and Carry" and "Lend-Lease" programmes, the destroyers made available as well as the Liberators and Flying Fortress bombers, and the American and Canadian participation in the convoys in various roles including the crucial escort duty. It must be said that the British returned the favour many fold with their provision of escorting armed trawlers, their experience of escort tactics, their Ultra intelligence information, and their HFDF (Huff Duff) high frequency direction finding technology.

The value and contribution of the very long-ranging aircraft equipped with new state-of-the-art radar cannot be overstated. It finally closed the gap in the mid-Atlantic, enabling the Allies to reach, locate, attack, and destroy the U-boats and surface warships of Germany anywhere in the vast seas. And with the variety of weather conditions prevailing along the shipping lanes, the proficiency and effectiveness of the new radar in the long-range bombers tipped the odds much more in the Allies' favour. Even so, the results showed that the "huff duff" technology and the human eye did, in fact, detect more enemy submarines than any other technologies of the period. Admiral Dönitz over-estimated the importance of the Allied radar, thanks mainly to being ill-advised by his scientists, and as a result took precautions against it that were largely ineffective. The combination of centimetric radar and the enormous and very timely growth of air power then turned the sea lanes into a U-boat killing ground.

Yet another vital contribution to the success of this major Allied campaign was that of Commander Frederick John "Johnnie" Walker, whose offensive team tactics against the U-boat wolfpacks had, by 1943, been adopted by the Royal Navy as well as the U.S. Navy's hunter-killer groups. For the sailors aboard Walker's *Black Swan-*

class sloops, high seas operations were often testing affairs (even the hardiest sailor could feel queasy in a sloop), but the vessels were highly manoeuvrable and, in action, reminded him of hounds on a scent. When his sloop, HMS *Starling*, sailed from the historic port of Liverpool, he had "A-hunting We Will Go" played loudly on the Tannoy to inspire the crew. In the course of the campaign, Walker's No 2 Support Group attacked and sank twenty-one U-boats, downing six of them in a single operation. He himself was credited with the destruction of *U-264*, the first snorkel-equipped U-boat to become operational.

Sharing kudos for their triumphs in the field of U-boat killing was Captain Donald Macintyre, some of whose efforts are described in another chapter, THE CAPTAIN.

Finally, the role of intelligence and the valuable contribution that was provided about the U-boat movements thanks in large part to the amazing cryptographers at the British Government Code and Cypher School, Bletchley Park, Buckinghamshire, must be acknowledged. Without question that contribution was absolutely key to Allied victory in the war. Ultra was the code-name for intelligence information that resulted from interpreting the high-grade codes and the cyphers collected, collated, and then disseminated by the Signals Intelligence Branch of GC&CS at Bletchley (now GCHQ in Cheltenham), which obtained the information by eavesdropping on enemy communications.

The challenge for the Signals Intelligence people was that security-graded radio traffic within the German armed forces was protected by the use of a sophisticated enciphering machine, Schlüssel M, also known as Enigma. In the use of Enigma, a message was typed on an ordinary keyboard and then passed through electrical circuits to three rotors which had separate contact points for each letter of the alphabet in a scrambled order. As the operator typed it, each letter of the message was transmitted in turn to the first, second, and third rotor, changing each time, until the enciphered letter to be used by the operator was displayed on a screen above the keyboard and then transmitted in Morse code. At the receiving end, an operator with a similar device and a list of the rotor settings for the day, simply went through the enciphering routine in reverse. As the rotors could be changed at will, and the number of electrical circuits could be increased, the variations possible verged on the infinite. The machine was compact and simple to operate, and the resulting code was virtually impenetrable.

Appropriated by the government for the duration of the war, the Bletchley Park House property incorporated a series of huts, Nissen and others, within the grounds and these were inhabited by the Bletchley code-crackers—academicians, crossword puzzle experts, chess players—who applied themselves hour after hour to the job of unscrambling the Enigma codes. They were initially unable to distinguish a pattern as they listened to the mass of German radio traffic. Not only did each branch of the enemy forces have its own Enigma rotor settings, the naval code, which was known as Hydra, was changed daily. The computer devices then available to the Bletchley folks, while enormous in physical size, were actually less powerful than most current laptops.

Help finally came, from Poland, where one of the early versions of the Enigma device had been built and the Polish intelligence service had monitored its development. They had supplied information about that development to the British government in London, but the Bletchley people desperately required more detailed information about Enigma's codes and rotors. To that end, the Royal Navy was assigned the task of capturing an enemy vessel with the Enigma device, codes, and any associated papers etc on board.

In February 1940, the Navy managed to capture the *U-33* which was mine-laying in the Firth of Clyde; that act produced three Enigma rotors. The incident was followed by one a month later when cipher papers and another rotor were confiscated from the armed trawler *Krebs*, and on 7 May 1941, when code settings for the coming three months were found aboard the weather ship *München*. After each of these incidents the government announced, for the benefit of German ears, that the ships had sunk before they could be boarded. But the important break for Bletchley came on 9 May when *U-110*, the U-boat commanded by Kapitänleutnant Fritz-Julius Lemp, chose to attack two merchant vessels off the coast of Greenland, with a fan of three torpodoes. Lemp is the U-boat commander who, as skipper of *U-30*, had been severely reprimanded after torpedoing and sinking the passenger liner *Athenia* on 3 September 1939, claiming later that he thought the ship was an armed merchant cruiser.

Lemp in *U-110* was just under the surface near the convoy when his periscope was spotted by a lookout on an escorting warship. The submarine was immediately attacked by the corvette HMS *Aubretia* with depth-charges and was forced to surface, where she received heavy gunfire from *Aubretia* and two other warship escorts. Lemp and most of his crew then abandoned the sub.

As the destroyer HMS *Bulldog* approached to ram the U-boat, her captain elected instead to capture it intact. He sent an armed boarding party aboard and they located and retrieved the Enigma machine and code books. King George VI later described the incident as "the most important event of the war at sea." With Enigma and many of its secrets now in the possession of staff at Bletchley Park, they were able to read the German Hydra naval code, but they were determined that the Germans *not know* they could read it, and all those who had been involved in the capture of *U-110* were sworn to keep silent about it, a silence which held for the next thirty years.

The Ultra intercepts were keeping the British informed and for the next nine months the positions of all operating U-boats were plotted in the Submarine Tracking Room of the Admiralty. In February 1942, however, the Hydra code was altered. It was simply a routine change and not because Dönitz suspected that the British had broken it. In the next three months, sinkings of Allied merchant ships doubled. Another change came about in spring 1943, when the Germans added a fourth rotor to Enigma, giving the Bletchley people a two-week headache while they struggled to cope with the new wrinkle. In that span, two convoys bound for Britain from New York lost a total of twenty-two merchant ships to the U-boats. From then on, though, the information provided by Ultra from Bletchley was magnificent. Churchill referred to Ultra as "the precious secret."

Now the days of U-boat success were indeed numbered. In the massive effort to overcome the German submarine menace, the Allies were investing more than a hundred thousand men, more than forty aircraft carriers, and hundreds of escorting destroyers, corvettes and sloops. And while Allied merchantman losses continued—twenty-four of the ships were sunk between September and December 1944—the action cost the Germans fifty-five U-boats. It didn't require much imagination for the surviving commanders of the Ubootwaffe to realise and accept that they were beaten.

The battle had been long, arduous, and costly to both sides, and both sides had fought bravely, steadfastly, and, in general, with a degree of honour. There were exceptions, however, such as an instance of a sinking U-boat's crew being fired on in the water by a British submarine, and another, in 1944, of a U-boat's guns being turned on the lifeboats of a torpedoed Greek freighter. For the two commanders who were responsible for these actions, the outcome exemplified the difference between being on the winning and losing sides in war: the Royal Navy officer received a decoration—albeit for another and more worthy feat—while the U-boat commander, Kapitänleutnant Heinz Eck, together with four of his crew, was tried by court martial, found guilty of a war crime and shot by a British firing squad on 30 November 1945.

The Royal Navy killings were largely forgotten, but the U-boat incident was turned into a *cause célebre*. Some believe that the British used it to try to convince the Nuremberg Tribunal that Admiral Dönitz had condoned such brutalities, and as such, was guilty of a war crime. The ploy, if that be true, did not work. The admiral was deprecating of the act and offered a reasonable excuse: his commanders were expected to eliminate the wreckage on the water (not the seamen), so that no trace would be left that might assist the escort warships to hunt down the U-boat. The tribunal judges weighed the evidence and, relative to the possible commission of a war crime, found in favour of the admiral.

There were also times when U-boat commanders came alongside a lifeboat to learn the name and tonnage of the vessel they had sunk, and then given sustenance to the survivors, in the form of cigarettes, cognac, and sometimes a course to steer for land. In his book, *Convoy*, Martin Middlebrook refers to an instance in which a U-boat surfaced and the men in lifeboats heard a voice through the darkness asking if they needed food. Wary of a trap, the seamen did not answer. Moments later, they heard the voice again. "Goodnight, British", Otto Kretschmer called, and *U-99* stole silently away. It was true that Admiral Dönitz had given his commanders orders that only downed airmen—who might give useful information—were to be rescued from the sea, and, considering the crowded conditions in a U-boat, this was reasonable enough, but there was never any proof that he approved the slaughter of survivors. Few U-boat commanders would attack an escort ship while it was picking up seamen from a stricken vessel, but this was not entirely for altruistic reasons: an escort so involved was one less available for offensive action.

In the dark night of 16 March 1942, the lone merchant ship SS *Allendi*, was steaming near the Ivory Coast of West Africa, making for Freetown to join with a convoy bound for Britain. The crew heard what they thought to be the sound of diesel engines and suspected it might be a surfaced U-boat charging its batteries. Early the next day their ship was struck by a torpedo and began sinking. Frank Lewis, Chief Radio Officer, SS *Allendi*: "The skipper came into the radio cabin and said it was time for us to get into the one remaining boat. We lost no time, for the ship was riding very low in the water by then. A good thing we did, too, because we had not pulled very far away when another torpedo struck her and she disappeared in just a few minutes. There we were, thirteen in a small jollyboat that was damaged and water-logged." The U-boat commander then came alongside and gave them the choice of staying where they were or being taken back to Germany as prisoners of war. Most of the men in the jollyboat were Merchant Navy officers and they decided to take their chances where they were. Lewis: "When the U-boat left us, she created such a wash that our boat overturned, and we were left swimming. We had just managed to clamber on to the upturned boat when the next wash came along, righted the boat and threw us back into the water." History showed that the Merchant Navy men made the right choice. They made their way to the Ivory Coast thirty-six hours later and eventually back to England.

The Allied invasion of the European continent in June 1944 was something less than the best kept secret of the war. Most Germans in the armed forces were well aware that it was in the offing and many had a pretty sound idea about where the Allies would likely be landing along the French coast. The more confident among them were persuaded that the Wehrmacht would be able to repel the invaders and shove them back into the sea before they could gain a foothold, and those who did manage to get ashore would be wiped out in the withering gunfire that would come from Hitler's vaunted Atlantic Wall defences along the coast. Those in the German High Command were less sure, however, about where the invasion forces would be landing and what the result might be. In the opinion of the German Army Commander in the West, Feldmarschall Karl Gerd von Rundstedt, the Allied forces would opt for the shortest route across the English Channel, to the Pas de Calais. Feldmarschall Erwin Rommel, who would command the German forces opposing the Allied cross-channel invasion, was convinced that the Normandy coast was where the action would occur. He was completely persuaded that the Allies must be beaten on the beaches or Germany would lose the war.

In numbers, von Rundstedt's command amounted to fifty-eight divisions spread along the coastline and behind it, from the hook of

Holland to the Spanish border. That number was an illusion though, as the enormous casualties the Germans had experienced on the Russian Front had effectively reduced his fighting strength to the equivalent of less than thirty divisions. What could the Germans hope to mount in the way of air defences? Due to several months of USAAF and RAF concentrated attacks, and the work of swarms of Allied fighters, the strength of the Luftwaffe was greatly reduced and it was desperately short of pilots, fuel, and serviceable aircraft. And with the weakening and downgrading of the German surface navy, Dönitz had to rely on what was left of his U-boat force to take up the slack and do its part in fending off the Allied effort. He later wrote in his memoirs: "Every vessel taking part in the landing is a target of the utmost importance which must be attacked regardless of risk. Every boat that inflicts losses on the enemy while he is landing has fulfilled its function even though he perishes in so doing." There was no denying that this newly dictated role for Germany's formerly key weapons of attack was the last gasp of warriors on the defence.

The Allied invasion of Europe was code-named Operation Overlord, and to oppose it, the surviving U-boats of Admiral Dönitz's force numbered sixty-one in the Bay of Biscay bunkers and twenty-two in the Norwegian fiords. Of the fifteen boats berthed in the pens at Brest that May, one was *U-415*, that of Oberleutnant Herbert Werner: "The order was to attack and sink the invasion fleet with the final objective of destroying enemy ships by ramming." At midnight on 6 June *U-415* was one of eight U-boats that slipped out of the huge Brest bunker and joined with an escort force of patrol boats and armed trawlers. Werner recalled that his orders were to proceed at top speed on the surface to the south coast of England, there to carry out the admiral's command, suicidally, if necessary. His boat would return to Brest two days later, badly damaged and one of only three boats to survive the mission. There had never really been much hope for the success of the small force of remaining U-boats against some 800 Allied warships and 4,000 landing craft. Werner later wrote: "By 30th June, U-boat operations since the invasion began were a full-fledged disaster. We had sunk five Allied cargo ships and two destroyers, and we had lost twenty-two U-boats."

To consider the capability and potential contribution of the U-boat fleet relative to the Allied D-Day cross-channel invasion, it is essential to remember that the U-boat was planned, designed, and constructed as a strictly offensive weapon and was never intended for defensive use. The primary focus of its mission in the war, as laid out by Admiral Dönitz, was the mid-ocean anti-convoy attack, preferably by wolfpack teams of U-boats. Substantial priority was not given to development of a specific submarine type or types dedicated to more tactical and defensive roles such as coastal ambush. Thus, when thrust into a defensive challenge in the months leading to the D-Day invasion, Dönitz and the men of the Ubootwaffe could no longer realistically anticipate victory, only the possibility of honour in defeat.

At 6:30 a.m., Tuesday, 6 June 1944, amphibious landings by Allied forces commenced along five key beaches of the Normandy coast. The landings were preceded with an airborne assault by 24,000 American, British, Canadian, and Free French troops shortly after midnight. A combination of inclement weather and a clever deception plan put into effect in the months preceding the invasion, aided the Allies in achieving the hoped for strategic and tactical surprise elements. Key to this was the effort to make the Germans believe that the invasion forces were to be led by General George Patton across the Straits of Dover to Calais. The ruse was so persuasively maintained even after the D-Day landings that Hitler was sufficiently convinced of that threat as to be unwilling to reinforce his troops in Normandy with forces positioned to defend the Pas de Calais.

The Allied command structure was in the charge of the American General Dwight Eisenhower, the Supreme Commander of the Allied Expeditionary Forces, with the British General Bernard Montgomery having overall command of the ground forces. It was the largest amphibious invasion in history, comprised of 73,000 American 61,715 British, and 21,400 Canadian troops, 195,700 Allied naval and merchant navy personnel, 4,000 ships and landing craft, and thousands of aircraft. The actual landings were made along a fifty-mile front, with the Americans assigned to Omaha and Utah beaches, the British to Gold and Sword beaches, and the Canadians to Juno beach. There were no U-boat attacks against Allied shipping on D-Day.

Effectively, U-boats were not involved in the English Channel on D-Day, and in the days that followed, were never able to impact the Allied effort. By late August, German emphasis was on saving the surviving U-boats by withdrawing them as much as possible to Norway and Baltic ports.

The rolling thunder of American tanks entering Brittany was joined by the pounding of R.A.F. bombs on the U-bunkers of Brest, St Nazaire, Lorient, La Pallice and Bordeaux. By September, Brest was under siege and surrounded by the American 6th Armored Division. Those U-boats remaining in the Biscay bases were dispatched on a hazardous six-week journey around the coast of Ireland, through the North Channel and past the Orkney and Shetland Islands, harassed all the while by Allied planes and warships, to eventually reach anchorage in the Bergenfiord on the southwest coast of Norway. Memories of the cafés and promenades and the sunshine they had left behind contrasted starkly with the glacial landscape, gloom, fogs and gray seas where they were now holed up, symbolic of the depressing decline in the fortunes of the Ubootwaffe. The retreat from France marked the end of their effective role in the Second World War.

The propaganda line out of Berlin trumpeted the great new assault by Germany's V-2 terror rockets on England, and coming soon to America as well, guaranteed to make the Allies sue for peace. More credible, perhaps, was the impressive December offensive by the Germans in the lush hills of the Ardennes in Belgium, France and Luxembourg on the Western Front, known today as the Battle of the Bulge. This massive German counter-offensive was aimed at splitting the British and American Allied line in two, capturing Antwerp, encircling and destroying four Allied armies, and then forcing the Western Allies to negotiate a peace treaty in favour of the Axis powers. Once accomplished, Hitler would then be free to refocus on Russia. Initially, circumstances favoured the Germans. Poor aerial reconnaissance due to exceptionally bad weather conditions, Allied overconfidence, and preoccupation with their own offensive tactics, left the Allies surprised by the enemy offensive even though intelligence personnel in Patton's Third Army had predicted it.

The then vastly superior Allied air forces had been grounded by the heavy overcast weather, but gradually the weather lifted and that, coupled with outstanding resistance around the town of Bastogne, and the renewed ability of the Allies to bring in supplies and reinforcements, turned the tide and ended the German offensive. It was the largest and bloodiest European land battle of the war.

Hitler took personal command of Berlin's defences in February 1945. In April the American president Franklin Roosevelt died and he was replaced by Harry Truman, who was no less dedicated to the defeat of Nazi Germany. On 1 May the death of Hitler was announced: "Our Führer, fighting to his last breath, fell for Germany in his Headquarters . . ." Days later, at the end of the war, the Nazis planned to scuttle their fleet (as they had done at the end of the First World War), including the remaining U-boats, but the British stipulated that no such action be taken, otherwise the bombing of strategic targets in Germany—or what remained of them—would go on. Dönitz was left with no choice, and on 5 May he ordered all U-boats to transmit their positions in plain language and sail to Allied ports: "Unbeaten and unblemished, you lay down your arms after a heroic fight without parallel."

At that point Germany still had more than 350 U-boats, including many new Type XXIs and XXIIIs, which had never been in action. The majority of these boats were in German ports or at anchor in the Norwegian fiords. Some remained at sea and of these, two were sailed to Argentina, while the rest went to Britain and America where they were surrendered. Nearly 200, however, in the hands of commanders who either did not believe the order of their Admiral, or refused to accept it, were scuttled by their crews. Of the 156 U-boats surrendered by September 1945, 110 were scuttled or sunk by Royal Navy gunfire off the coast of Northern Ireland. Nearly 30,000 of the 39,000 German sailors who went to sea in the U-boats never returned.

"Boys are the cash of war. Whoever said 'We're not free-spenders' doesn't know our likes."
—John Ciardi

BIBLIOGRAPHY

The author is grateful to the following people for their kind, generous assistance in the research, preparation, and development of this book: William Anderson, Fiona Andrews, Jack Armstrong, Brooks Atkinson, Robert Atkinson, J.J.Banigan, Brian Barber, Malcolm Bates, Lance Bauserman, Susan Bergquist, Beverley Brannan, Horst Bredow, Joann Bromley, Geroffrey Brooks, R.M. Browning Jr, Piers Burnett, Brian Burns, Samuel Butler, Tami Calhoun, Joyce Camiel, Liz Campbell, Joseph Cereola, Debby Comer, Jane Constantini, Harry Cooper, Brian Coval, Jack Currie, Peter Donnelly, A.C. Douglas, Andy Duff, Rob Dunn, C.B. Eagye, Gary Eastman, Lee Edwards, Charles Eshelman, Harry Farmer, Gary Fisher, Malcolm Fisher, Jan Friedman, David Garetson, Florence Garetson, James Gibson, Keith Gill, Charles Graves, Peter Guy, Betty Hamilton, Peter Hamilton, H.G. Hall, Patrick Hannafin, Cyril Hatton, Thom Hendrickson, John Hersey, Charles Hill, William Hoeft, Eric Holloway, Ed Holm, Franc Isla, David Jones, Claire Kaplan, Hargita Kaplan, Joseph Kaplan, Margaret Kaplan, Neal Kaplan, Paul Kemp, Michael King, Albert Konetzni, John Lester, Steven Levingston, Peter Lewis, John Lily, Peter Macdonald, Otto Marchica, Edwin Markham, Wilson McArthur, Elise McCutcheon, Judy McCutcheon, Richard McCutcheon, Hans Milkert, Steve Nichols, David Noel, Michael O'Leary, Merle Olmsted, Peter Padfield, A.H. Pierce, Doug Prince, C.H. Rayner, Phil Richards, Francis Rockwell, Jim Roderick, Andy Rooney, Thomas Rowe, Owen Rutter, Leonard Sawyer, Vern Schwartz, Brian Sewell, Frank Shaw, Wendy Shaw, Christy Sheaff, Doug Siegfried, Susan Sirota, Mike Sizeland, Mark Stanhope, Ron Steed, Kevin Stephens, Lloyd Stovall, Mary Beth Straight, Jeff Tall, Mark Thistlethwaite, Gertrude Thaler, Neil Thomson, Jack Thompson, Nancy Turner, William Walders, Heather Walders, Peter Wakker, Robin Watson, Colin Watts-Tucker, Colin Way, Norm Wehner, David Werner, Herbert Werner, Robert Westall, James White, W. Whiting, J.W.S. Wilson, Roger Wise, E. Withers, Chris Worton, Peter Wright, Dennis Wrynn, John Zinner.

Many thanks to the following people for the use of extracts from their published and unpublished texts: Joseph Addison, Ronald Bailey, Douglas Botting, Lothar-Günther Buchheim, James L. Cate, Winston Churchill, John Ciardi, Wesley F. Craven, Miles Delap, Karl Dönitz, James Doolittle, Bernard Edwards, Roger Freeman, Daniel Gallery, James A. Goodson, Peter Guy, Arthur Harris, Cyril Hatton, William Hazlitt, Thom Hendrickson, John Hersey, HMSO, Otto Kretschmer, Frank Lewis, Harry Ludlam, Paul Lund, Donald Macintyre, Henry Miller, Nicholas Monsarrat, Peter Padfield, Barrie Pitt, Günther Prien, Terence Robertson, Eric Sauder, Jak P. Mallman Showell, Michael Sizeland, Peter Wakker, William Walders, John Waters, Colin Watts-Tucker, Colin Way, Herbert Werner

BIBLIOGRAPHY

Bailey, Chris, *The Battle of the Atlantic, The Corvettes and their Crews*, Alan Sutton Publishing Ltd., 1994
Beaver, Paul, *U-boats in the Atlantic*, Patrick Stephens, ltd, 1979
Bekker, Cajus, *The German Navy 1939-1945*, Dial Press, 1974
Bishop, Chris, *Firepower Sea Warfare*, Grange Books, 1999
Blair, Clay, *Hitler's U-boat War*, Cassell, 1998
Blake, Bernard, *Jane's Underwater Warfare Systems 1990-91*, Jane's Information Group, 1990
Botting, Douglas, *The U-boats*, Time-Life Books, 1979
Breyer, Siegfried and Koop, Gerhard, *The German Navy at War 1939-45*, Schiffer
Brooks, Ewart, *The Gates of Hell*, Arrow Books, 1973
Broome, Jack, *Convoy Is To Scatter*, William Kimber, 1972
Buchheim, Lothar-Günther, *The Boat*, William Collins, 1976
Burn, Alan, *The Fighting Commodores*, Leo Cooper, 1999
Cameron, Ian, *Red Duster, White Ensign*, White Lion, 1974
Cantwell, John, *Images of War—British Posters*, HMSO
Churchill, Winston S., *The Second World War*, Houghton Mifflin, 1948
Clancy, Tom, *Submarine*, Berkley Books, 1993
Compton-Hall, Richard, *Submarine Boats*, Windward, 1983
Cope, Harley F., *Serpent of the Seas*, Funk and Wagnells, 1942
Costello, John and Hughes, Terry, *The Battle of the Atlantic*, Fontana Collins, 1977
Crane, Jonathan, *Submarine*, BBC, 1984
Cremer, Peter, *U-boat Commander*, Naval Institute Press, 1985
Crowther, J.G. & Whiddington, R., *Science At War*, HMSO, 1947
De Launay, J., and De Schutter, J., *Arromanches 44 The Normandy Invasion*, Editions J.M. Collet, 1984
Desquesnes, Rémy, *Normandy 1944*, Editions Ouest-France Memorial De Caen, 1993
Dickison, Arthur P., *Crash Dive*, Sutton Publishing, 1999
Dönitz, Karl, *Memoirs*, Greenhill Books, 1990
Edwards, Bernard, *Under Four Flags*, Percival Marshall, 1954
Edwards, Bernard, *The Merchant Navy Goes To War*, Robert Hale, 1990
Edwards, Bernard, *Dönitz and the Wolf Packs*, Cassell, 1996
Enever, Ted, *Britain's Best Kept Secret—Ultra's Base at Bletchley Park*,

Alan Sutton, 1994

Farrago, Ladislas, *The Tenth Fleet*, Drum Books, 1962

Frank, Wolfgang, *The Sea Wolves*, Mann, 1973

Franks, Norman, *Dark Sky, Deep Water*, Grub Street, 1997

Friedman, Norman, *Submarine Design and Development*, Naval Institute Press, 1984

Gabler, Ulrich, *Submarine Design*, Bernard & Graefe Verlag, 1986

Gallery, Daniel V., *Twenty Million Tons Under The Sea*, Regnery, 1956

Gannon, Michael, *Operation Drumbeat*, Harper Perennial, 1990

Giese, Otto, *Shooting The War*, Naval Institute Press, 1994

Graves, Charles, *Life Line*, William Heinemann, 1941

Gray, Edwin, *The Killing Time*, Scribners, 1972

Gray, Edwin, *The Devil's Device*, Seeley, Service and Co., 1975

Gretton, Peter, *Crisis Convoy*, P. Davies, 1974

Guske, Heinz, *The War Diaries of U-764*, Thomas Publications, 1992

Hadley, Michael L., *Count Not The Dead*, Naval Institute Press, 1995

Hampshire, A. Cecil, *The Blockaders*, William Kimber, 1980

Harris, Arthur, *Bomber Offensive*, Collins, 1937

Harris, Arthur, *Bomber Offensive*, Collins, 1947

Hervy, John, *Submarines*, Brassey's, 1994

Hickam, Homer H., *Torpedo Junction*, Naval Institute Press, 1989

Hill, J.R., *Anti-Submarine Warfare*, Ian Allen, 1984

Hirschfeld, Wolfgang, *Modern Sub Hunters*, Cassell, 1996

HMSO *The Battle of the Atlantic*, 1946

HMSO *Coastal Command*, 1942

HMSO *We Speak From The Air*, 1942

HMSO *The U-boat War in the Atlantic*, 1989

HMSO Merchantmen at War, 1942

HMSO Fleet Air Arm, 1942

Holmes, Harry, *The Last Patrol*, Airlife, 1994

Hough, Richard, *The Longest Battle*, Weidenfeld & Nicholson, 1986

Horton, Edward, *The Illustrated History of the Submarine*, Sidgewick and Jackson, 1974

Hoyt, Edwin P., *The U-boat Wars*, Robert Hale Ltd, 1984

Humble, Richard, *Undersea Warfare*, New English Library, 1981

Humble, R. & Bergin, M., *A WWII Submarine*, Naval Institute Press, 1991

Hurd, Archibald, *The Battle of the Seas*, Hodder & Stoughton, 1941

Hutchhausen, Peter, *Hostile Waters*, Arrow, 1997

Ireland, Bernard and Grove, Eric, *Jane's War At Sea 1897-1997*, Harper

Collins, 1997

Jackson, G.Gibbard, *The Romance of a Submarine*, J.B. Lippincott, 1931

Jenkins, Goeffrey, *Hunter Killer*, Fontana Collins, 1966

John Jahr Verlag, *Waffen im Einsatz*, 1976

Jones, Jeffrey, *Defeat of the Wolf Packs*, William Kimber, 1986

Jones, Jeffery, *Submarines Versus U-boats*, William Kimber, 1986

Kemp, Paul, *Convoy Protection*, Arms & Armour, 1993

Kemp, P.K., *H.M. Submarines*, Herbert Jenkins, 1952

Knox, Collie, *Atlantic Battle*, Methuen & Co., 1941

Lamb, Charles, *To War in a Stringbag*, Nelson Doubleday, 1977

Lavo, Carl, *Back From The Deep*, Naval Institute Press, 1994

Lawliss, Chuck, *The Submarine Book*, Burford Books, 1991

Lewin, Ronald, *Ultra Goes To War*, McGraw-Hill, 1978

Lund, Paul and Ludham, Harry, *Night of the U-boats*, NEL, 1974

Maas, Peter, *The Terrible Hours*, Harpertorch, 1999

Macintyre, Donald, *The Battle of the Atlantic*, Pan Books, 1961

Macintyre, Donald, *The Naval War Against Hitler*, Batsford, 1971

Margolin, V., *Propaganda: Persuasion in World War II Art*, Chelsea House, 1976

Mars, Alastair, *Unbroken*, Pan Books, 1953

Mason, David, *U-boat: The Secret Menace*, Ballantine Books, 1968

Miller, David and Jordan, John, *Modern Submarine Warfare*, Salamander Books, 1987

Messenger, Charles, *World War II in the Atlantic*, Warfare Books and Toys Ltd., 1990

Metson, Graham, *An East Coast Port: Halifax at War 1939-1945*, McGraw-Hill Ryerson, 1981

Middlebrook, Martin and Everitt, Chris, *The Bomber Command War Diaries*, Penguin, 1990

Middlebrook, Martin, *Convoy*, Penguin Books, 1978

Monsarrat, Nicholas, *The Cruel Sea*, Penguin, 1951

Morison, Samuel Eliot, *The Battle of the Atlantic*, Little Brown, 1947

Morison, Samuel Eliot, *The Two-Ocean War*, Atlantic Little Brown, 1963

Mulligan, Thomas P., *Lone Wolf Werner Henke*, Praeger, 1993

Murrow, Edward R., *This Is London*, Shocken Books, 1941

Neitzel, Sonke, *Die Deutschen Ubootbunker und Bunkerwerften*, Bernard & Graefe Verlag, 1991

Padfield, Peter, *War Beneath The Sea*, Pimlico, 1995

Parker, Mike, *Running the Gauntlet*, Nimbus Publishing, 1994

Pitt, Barrie, *The Battle of the Atlantic*, Time-Life Books, 1977

Preston, Anthony, *Flower Class Corvettes*, Bivouac Books, 1973
Prien, Günther, *U-boat Commander*, Tempus Publishing
Robertson, Terence, *The Golden Horseshoe*, Evans Brothers, 1955
Rogers, Stanley, *Sailors At War*, George G. Harrap, 1942
Rossler, Eberhard, *The U-boat*, Naval Institute Press, 1989
Runyan, Timothy & Copes, Jan, *To Die Gallantly*, Westview Press, 1994
Rutter, Owen, *Red Ensign*, Robert Hale, 1942
Shaw, Frank, *The Merchant Navy at War*, 1944
Schofield, B.B., *The Russian Convoys*, B.T. Batsford, 1964
Showell, Jak P. Mallmann, *U-boats Under the Swastika*, Naval Institute Press, 1989
Showell, Jak P. Mallmann, *The German Navy in WWII*, Naval Institute Press, 1991
Showell, Jak P. Mallmann, *U-Boats Attack!*, Spellmount, 2011
Smith, P.C., *Arctic Victory*, Kimber, 1975
Smith, P.C., *Pedestal—The Malta Convoy of August 1942*, Crecy Books, 1994
Syrett, David, *The Defeat of the German U-boats*, U. of South Carolina, 1994
Tarrant, V.E., *The U-boat Offensive 1914-1945*, Naval Institute Press, 1989
Terraine, John, *Business in Great Waters*, Leo Cooper, 1989
The U-boat Commander's Handbook, Thomas Publications, 1989
Vause, Jordan, *U-Boat Ace: Wolfgang Luth*, Naval Institute Press, 1976
Warlimont, Walter, *Inside Hitler's Headquarters 1939-45*, Presidio Press 1993
Waters, John M., *Bloody Winter*, Naval Institute Press, 1967
Werner, Herbert, *Iron Coffins*, Holt, Rinehart & Winston, 1969
Westwood, David, *The Type VII U-boat*, Naval Institute Press, 1984
Williamson, Gordon, *U-boat Crews*, Osprey, 1995
Winterbotham, F.W., *The Ultra Secret*, Future Publications, 1976
Winton, John, *Ultra At Sea*, Leo Cooper, 1988

WHY DO THEY DO IT?

"Why did I join the submarine service? I am not quite sure. In our centenary year we now have several fourth-generation submariners who have followed their fathers into submarines, but I am not one of these. I was not entirely a volunteer either, but there was a distinct shortage of submarine officers when I did my training back in 1957 as an entire training class of seamen and technical officers had perished when HMS *Affray* went down in 1951, and this deficiency ran on for several years. I was easily persuaded and have not regretted this decision for one moment. It certainly wasn't for the money (half a crown [12 1/2 pence] a day extra pay in those days).

"Responsibility at an early age, the opportunity to command as a Lieutenant, small ship comradeship with each depending on the other. Tremendous 'regimental' pride and lifelong friendships extending to an international brotherhood of those who do their business beneath the surface. Operational professionalism of the highest order, quite a bit of excitement and, of course, a touch of glamour—but I was very fortunate to have served when I did as the advent of the larger, comfortable nuclear submarine made the service a little more impersonal despite the huge technical challenge. What a lucky fellow I am to have served when I did, starting in conventional / diesel submarines, spending most of my time abroad, and eventually graduating to an SSN."
—Commander Mike Sizeland, Royal Navy (Ret)

"We operate with impunity in virtually any body of water we choose to go in. That's what attracted me to submarines as a midshipman, and the opportunity to do real-world things instead of just practicing with other members of the U.S. Navy. I wanted to go against the real opponent in the real environment, and that's exactly what I've gotten the opportunity to do in the last four years, and after four years of doing the attack submarine business I'm very confident in our ability to go where we want without anyone finding us.

"My mother was a Navy brat. Her father was a captain and her brothers were all officers in the Navy. All three of them were graduates of the Naval Academy. As a little kid I used to visit my grandparents in Key West, Florida. There was a submarine base there at the time and my grandfather, who had been on submarines in the 1920s, took me on tours of the submarines. He had the book *Submarine Operations in World War II*, by Theodore Roscoe, the authoritative history of sub operations in that war. I would lie there on the floor looking at the pictures in it every time I visited them. That stuck in the back of my mind. When other kids got spacecraft toys, I got submarines that would shoot missiles and torpedoes and you could take them in the pool.

"I always wanted to go to the Naval Academy, and once I got there I pretended that I was going to be open-minded, but in fact, it was a foregone conclusion that I wanted to go into submarines. I never doubted that decision. I look back on my career with absolutely complete satisfaction. I've gotten to go everywhere, operate in evey body of water, to do every one of the submarine operations. I've had all the moments of excitement that I hoped I would.

"In the submarine business, you are an independent operator, on your own. You have to solve your own problems. You don't get on the radio, call home and ask them for help with a technical problem, fixing a piece of equipment. 'What do you want me to do now, boss?' You can't have a helicopter fly in a part to you. You can't get the technical representative to fly out to the ship to help you. You can't get any prints or drawings that you don't have. You have to figure it out yourself. The 23-year-old kids on your ship have got to sort out the problem, figure out how to fix it. Very often they have to figure out how to use parts that were meant to do something else; how to put them together to serve the function in the piece of gear that we don't have parts for. That kind of creativity, self-sufficiency and resourcefulness—you're out there on your own and you have to solve the problem yourself. It's been very satisfying. You can't do that without a great bunch of guys. I was told before I came into submarines that I would work with the cream of the crop of sailors. The enlisted guys, and the officers, are super-aggressive, hard-working, smart and dedicated. I found that to be true. It's very easy to do a hard job like this when there is no question that everyone is pulling on the same end of the rope. I don't look forward to going into the private sector one day and having to worry about who is on my side, competing with people in my own company. On a submarine there is no doubt that everybody is on the same side and that everyone wants the right thing to happen. They don't worry about who gets the credit. They just do the right thing. It's a fantastic environment.

"My own experience has all been attack submarines and I'm very proud to have been on them. It's a harder job [than on missile subs];

everyone will tell you that it's a harder job. The schedule is more flexible, constantly changing. The operations are more intense and demanding. The amount of space in the boat is much more compressed. It's harder: harder on the sailors, harder on the officers. There is no question but that some guys flourish in that kind of environment. That's what I like. That's what I came in for, the challenge. You've got to bob and weave with the problem, sort it out on the fly, that kind of thing. That's the stuff I love about this business. I don't think I would enjoy being on a ballistic missile submarine, where the schedule is predictable, where they can get something set up and go for a fixed period of time, that works out best for them. That's great. I think that probably more than half of the boomer guys will recirculate back to a boomer. Certainly more than half of the attack submarine guys will recirculate back to an attack submarine. Probably one-fourth of one's career will be on the other kind of ship than the one that you spend most of your time on. I'm an oddball because I have been on attack submarines for all four of my tours. That's very unusual. Less than ten percent of submariners are in that situation, spending all of their tours on one type or the other. I wear some kind of warped 'badge of honor' that I've done the hard job for four consecutive tours."

—Commander William Hoeft, skipper, USS *Salt Lake City*, SSN 716

"When I joined the Navy in 1970, the training package was that you spent a year at Dartmouth [Britannia Royal Naval College], then a year at sea as a midshipman. Then you went back again into the Navy for a year's worth of academics before you had to make a decision as to which branch you would go into, even though you wouldn't necessarily go straight into that branch.

"In 1970 the Fleet Air Arm in the British Navy was declining. The decision had been made in 1969 that fixed-wing flying was no longer going to be part of the Navy, eliminating that as a good route through the Navy. To my mind, submarines, especially the SSN fleet, represented the battleships of the future. It was a growing force. We had a large number of conventional submarines and the nuclear submarine was coming on line in a big way. The attraction of early command was significant in that you could take command of a conventional submarine at age 28 or 29, if you were moving, and a conventional submarine was a fairly potent weapon. It was certainly more impressive than a mine-sweeper, which is the equivalent of what I would have got if I had stuck in the flotilla. So, early command, early responsibility, and an attraction to what appeared to me to be the expanding branch of the Navy, in a business which was expanding, were very much the driving forces [behind my choice of submarines.]

"I went to sea from Dartmouth in a conventional submarine just for a day to give me an insight into it, and it all looked good to me. It's a very different life. I read physics at university. Physics was the only subject I was ever any good at and the nuclear aspects of it were the spark that tied very neatly into my career. I was ambitious enough to think that this degree would be useful to my career. I then went back into the Navy and did some courses, and went into the submarine world joining HMS *Swiftsure* in 1976. I served with her much longer than normal, until 1979, and during that time I qualified as a submariner and got these submarine brooches [dolphins], and I remember the enormous pride in getting them. I then went back into the conventional submarine world in HMS *Orpheus*, which was an odd route. Most people had grown up through the conventional submarines. I was the Sonar Officer. During my time in *Swiftsure* I was the Torpedo Officer and then the Communications Officer. After *Orpheus* I went back to another S-boat, *Superb*, for about two years as the Torpedo and Anti-Submarine Officer, and I went straight from there to the Perisher Course. I then was given HMS *Orpheus* to command just after the Falklands War, and took her down to the Falklands. From there I went to Captain Submarines Sea Training Organization as one of the training staff. I then got promoted to Commander and was given HMS *Splendid*, in command for two years. I went from there to become the teacher of the commanding officers qualifying course [Perisher] for two years. Then, after nine months in the Ministry of Defence, I went to become Captain Submarine Sea Training, in charge of the workup of all our submarine fleet."
—Admiral Sir Mark Stanhope, Royal Navy [In 2009 Admiral Stanhope became First Sea Lord and Chief of Naval Staff]

"I had read all this stuff about the World War II submarines and the concept of how the machines worked. That's why I came in. The machine is cool. The mechanics of it have always impressed me. When you get something that's designed to take the pressure and the abuse that this thing takes, and it still works time and time again, that's like, wow! They say that the most complicated piece of gear in the world is the space shuttle. The second is the submarine.When you thing that you have all of these systems that work together, computer stuff, the reactor, all that stuff back aft, its all got to work together to make this thing go forward,

INDEX